HOW TO
~PLAN~
PREPARE
AND SUCCESSFULLY COMPLETE

. . . .

YOUR SHORT-TERM MISSION

For Volunteers, Churches, Independent STM Teams
and Mission Organisations: The Ultimate Guide to Missions

MATHEW BACKHOLER

How to Plan, Prepare and Successfully Complete Your Short-Term Mission – For Volunteers, Churches, Independent STM, Teams and Mission Organisations, The Ultimate Guide to Missions: For Individuals, Leaders, Teams and those Planning a Christian Gap Year: The Why, Where and When of STMs

UK ISBN 978-1-907066-05-4
British Library Cataloguing In Publication Data
A Record of this Publication is available from the British Library.
First Published in April 2010 by ByFaith Media in Association with www.MissionsNow.co.uk. Updated in 2012, 2014 and 2016.
This book is also available as an ebook.

- Jesus Christ is Lord -

'The Lord gave the Word; great was the company of those who proclaimed it' (Psalm 68:11).

'As cold water to a weary soul, so is good news from a far country' (Proverbs 25:25).

'To him who knows to do good and does not do it, to him it is sin' (James 4:17).

Contents

Contents

Jesus said, "Go into all the world and preach the gospel to every creature. He who believes and is baptised will be saved; but he who does not believe will be condemned" (Mark 16:15-16).

Jesus said, "Go therefore and make disciples of all the nations ...teaching them to observe all things that I have commanded you; and lo, I am with you always, even to the end of the age" (Matthew 28:19-20).

Preface

'As cold water to a weary soul, so is Good News from a far country' Proverbs 25:25.

'To him who knows to do good and does not do it, to him it is sin' James 4:17.

The author has been on more than thirty short-term missions (STMs) in over forty nations of the world, spanning three decades. *How to Plan, Prepare and Successfully Complete Your Short-Term Mission – For Volunteers, Churches, Independent STM teams and Mission Organisations* has been written from first-hand experience. The author's aim is that this book will aid you in your STM, whether you are an individual exploring the options at home or abroad, or a church leader planning to take a group. You may have two weeks free or be taking a gap year; you may be drawn towards a particular people group or country, or are just looking for the right mission organisation to join. This book will assist you in these areas, give your firm biblical foundation for STMs and will guide you through the process, before, during and when you return home, and includes many valuable insights. The application of the truths within this book will greatly help you on your journey of discovery and exploration into new lands and cultures on your STM.

In some chapters, the author refers to 'we,' this is himself and any other members of the STM team whom he was travelling with or leading. The boxed testimonies are all real events, though some of the names have been changed (even if just to protect from embarrassment!). Throughout the book, prices of items are stated in both British pound sterling (£) and American dollars ($) which at the time of writing was $1.6 to £1.00. Some prices are rounded-up (or down) to the nearest whole figure. Scriptures in italics are the author's own emphasis. Square brackets [these things] indicate where the author has added additional information within a quote.

The author has a heart for the Great Commission at home and abroad and desires to glorify Jesus Christ, the Son of God through his daily living and writings. As a missionary evangelist (amongst many other duties and responsibilities), the author in his labour towards the Great Commission has met, interviewed, led, worked alongside, sat under and interacted with numerous Christian workers with a variety of callings and giftings from different denominations in many countries on several continents. These individuals have been friends, associates, contacts, advisors, team leaders, team members, fellow labourers on STMs, as well as workers in mission agencies; founders of organisations and ministries, including staff from mission training organisations. This global interaction has enabled the author to draw from a deep mine of knowledge that has helped in the production of this book. Thanks for all your testimonies!

The Son of God became the Son of man in order that the sons of men might become the sons of God. He came to do for us what we could not do for ourselves – Selwyn Hughes.[1]

Paul Backholer (the author's brother) in *How Christianity Made the Modern World* wrote: 'The question that every believer must ask themselves is, 'Am I using my influence for Christ?' What if every Christian today put their influence into action for the Kingdom of God, instead of indirectly supporting another kingdom by inaction? This is not only a challenge to us all, but an opportunity. This is a chance for us to leave a legacy outside of our immediate home, a chance for us to make our lives count and to know that our existence has meaning and purpose. Today is our opportunity to act and leave a legacy!'[2]

Mathew Backholer – March 2010.

Since the Arab Spring, which began in December 2010 in Tunisia, North Africa, much of North Africa and the Middle East has undergone dramatic change and seen much turmoil over the past six years. With the rise of the Islamic State (IS) (also known as ISIS, ISIL, Daesh and Daish) in 2014, sweeping into and taking control over large swathes of Iraq, Syria and other parts of the Middle East; with affiliated groups in pockets in North Africa and northern Nigeria etc. These are the countries that you should avoid on your STM. Terrorist attacks have also been against tourists/foreigners in Tunisia, Egypt and Mail in West Africa. In November 2015, 130 people were killed in Paris, France, and around 300 were injured in simultaneous terrorist attacks. These included gunmen/women and suicide bombers. Islamic terrorists have also struck in many other countries from Pakistan to Indonesia. January 2016.

Chapter One

The Importance of the Great Commission

Jesus said, "Go into all the world and preach the Gospel to EVERY CREATURE" Mark 16:15.

Jesus said, "All authority has been given to Me in heaven and on earth. Go therefore and make disciples of all the nations, baptising them in the name of the Father and of the Son and of the Holy Spirit, teaching them to observe all things that I have commanded you; and lo, I am with you always, even to the end of the age" Matthew 28:18-20.

The Great Commission

Jesus' parting Words to His disciples, before He ascended into heaven, revealed His most passionate desire to reach the lost – the Great Commission – "Go therefore and make disciples of all nations..." This VERY important message which was entrusted to them was to be passed on from generation to generation (being practically outworked and fulfilled) because Jesus came to 'seek and to save' those who are lost (Luke 19:10), for 'there is no other name under heaven given among men by which we must be saved' (Acts 4:12).

God's love for mankind is immense and is documented in the most famous verses of the Holy Bible: 'For God so loved the world that He gave His only begotten Son, that whoever believes in Him should not perish but have everlasting life' (John 3:16). 'For God did not send His Son into the world to condemn the world, but that the world through Him might be saved. He who believes in Him is not condemned, but he who does not believe is condemned already' (John 3:17-18). Jesus came to heal the broken-hearted, to bind up their wounds and to set the captives free, because the Spirit of the Lord was upon Him to preach the Good News to the poor (Luke 4:18-19) and we are called to follow in His footsteps.

Short-term missions (STMs) are a great way to be part of the Great Commission. Those that go often use their holiday (vacation) time, take a gap year or go outside of term time when colleges and universities have broken up.

In 1910, Bishop Ingham, Home Secretary of the Church Missionary Society, wrote: 'When...Church members, whether they be administrators or soldiers or merchants or mechanics or clerks, are sent forth to their sphere of work to make them into spheres of influence – then and only then will the world see the sort of witnesses our Lord meant when He said, "Ye shall be witnesses unto Me," and then will the Churches know as never before the real presence and power of the Lord."[1]

Thirteen Waves of Christian Missions

Historically, there have been at least thirteen distinct waves of Christian missions with new missionaries being raised up and sent forth:

1. After the ascension of the Lord Jesus Christ; at Pentecost when the Holy Spirit was outpoured and those present in the Upper Room received power from on high (Acts 1:8-14 and 2:1-4). The disciples and the apostles went into all the world and proclaimed the Good News beginning in Jerusalem.

2. During the third to the sixth centuries much of Europe received the Good News, whilst in key locations there sprang up mission sending centres with missionary-minded monks.

3. During the Middle Ages when from AD 1100 to AD 1300, hundreds of Franciscans and Dominican monks went to evangelise the Muslims in North Africa, which had been a centre of Christianity in the second and third centuries. The Franciscan Revival (c.1209-1220), in Italy, gave extras impetus to the work, though in the span of two hundred years, two hundred monks from both the Franciscans and Dominican orders lost their lives in this missionary advance; many were martyred.

4. The fourth wave of missions came out of the Moravian Revival (1727), when in 1731, the Moravian Mission was founded and the small church at Herrnhut, (in modern day Germany), sent more missionaries in twenty years than Protestant Christians had done in the past two centuries!

5. The fifth wave sprang out of the Evangelical Revival (1739-1791), at the end of the eighteenth century and rolled into the twentieth century. Missionaries sailed to the farthest part of the world; largely to the colonies of European nations, but also to the unevangelised around the Pacific Islands, Asia and Africa. The Baptist Missionary Society was birthed in 1792. The non-denominational London Missionary Society was founded in 1795. The Anglican Church Missionary Society began in 1799 and the British and Foreign Bible Society was formed in 1804, though its

beginnings were birthed in 1787. John Wesley of England, a former missionary to the American Indians (1735-1737), had encouraged missions all his life. Wesley's right-hand man, Dr. Thomas Coke, officially inaugurated Methodist Missions in 1787 and became known as the Missionary Bishop of Methodism. He crossed the Atlantic to America eighteen times whilst the Wesleyan Missionary Society began its work in 1817.

6. The American Board of Commissioners for Foreign Missions (1810), was the direct outcome of the Haystack Revival of 1806, which broke out at Williams College in America, touching other colleges and became the sixth wave of missions.

7. The seventh wave came out of the 1857-1860 revival that began in New York, America, and went worldwide. This led to an estimated 5 million converts and more people were called into missions. On David Livingstone's return to Britain in 1856, from seventeen years in Africa, he gave new impetus to the cause of missions as he spoke at a number of universities (again on his return in 1864-65) and on the news of his death in 1873. Hudson Taylor, missionary to China was encouraged with the revival in Britain (1858-60) and believed that God would bless the mission field. He founded the China Inland Mission (CIM) in June 1865.

8. The eighth wave came from the Student Volunteer Movement which in forty years (1888-1928), led to an estimated 20,000 students becoming missionaries! This began when the Cambridge Seven joined the CIM and before sailing to China in Feb. 1885, spoke at a number of influential British universities, challenging the students to do something with their lives.

9. The Welsh Revival of 1904-1905 led to more than a dozen revivals around the globe and the ninth wave sprung from the campuses revivals of 1905 (largely in America), which led to an estimated 10,000-15,000 students becoming missionaries!

10. The tenth wave of missions began in the late 1920s, the native missionary movement, when Andrew Gih was touched by the Shanghai Revival (1925)[2] and began the Bethel Evangelistic Band / Bethel Mission where Chinese Christians formed teams and began mass evangelism, first in China, then across Asia. However, during the Pyongyang Great Revival (1907-1910)[3] Koreans began mass evangelism campaigns such as the 'Movement of Saving One Million Souls for Christ' which began in the autumn of 1909. The Oriental Missionary Society (OMS) was founded in 1902 and in 1912, the 'Great Village Campaign' began where all 10.3 million homes in Japan were given a Gospel booklet and was completed by 1918! By 1923, the Tokyo

Bible Training Institute had trained no less than one thousand national preachers and by 1925, OMS had 201 mission stations and an equal number of itinerary points had been opened.[4]

11. The eleventh wave of missions began in the late 1950s / early 60s when lay personnel took time out from work and went on STMs. These increased in strength as new mission agencies such as Youth With A Mission (YWAM), Campus Crusade for Christ (CCFC) and Operation Mobilisation (OM) were birthed giving the opportunity for a layperson to "Go," even if just for a few weeks.[5] See page 148, From Missionary Artisans to STMs.

12. From China in the 1920s came the vision of 'Back to Jerusalem;'[6] Chinese Christians evangelising along the old Silk Road (which lies along the 10/40 window — the least evangelised countries of the world situated at the 10-40 latitude), which was re-birthed in the 1980s. Since the 1980s, the native missionary movement from developing countries within the continents of Asia and Africa have mobilised to take the Good News to the nations along the 10/40 window of which Gospel for Asia (GFA) is very prominent.[7]

13. From the 1990s onwards, but especially in the twenty-first century, millions of Americans (and those of other nationalities) have accepted the call to their short-term mission.

American Short-Term Mission Statistics

The leader in the world for STMs are North Americans, whilst America is also the biggest full-time missionary sending nation in the world, followed by South Korea and then the United Kingdom.

In 1965, only 540 individuals from North America were involved in short-term missions. In 1975, 6,000 people from the USA went on a STM. By 1987, this figure increased to over 60,000. Between 1979 and 1989, the annual number of participants in STMs rose from just over 25,000 to approximately 120,000. By 1992, there were more than 250,000 short-term missioners (STM-ers). By 1998, there were 450,000 STM-ers. In 2003, there were an estimated one million STM-ers sent out. In 2004, data suggested the number could be as high as four million STM-ers. In 2005, 1.6 million U.S. church members went on a STM. In 2008, it was reported that 8 million U.S. adults went on a STM trip in the last five years, though 33 percent of the STMs were locations within the U.S. In 2009, statistics revealed that more than 2 million U.S. citizens went on a STM the previous year. See Appendix A.

Every Tribe, Nation and Tongue

The disciples of Jesus Christ were commissioned to preach and teach about the Kingdom of God; to proclaim the Good News of salvation, to make disciples, to cast out demons, to heal the sick and raise the dead (Matthew 28:18-20 and Mark 16:15-18) – all in the mighty name of Jesus Christ, the Son of God, the Saviour of the world. These commands of Jesus Christ, spoken nearly two thousand years ago, are just as binding to us, as to the early disciples. They are passed from one generation to the next until every tribe and tongue has heard the glad tidings – 'as a witness to all nations' and then, and only then, will Jesus come again (see Matthew 24:14, Revelation 5:9 and Revelation 7:9). However, remember, that Peter in relation to the Day of the Lord (the end times), reiterated that we have our part to play – our responsibility and duty towards mankind. God is 'longsuffering towards us, not willing that any should perish but that all should come to repentance' and that we should be 'looking for and *hastening* the coming of the day of God' (2 Peter 3:9-12). This is when we fulfil our vital role in the Great Commission to: 'Go into all the world and preach the Gospel to EVERY CREATURE' (Mark 16:15).

Mission Related Scriptures

- Thus says the Lord God, "When I say to the wicked, 'You shall surely die,' and you give him no warning, nor speak to warn the wicked from his wicked way, to save his life, that same wicked man shall die in his iniquity; but his blood I will require at your hand" (Ezekiel 3:18).
- The apostle Paul declared to the Ephesian elders that he 'kept back nothing that was helpful, but proclaimed it' and was 'innocent of the blood of all men' because he did 'not shun to declare the whole counsel of God.' For three years he warned them night and day with tears (Acts 20:20-27 and 31).
- Jesus said, "Go out into the highways and hedges [byways] and compel them to come in, that My house may be filled" (Luke 14:23).
- Jesus said, "...I chose you and appointed you that you should go forth and bear fruit and that your fruit should remain" (John 15:16).
- Jesus said, "...As the Father has sent Me, I also send you" (John 20:21).

- Jesus said, "...You shall be witnesses to Me in Jerusalem and in all Judea and Samaria and to the end of the earth" (Acts 1:8).

The Father of Modern Missions

Towards the end of 1786, twenty-five year old shoe-maker, William Carey, accompanied by another minister went to a meeting of ministers at Northampton, England, where towards the end, the two men were told to propose a question for general discussion. Carey pleaded many excuses, until he finally gave in and asked, "Whether the command given to the apostles to 'teach all nations,' was not obligatory on all succeeding ministers to the end of the world, seeing that the accompanying promise was of equal extent?" The ministers were not impressed with his question or his observation!

Within two years, William Carey read a publication by Jonathan Edward, *A Humble Attempt To Promote Explicit Agreement and Visible Union of God's People in Extraordinary Prayer for the Revival of Religion* and the *Advancement of Christ's Kingdom on Earth* (1747). The second work (a pamphlet) was by Andrew Fuller, entitled *The Gospel Worthy of all Acceptation* (1785), which led to the ministers of the Northamptonshire Association in England, holding a monthly prayer meeting for the unreached people of the earth. Carey came to the conclusion that, "If it be the whole duty of all men, where the Gospel comes to believe unto salvation, then it is the duty of those who are entrusted with the Gospel to endeavour to make it known among all nations for the obedience of faith."

On 2 October 1792, at the first available meeting of ministers at Kettering, England a plan had been prepared 'for the purpose of forming a society for propagating the Gospel among the heathen.' The Society and its motto were: 'Expect great things from God – Attempt great things for God,' inspired by the verses from Isaiah 54:2-3 in the Authorised Version of the Holy Bible. Thus, the Baptist Missionary Society was founded and William Carey on sailing for India in June 1793, became the 'Father of Modern Missions.' He had told his friends and fellow ministers that he expected them to "hold the ropes" – in prayer and finances and Andrew Fuller became the first secretary of the Baptist Missionary Society.[8]

> Dr. David Livingstone, said, "God had an only Son and He made Him a missionary."

Chapter Two

Why Should I GO on Short-Term Missions (STMs)

'Now in the church that was at Antioch there were certain prophets and teachers...As they ministered to the Lord and fasted, the Holy Spirit said, "Now separate to Me Barnabas and Saul for the work which I have called them" ' Acts 13:2.

'Whatever your hand finds to do, do it with all your might...' Ecclesiastes 9:10a.

Why Should I Go?
Have you ever heard the following question or asked it yourself, "Why should I go on a short-term mission (STM)?" The simple answer is because Jesus told us to, "Go into all the world and to preach the Good News to all nations" – this is the Great Commission and we can all participate if we go on a STM.

The Great Commission is not a request to be slotted into a busy schedule of our own life's pleasure and desires, but a command to be obeyed, and STMs help us work towards that aim. How will people hear the Good News if we do not go and tell them about it, showing them the love of Christ in action? If we do not go on a STM soon, when will we, if ever at all?

J. Hudson Taylor, the founder of the China Inland Mission said, "The Great Commission is not an option to be considered, it is a command to be obeyed."

Campus Crusade for Christ
Bill Bright was the founder and leader of Campus Crusade for Christ (CCFC). In the year of his death in 2003, CCFC had 26,000 full-time staff and more than 225,000 trained volunteer staff in 191 countries, in areas representing 99.6% of the world's population. From 1953-2003, CCFC had given approximately 6 billion exposures to the Gospel worldwide, through various means and methods. Bill Bright said, "There is no higher calling or greater privilege known to man than being involved in helping fulfil the Great Commission," and STMs fill this gap.

Bill Bright said on one occasion, "My brothers and sisters in Christ, we have been bought with a price: the blood of the holy Creator God of the universe. We are called by God to maintain our first love, to obey His commands to love others, and to tell others how much He loves and cares for them. The God-man, Jesus of Nazareth, has commissioned us to help take His Gospel to the ends of the earth. Let us fulfil the Great Commission..."

Bill Bright was focused on Jesus Christ and the Great Commission and he never strayed from that heavenly vision. He said that when he got up each morning, he evaluated all the potential activities of that day based on the question: "Will it help fulfil the Great Commission?" He was a workaholic for Jesus until the end. He was never concerned about dying and always said it was a "win-win" situation for him. He said, "If I stay, I will continue to be able to serve my Lord, and if I leave, I will be with Him." For most of his life, he signed every piece of correspondence with these words: "Yours for fulfilling the Great Commission in this generation."

Why Go on STMs?

There are many reasons why people go on a STM and some are better than others. Let's take a look at them.

Personal Reasons to Go on a STM:
- The Call – to go.
- The Command – be obedient.
- Concerned – for the lost.
- Compassion – on those who have never heard.
- Compelled – 'Woe [intense mournfulness] is me if I do not preach the Gospel' (1 Corinthians 9:16).

I was studying at a Bible College in the UK and during the Christmas holidays, I had the opportunity to go on a humanitarian mission to Eastern Europe. We travelled in an old school bus and went through at least six or seven countries and what an experience it was. Donald – Bulgaria.

The Reasons why People Go on a STM
- Concern for the Great Commission.
- Adventure (see new places & time out from the routine).
- Gap year (often between college and university).

- Escaping from problems / heartache at home.
- To evangelise or civilise! (Though the former is correct).

The aim of Tim Dearborn's *Short-term Missions Workbook* was to 'protect us from being mission tourists and propel us into lives of global citizenship' – because 'our funds and lives must be invested wisely for the Kingdom and not merely for spiritual adventurism.' Tim Dearborn also noted that: 'God will never call us into a ministry without providing the abilities we need to participate in God's purpose in it.'[1]

> A mission trip not only assists and can change the lives of those to whom you serve, but can be life changing for the one who went to serve.

STMs can be Life changing

STMs change not only the ones to whom they serve, but the person who goes. A mission trip is part of the college of life, it aids Christian discipleship, is educational and opens the world to others in far greater need than ourselves – it makes us think less of self and more of others, less of my problems and more on my blessings. It personally challenges us to pray for and to give more towards the Great Commission at home and abroad, and makes it personal, rather than distant. If you are overweight, you may also lose a few pounds (in weight); so that cannot be bad!

> I am halfway through my gap year (my first STM) and am working with a Christian drama group. I spend most mornings and many afternoons performing before schoolchildren at their assemblies, and as a team, we participate in lots of Bible studies. It is great being in a Christian environment and I have grown up so much. Merriel – England.

What you can Learn on your STM
- About yourself, what is important and what is not, and what you can live without.
- About others, their needs, concerns, language, lifestyles and culture.
- Insights into your own culture and other cultures.
- Your strengths, weaknesses, character (the good and bad), giftings, talents and deficiencies.

- The generosity of those who have so little.
- The importance of evangelism, world missions (at home and abroad) and the worldwide body of Christ.
- A greater love for Jesus, the importance of the Holy Spirit to empower and the Father heart of God.
- That "church" is done differently in other cultures with local expressions of worship and preaching.
- The importance to read and apply the truths of the Holy Bible. Memorisation of key Scriptures (especially evangelistic ones) are very beneficial when sharing the Good News and will be recalled from your memory.
- The world is bigger than you thought and very diverse.
- Working together as a team and having individual responsibilities and duties.
- Your STM can be the beginnings of God's bigger plan for your life – perhaps your future vocation, an adjustment of priorities, evaluation of finances, giftings and talents or taking your eyes off self and looking to the needs of others – the possibilities are endless.

Working for God

J. Hudson Taylor, after he founded the China Inland Mission, was giving advice to a group of pioneers who were under his leadership and reminded the group that there are several different ways of working for God. He said, "One is to make the best plans we can and carry them out to the best of our ability. This may be better than working without a plan, but it is by no means the best way of serving our Master. Or, having carefully laid our plans and determined to carry them through, we may ask God to help us and to prosper us in connection with them. Yet another way of working is to begin with God; to ask His plans and to offer ourselves to carry out His purposes."[2]

Oswald Chambers wrote: 'It is easier to serve God *without* a vision, easier to work for God *without* a call, because then you are not bothered by what God requires; *common sense* is your guide, veneered over with Christian sentiment. But if you receive a commission from Jesus Christ, the memory of what God wants will always come like a goad [a stab] and you will no longer be able to work for Him on the *common sense* basis.'[3]

Chapter Three

Should I Go on a Mission Trip?

'The Lord gave the Word; great was the company of those who proclaimed it' Psalm 68:11.

Jesus said, "He who is faithful in what is least is faithful also in much; and he who is unjust in what is least is unjust also in much. Therefore if you have not been faithful in the unrighteous mammon, who will commit to your trust the true riches? And if you have not been faithful in what is another man's, who will give you what is your own?" Luke 16:10-12.

Who Should Go – or Not Go?

The reason people go on short-term missions (STMs) is primarily to obey the command of Jesus – the Great Commission (see Matthew 28:18-20 and Mark 16:15-18).[1] The question has been asked on many occasion, "Can anybody go on a STM trip?" The answer to this is firstly yes, and secondly no. J. Hudson Taylor, founder of the China Inland Mission, said, "The Great Commission is not an option to be considered but a command to be obeyed." Secondly, people may have natural limitations or a disability that may make it very difficult in some places, whilst other people may be a liability. Age, as well as existing health issues can be a factor in some places. An unfortunate individual may have just broken their leg or recently had major surgery, and these factors need to be discussed with your doctor and any mission organisation or church before you depart.

God can use anybody who is willing to go on a STM as it is not your ability, but your availability. Jesus did not say to the disciples, "Friends, I'm leaving you all, have a great pleasure-filled life and remember to be good." Instead, He told them to go forth and proclaim the Good News of His Kingdom, preaching repentance and the forgiveness of sins in His name. Go and make disciples of all the nations and teach the new converts how to live, cast out demons, lay your hands on the sick and raise the dead. You will speak with new tongues, serpents will be unable to harm you and if you accidentally drink anything deadly, you will be safe (see Mark 1:15, Mark 16:15-18 and Luke 12:47).

There is an open call from God to all believers in Christ to be a part of His Great Commission and that includes being fully surrendered to the Holy Spirit (Romans 12:1-2), so as to be able to respond to the call of God, "Who will go?" (Isaiah 6:8) or, "Who will stand in the gap?" in prayer (Ezekiel 22:30). The apostle Paul wrote: 'Woe is me if I do not preach the Gospel' (1 Corinthians 9:16). He intended to visit Asia (Minor) on a STM but had a vision, a calling to Macedonia, where he saw a man pleading, "Come and help us" (Acts 16:6-10) and so he went.

> George Verwer, founder of Operation Mobilisation said, "The devil would love to convince you that all this mission stuff isn't for you. The devil is a liar and you know it!"

Dave Davidson a mission mobilizer spoke of a giving a tithe of one's life to be involved in missions. He said, "Let's estimate an average 70 year life span and consider tithing a minimum of 10% of your life to God for cross cultural mission work. Refunding the first 20 years for training, 10% of 50 years is 5 years of mission work over a 70 year life span. Consider serving 3 years after retirement, leaving a timely 2 year term right now wherever you are in life to go and serve God in missions."[2]

I Cannot Go – Or Can I?

There are many reasons why some people think that they cannot go on a STM. For some it is: I'm too young, I'm not ordained, I have never preached / given my testimony, I have no qualifications, I have no spare money, or I'm useless.

Jeremiah was called by God as a young man and said, "Ah, Lord God! Behold I cannot speak, for I am a youth." But the Lord said, "Do not say 'I am a youth,' for you shall go to all whom I send you...do not be afraid of their faces for I am with you..." (Jeremiah 1:6-7).

The apostle Paul wrote to Timothy: 'Let no one despise your youth, but be an example to the believers in word, in conduct, in love, in spirit, in faith, in purity' (1 Timothy 4:12).

Moses had a stutter and was afraid to go on his mission to speak to Pharaoh, but God undertook for him and gave him the confidence he needed and Aaron was there to assist him. Moses went on to become the leader of the nation of Israel.

Some of the twelve disciples were fishermen but they had no certificate from the Guild of Fishermen, whilst Peter and John were noted as 'uneducated and untrained,' yet those who heard them preach 'marvelled...[and] realised that they had been with Jesus' (Acts 4:13). The disciples had not been ordained by a denomination, but had been commissioned by Jesus to "Go," and they did, and saw great things for the glory of God.

It is important that none of us look down upon ourselves (or on others) and you should not let anyone look down upon you because of your age or gender. If you have a testimony (Jesus has saved me) and a willing heart to go on STM then your are qualified and ready.

At the beginning of the twentieth century, an Indian convert approached a missionary and asked to be employed by him to preach the gospel. The missionary had no money, but the man pleaded for a job. Finally, the missionary stated that if he could live off one U.S. dollar a month, then he would employ him out of his own pocket. The worker it appeared was too ignorant to earn the one dollar (was not good at preaching) and was dismissed from service. Then the Hindus came in from the village and said, "Where is the man who loved us; will you not send him back?" The local missionary retelling the story to a fellow labourer, with tears in his eyes said that the Indian worker had seen five hundred conversions to Jesus Christ! His salary doubled to two dollars a month.[3]

Family Ties and Work Responsibilities

There are those with a family to look after and you cannot just run off and leave your spouse, the children, or ageing parents (if you are their carer) to go on a STM. If you are married, is your spouse in full support? If you have children what will happen to their schooling if they come with you, or if they stay home with one parent? What about pre-existing health issues? A person may have a work commitment (such as a teacher or a nurse with a six month or a years contract) which would prevent them from going away immediately on a STM.

My husband went to Asia to be a missionary and left our young children and myself at home. I was in agreement with him going, after all, once settled, the children and I were going to join him. Whilst in Vietnam he deserted us – we are no longer married. Dorothy – England.

Financial Obligations

If you are in serious debt and struggle to pay off your loans and credit cards then your financial obligations will hinder you going on a STM; especially if you have a mortgage. The Bible tells us that we are to 'owe no one anything, except to love one another' (Romans 13:8), therefore you are duty bound to pay off your debts as defaulting on your payments is wrong.

Creditors will perceive any STM as a holiday abroad and defaulting on your payments is dishonourable and will land you in trouble. If you are taking a year out and have a student loan then the repayment issues will vary because you have zero income. If you have made bad financial choices in the past, is it right to get people to part with their money (individuals or your church) for you to go on a STM, when you have not been responsible for the little you have had? If you have not proved faithful with your own money, you will not be faithful with others (see Luke 16:10 and Luke 19:11-27), and we must all take responsibility for our actions.[4]

It is also not advisable to finance your STM on borrowed money, because where God guides, He provides, as God pays His own invoices. See also Chapters Fourteen and Fifteen, Financing your Short-Term Mission and Finances – Trusting God.[5]

Health Issues and Disability

Do you or any members of your team have any pre-existing health issues? The medicine may not be available where you are going on your STM and the nearest hospital may be days away. Before you depart on your STM, stock up on your prescription medicines, keep them in their original packaging and get a note from your doctor because at customs you may be perceived as a travelling pharmacist!

A disability may not eliminate those who desire to go on a STM, but certain locations may not be appropriate. Some mission organisations or agencies may not be able to give the assistance they need or feel unable to accept those with a disability due to various risk factors or logistical issues.

Any Cog in the Machinery

More than seventy-five years ago, a special visitation of the Holy Spirit came to the Bible College of Wales (BCW), which had been founded by Rees Howells. He was a former coalminer turned missionary to Gazaland, (modern day Zimbabwe), who had seen revival at his mission station, and in dozens across Southern Africa, in five different nations. In 1936, the Holy Spirit had touched both students and staff whose focus was for EVERY CREATURE to be reached with the Gospel (Mark 16:15).

Dr. Kingsley C. Priddey, a staff member of BCW noted that in the previous year, '...Many had put their all on the altar for the sake of giving the Gospel to every creature. We had become willing to be any cog in the machinery that God needed to put that through in our generation....'[6]

For some, they went into different countries on their missions; others stayed behind and interceded for those who went (prayer partners), whilst many continued to train those who would go to the mission field.

> 'Do not withhold good from those to whom it is due when it is in the power of your hand to do so' Proverbs 3:27.

C. H. Spurgeon, the famed London preacher in Victorian England, said, "There are three kinds of people in the world: the wills, the won't and the can'ts. The first accomplish everything, the second oppose everything; the third fail in everything."[7]

Go, Pray and Give

David Livingstone was in Nottingham, England, in September 1864, where he spoke at the Society for the Propagation of the Gospel in Foreign parts. In part of his speech, relating to his travels through Southern Africa, he said, "They think the white people will eat them. They look upon us as cannibals, and we look upon them as savages. If we knew each other better we should find that we are very much better than we suppose each other to be. This is the case with different bodies of Christians; one body thinks themselves better than any other body; but when they meet together to pray, they have all the same object in view. They wish to bring others into the same blessed state as they are in themselves. This is the nature of Christianity – to impart the same blessing to others that we enjoy ourselves; and all who acknowledge the claims of Christianity believe that they ought to obey the command of our Saviour to go into all the world and proclaim the Gospel to every creature. I do not mean that you all ought to go and preach the Gospel to these Africans where I have been; but everyone is bound to obey this command. If he cannot do this himself, he must do it as a substitute; just as, in the defence of the country, all cannot go and fight and defend the country. Some people may become volunteers, but many others can aid and encourage the volunteer movement. So, many who cannot become missionaries themselves may encourage and aid the missionaries scattered throughout the world by their prayers and contributions."[8]

> Someone once said, "No one ever said that short-term missions are the way to evangelise the world, but they are a good way to get started!"

Georgina A. Gollock in *Candidates in Waiting – A Manual of Home Preparation for Foreign Missionary Work* (1892) wrote: '...An individual missionary call does not of necessity mean bodily presence in the foreign mission field. It seems as if some were called to China, or Africa, or India, *for God*, and others were called, no less truly, *to God* for China, or Africa, or India, or rather for the world. Their place is *at home*, their work is *for the world*, and they are kept here to kindle the flame of love and longing in other hearts. They are the instruments of God the Holy Ghost in His great work of calling out missionaries; they are the intercessors on the mountaintops, strengthening the warriors in the field. They are truly called, not only as the whole Church is called, but in a special sense, and they have a special and glorious service of their own. These words may come as a light to someone whose heart God has touched, but whose way He has completely closed. Be not cast down; pledge yourself fearlessly to Him for the evangelisation of the world, and He will not only use you *in* the work at home, but *for* the work abroad.'[9]

> William Carey, missionary to India and the Father of Modern Missions, said, "Few people know what may be done till they try and persevere in what they undertake."

Whatever your circumstances, everyone can still pray for world missions, others are able to go on a STM and others will be able to give financial support (Matthew 9:35-38). For some, their obstacles in preventing them from departing may dissolve within a year or two (or even quicker), as God moves in mysterious ways. With God, nothing is impossible and have faith, but do not try to squeeze God into your plans, fit into His!

Chapter Four

My Call or God's Call?

'Whatever your hand finds to do, do it with all your might...'
Ecclesiastes 9:10a.

'Now when they [Paul and Timothy] had gone through Phrygia
and the region of Galatia, they were forbidden by the Holy Spirit
to preach the Word in Asia. After they had come to Mysia they
tried to go to Bithynia, but the Spirit did not permit them' Acts
16:5-6.

Plans and Ideas
In the Old Testament, we can read about a situation where the
prophet Nathan said to King David, "Go, do all that is in your
heart, for the Lord is with you." But in the night the Word of the
Lord came to Nathan and he informed King David that it was not
God's will for him to build a temple for Him to dwell in (2 Samuel
7). However, he was permitted to prepare the building materials
for his son Solomon who accomplished the task (1 Chronicles
22 and 1 Kings 5 and 6). The story reveals to us that we can
have great plans and ideas, but that they may not be of God – or
not God's best for us. On the other hand, the timing may be out
or other factors are involved and this can be the same with
short-term missions (STMs).

God's Blessing and God's Anointing
There is a big difference between God *blessing* a work and
God *anointing* a work and this is true of all who go on a STM. If
we are the masters of our own money then we can go when and
where we want to, but if *God* is the Master of the money (which
we hold in stewardship) then we had better not squander it on
extravagant living. Jonah had his own money and so was able to
flee when he was told to go on his STM to Nineveh. Thankfully,
and mercifully for the Ninevites, Jonah though reluctant, did go
and the city saw revival, as its citizens turned to the Lord when
he told them to repent or the judgment of God would be seen
within forty days! (Book of Jonah).

After Jesus, the apostle Paul was probably the best missionary ever and went on three major mission trips, all of which lasted for a considerable time as he moved from city to city in various countries and regions.

Paul was always part of a mission team and had various helpers and assistants along the way. With Timothy, 'they were forbidden by the Holy Spirit to preach the Word in Asia' (a Roman province, Asia Minor), and 'after they had come to Mysia they tried to go to Bithynia, but the Spirit did not permit them' (Acts 16:6-10). So they came down to Troas and it was here that Paul had a vision of a man saying, "Come over to Macedonia and help us." When they arrived, God had prepared the heart of Lydia, a seller of purple cloth and she and her household believed and were baptised (Acts 16:9-15).

It was not that God did not want those in Asia to hear the Good News, but that the timing was incorrect, for within five or six years, Paul visited the region. After two years of teaching and preaching 'all who dwelt in Asia heard the Word of the Lord' (Acts 19:10) and the verse following informs us that God worked 'unusual miracles by the hand of Paul' because he was anointed for the work, he was in the will of God and the timing was correct.

Seek Guidance From God

Missionary to China, J. Hudson Taylor, wrote to a friend who needed guidance: 'Light will no doubt be given you. Do not forget, however, in seeking more, the importance of walking according to the light you have. If you feel called to the work, do not be anxious about the time and way. He will make it plain...I desire increasingly to leave all my affairs in the hands of God, who alone can and who assuredly will, lead us aright if humbly and in faith we seek His aid.

'...I urge on you...the importance of seeking guidance from God for yourself personally apart from the movements of others. ...But let us seek to see our own way clearly in the light of His will and then in trial and perplexity we shall be 'steadfast, unmoveable,' not having trusted to an arm of flesh. The Lord guide and bless you and give you ever to lean unshaken on His faithfulness.'[1]

Steps of Obedience for God's will to be Revealed:
- Move in step with God, not too quick or too slow (Psalm 32:9 and Galatians 5:25).

- Fear God and He will teach you the way to go (Psalm 25:12). C.f. Proverbs 1:7a, Proverbs 8:13a & Prov. 9:10.
- God's timing is always critical and essential for any work (Acts 16:5-10 and Acts 19:8-10). C.f. Acts 13:1-5.
- Trust God entirely (Psalm 37:4-7, Psalm 37:22, Proverbs 3:5-7 and Matthew 6:25-34).
- Yield yourself fully to God that you will know His will (Romans 12:1-2 and 2 Corinthians 5:15). C.f. John 4:34.
- And remember to obey God completely when He makes His will known to you (Acts 16:10).

I had my heart set on going to a certain Bible College, but they were never able to send me the information I requested. Even when I visited the church out of which the Bible College sprang, there was no prospectus and nobody was able to help me in my enquires. I concluded that this Bible College was not the will of God for me (because the door closed), but was led to another one. Jeffrey – England.

Go because I am Called

Many people go on a STM because they have received a direct Word from the Lord – they are called of God. God may not grab your attention like Moses at the burning bush (Exodus 3:1-4), or Elijah at the mountain of God where an earthquake and then a fire got his attention (1 Kings 19:11-12), but God spoke through a still small voice. In your quiet time, God may have spoken to you about the needs of a certain people group or country, or you feel burdened or concerned about those who have never heard the Good News. Others have been reading the Holy Bible, watching a documentary on television or reading a magazine or book and they just 'know' that God is leading them towards a certain place (country or people), as something just 'jumps out' and grabs their attention. Your church may be organising a STM and you feel that God is prompting you to sign up, or a visiting preacher or missionary has highlighted the needs of a certain area or people and it speaks deeply to your heart.

Terrible Statistics

It has been estimated that 168,000 people die everyday (7,000 an hour) who did not trust Jesus Christ as their Saviour (the ONLY way to heaven, see Acts 4:12) and thus are ushered into hell where there will be 'weeping and gnashing of teeth' (see

Matthew 8:12, Matthew 13:41-42 and Matthew 22:13-14). Many of these would have never have had the Good News preached to them – all were entitled to. A mission founder, after stating the statistics of his mission over the past three decades also declared with a heavy heart, that in the same time period, 300,000,000 unconverted of the population had passed into eternity from his field of labour alone!

The mission founder said, "To all Christ commanded that it should be given. What shall we say to the Master when He asks us about them? His brow as pierced with thorns, His hands and feet by the nails, His side with the spear, to purchase redemption for us and for them. What have we suffered to give these people the glad tidings? What are we doing now, that costs us pain to prevent the ceaseless stream of souls from following them, un-rescued, into eternity?"[2]

Multitudes of people have never heard the Good News, yet the command to preach the Gospel to every creature has never been cancelled. The question is: 'What am I doing about it?' Are we constrained by the love of Christ and the hope of His coming to obey His last command? Or do we live for self with no thought, care or concern about those, for whom Christ came to save?

Swedish missionary, Jane Guinness wrote: 'A great *without* has been written upon heathenism. Men and women are toiling without a Bible, without a Sunday, without prayer, without songs of praise. They have rulers without justice and without righteousness; homes without peace; marriage without sanctity...poverty without relief or sympathy; sickness without skilful help or tender care; sorrow without any to bind up the wounded hearts; sin, lying and crime without a remedy and worse of all, death without hope.'[3]

Remember you can accept or reject the call of God (for your STM), but you will have to eternally live with the consequences of any disobedience.

See also Chapter Ten, The Will of the Lord / God's Guidance.

Chapter Five

Are Short-Term Missions a Waste of Finances?

Jesus said, "My food is to do the will of Him who sent Me, and to finish His work...look at the fields, for they are already white unto harvest. And he who reaps receives wages and gathers fruit for eternal life, so that he who reaps may rejoice together. For this saying is true, 'One sows another reaps' " John 4:34-37.

'For the redemption of their souls is costly...' Psalm 49:8a.

A Waste of Finances

A minority of Christians claim that short-term missions (STMs) are a waste of finances. There are many and varied reasons why some hold to this point of view, but can we quantify a price for a soul? We should be wise and good stewards of our resources and if we are *only* focussing on development aid then it is understandable why the argument, "waste of finances" is heard from some quarters. A 2006 study in Honduras found that STM teams spent an average of $30,000 (£18,700) on their trips to build one home that a local group could construct for $2,000 (£1,250). Kurt Ver Beek, a professor of sociology at Calvin College who conducted the research said, "To spend $30,000 to paint a church or build a house that costs $2,000 doesn't make a whole lot of sense."[1]

Some would say that money spent on STMs takes essential resources away from traditional mission organisations or diverts funds away from a missionary who was sent out by their local church. This is not true as new money is released and not diverted from other causes. In reality, new funds are created to finance those who go on a STM which otherwise would have been spent on other things: a car, a holiday / vacation, new TV or mobile / cell phone, and without the STM, would never have filtered into the mission field. Research reveals that those who have gone on STMs are more likely to pray more and to give more towards world missions than those who have never gone, so STMs increases the level of financial giving! See Appendix B.

The exception may be if the church finances the STM in its entirety, which personally, I think is unwise, because if it costs the STM-er nothing, they will generally give less of themselves than if it came out of their own wallet, and not appreciate the hard toil (or sacrifices made) in obtaining those funds. There is always a danger that those with an adventurous spirit and those who wish to take a gap year, will always jump at the chance of a STM when the financial responsibility is not with them.

Nobody bats an eyelid when a family from the church flies off to another continent on a two-week holiday – in fact it is deemed quite normal. The holiday of mum (mom), dad and two children over eight years of age would have cost a minimum of £2,000 ($3,200) but could be considerably higher. So is it reasonable to say STMs are a waste of finances whereas they are of Kingdom value and a holiday is not? In fact, this two-week holiday if perpetuated for the year would cost £52,000 ($83,200) or £13,000 ($20,800) per head, so is £4,000-£5,000 ($6,400-8,000) so unreasonable for a committed member of your church to go on a STM for six months or double that amount for a year? The cheapest STM for one year I have come across is £3,000 ($4,800).[2]

There are some who say that the finances used for a STM could be better stewarded to produce a greater harvest in other areas. That may be so, but has your church used that same amount of money and produced a harvest or is it just an untested theory? Perhaps we should look at how much is expended on flowers per week; just £15 ($24) per week is £780 ($1,250) per annum. An Indian pastor informed me that that amount could finance three indigenous workers in India for a year! How many souls are saved within your church building per annum and stay true to the faith within a year? How much did the evangelistic campaign cost (how many months of preparation were involved) and what fruit was born – if any?

A STM is not about statistics, but it is a life changing experience and an *investment* into the Kingdom of God. STMs can lead to long-term fruit in the person who has gone – praying for missions, financially supporting and mission mobilizing (encouraging others and raising awareness).

Thirty years ago, when I was a student, I went on a short-term mission as part of a team – it changed the course of my life! We went to Muslim North Africa, and though I had no knowledge of Islam at that time, and no thought of being a missionary, from the moment we entered North Africa, my heart was captured.

The eyes of the women and the children seemed to hold an appeal, and the first night I slept on African soil (literally, we were camping under the stars), their call echoed loudly in my heart. By the end of the trip, I knew that my future was linked with that nation. Over the next couple of years as I finished my studies, the Lord confirmed his call to me in so many ways. I went on to work in that nation for five years, and am now involved in training people, many of whom go into the Muslim world. G— Wales.

Full-time Missionaries and STMs

Some full-time missionaries say that a team of STM-ers can cause problems, and I don't deny that, but even the Scriptures declare, 'Where no oxen are, the trough is clean, but much increase comes by the strength of an ox' (Proverbs 14:4), and who is to say that these same missionaries have not caused problems? We all make mistakes; it's part of life and let us learn from them!

STM teams reveal the principle of synergism, where the combined power (of two) increases, as opposed to an individual going it alone on the same objective, because 'two are better than one, because they have a good reward for their labour...and a threefold cord is not quickly broken' (Ecclesiastes 4:9-12).

In the 1980s, New Tribes Mission (NTM) began Summit Assist teams where STM teams assist NTM missionaries around the world with major building projects such as building missionary homes, airstrips, water systems and clinics.[3] These STMs are from 3-4 weeks in duration. NTM (UK) wrote: 'One Assist team can accomplish 2,000 hours of physical work. It takes a missionary at least 2,000 hours to learn a tribal language. One team can save career hours of labour that would otherwise take them away from their ministry. Each team has frequent team meetings, which gives both missionaries and the team leader's opportunity to share from the Word and speak of their ministries.'[4]

Leaders must also remember that the missionary you may be working alongside (with your STM team) has their own duties to fulfill and so may not be able to supervise or be present at every meeting. The missionary may have permitted your team to stay at his or her home or have arranged meetings for you out of courtesy, or under obligation to his or her denomination or superiors. This does not make the missionary, your maid, cook, driver or personal assistant. Whilst they are probably delighted with your presence and will assist you as much as they can, respect their home, time, and duties. Don't be a burden, but a blessing!

Sowers, Reaper and Builders

The Bible speaks of sowers, reapers and builders, and in the Kingdom of God we all have our part to play (see Matthew 13:3-9, John 4:37-38, 1 Corinthians 3:3-17 and 2 Corinthians 9:10). David Hill, missionary to China in the nineteenth century, noted that the Sowers field of labour 'is the most extensive,' those who sow the good seed of the Gospel. Reapers, he wrote: 'Seek to gather into one visible body, one elect community,' (the new converts becoming the local church), whilst the Builders are 'elders ordained out of every city, whose province is to build up those gathered into the Church,' (to make strong and healthy disciples).[5]

The apostle Paul wrote: 'I planted, Apollos watered, but God gave the increase. So neither he who plants is anything, nor he who waters, but God who gives the increase. Now he who plants and he who waters are one, and each one will receive his own reward according to his own labour' (1 Corinthians 3:6-8). Thus with different talents, callings and giftings, we work together for the common good of mankind to build the Kingdom of God and be faithful to serve our generation as King David did in his generation (see Acts 13:36).

Globalisation

We live in an age of globalisation whereas in previous centuries; missionaries had to stay in one place for several years to learn the language, to build a home, to till the land and to interact with the people who were as alien to the missionaries as they were to the locals. But in the twenty-first century, you can go to most countries in the world and find English speaking people. At least half the world have access to a mail box or the internet. Therefore, Bibles, Gospels, portions of Scripture, tracts and training materials etc. are available in more than 2,200 languages of the world and so the time needed in one place is very different for a STM-er as opposed to one who had been called to give their entire life to a particular field of service.

STMs in no way replaces the traditional missionary but are often there to assist them in their ministry for a shorter period and to open to the STM-er the world of missions, and sometimes, God's will for their lives. For many full-time missionaries their job function is to establish or plant a local church (translate the Bible etc.), whereas STMs are designed to support local churches and to work in partnership with them.

- 'Why should so few hear the Gospel again and again when so many have never heard it once?' – Oswald J. Smith.
- 'As long as there are millions destitute of the Word of God and knowledge of Jesus Christ, it will be impossible for me to devout my time and energy to those who have both' – J. L. Ewen.

In 1832, Daniel Wheeler (1771-1840) a Quaker, (a Christian sect which used to be Christian!), with a large missionary heart was led of the Holy Spirit to the South Sea Islands in the Pacific. He departed in a Quaker owned ship in 1834 where he would minister from island to island, for up to three months at a time, though it was often just weeks. He ministered in Rio de Janeiro, Tasmania, the Society Islands, Tahiti, Huahine, Raiatea, Tahaa, Bolabola, Eimeo, Hawaii; left the Friendly Isles, onto the Sandwich Isles of which Rarotonga is the largest. From there he sailed to the Hervey Islands; Vavau being the most northerly visited and in 1836, sailed to New South Wales, New Zealand and back into Tazmania and then on to Australia.[6]

More than a hundred years ago, August Diamond who documented the life of Daniel Wheeler wrote: 'A Question is sometimes raised as to the relative usefulness of the continuous work of the resident missionary and the evanescent [tending to vanish like vapour] character of the flying visits of these ambassadors of Christ. But each work has its place; one plants, another waters, the same Divine Master owned the work of the one and sent the other to strengthen, encourage and confirm. The only thing is to be faithful to the call that comes.'[7]

August Diamond also correctly and wisely noted: 'In telling the stories of these Quaker worthies, our desire is not to glorify them or the Society [of Friends] that they loved, but to show that under all circumstances the Gospel of the Lord Jesus Christ is the power of God unto salvation to everyone that believeth, and wherever it is faithfully proclaimed in the power of the Holy Spirit, it finds hearts willing to receive it.'[8]

In the last decade of the nineteenth century, Dr. Griffith John addressing a group of men who were in training for the ministry said, "It is not my habit to say anything to induce young men to devote themselves to this work, for I have a wholesome dread of man-inspired missionaries. But...I thank God...that I am a missionary. I have never regretted that step I took many years ago in opposition to the strongly expressed wish of my best friends; and if there is a sincere desire burning within my breast, it is that I may die in labouring and suffering for Christ among the heathen. Oh, it is a glorious work! I know no work like it, so real, so unselfish, so Christ-like.... The world for Christ! ...Oh young men think of it, dwell upon it and if you hear the voice of God bid you go, manfully take up your cross and go, and you will never cease to thank Jesus Christ our Lord for counting you worthy to be missionaries."[9]

Without Excuse
The Bible explains to us that non-Christians are without excuse because creation is a witness for the existence of God (Romans 1:20-21), but also, there is no excuse for Christians who refuse to share the Good News by their lips and testify by their changed lifestyle. '...How shall they hear without a preacher? And how shall they preach unless they are sent?' (Romans 10:14-15). Will you support STMs (by your money, prayers and your self) as an investment into the Kingdom of God?

Evan Roberts of the Welsh Revival (1904-1905) said, "How shall the heathen [unevangelised] warm himself by the eternal fires of God's love, if we not give the money for the fuel?"[10]

Missionary to India, William Carey said, "If Christ could stoop so low as to visit our...sinful world and be moved with compassion upon the most undeserving and guilty, the most sinful and depraved...in what better way could we demonstrate that we are partakers of His grace than by earnest endeavour to imitate His example...by labouring to promote the salvation of the most ignorant and helpless of mankind?"

Chapter Six

Motives for Going on a Short-Term Mission

'The heart is deceitful above all things, and desperately wicked; who can know it? I, the Lord, search the heart, I test the mind to give every man according to the fruits of his doings' Jeremiah 16:7.

'Every way of a man is right in his own eyes, but the Lord weighs the hearts' Proverbs 21:2.

My Motive for Going on a STM

Be aware of peoples' motives for going on a short-term mission (STM), as they may not be as pure as you think they are – what are they? Be honest and ask yourself these questions. Is it: To feel good, the command of Christ, the call of God, the advice of their pastor or youth leader, frustrations at home, adventure (itchy feet), to look good, the need to help others, to win the lost, to serve, to delay their further education or to put off the inevitable of getting a job etc.?

Jesus condemned the scribes and Pharisees saying, "Woe to you, scribes and Pharisees, hypocrites! For you travel land and sea to win one proselyte [single convert, NIV], and when he is one, you make him twice as much a son of hell as yourselves" (Matthew 23:15). Here were the religious rulers of the day, going on STMs, yet they themselves were not right with God! From the Old Testament: '*I have not sent* these prophets, *yet they ran.* I have not spoken to them, yet they prophesied' (Jeremiah 23:21).

Are they a disciple of the Lord Jesus Christ? Are they "born again" as Jesus said in John 3:3? Have they repented of their sin, forsaken them and put their trust and faith in the finished work of Jesus Christ? – The Son of God and Saviour of the world, who died at Calvary and rose again! See Appendix C.

Some may find it hard to conceive that people go on STMs with ulterior motives, (which may be unbeknown to them), because of the deceitfulness of their own heart, whilst some wilfully join up with a mission agency or organisation, or become part of the church mission team knowing their own deceitfulness. The apostle Paul writing to the Philippians noted both types of people: 'Some indeed preach Christ, even from envy and strife, and some also from good will; the former preach Christ from selfish ambition, not sincerely, supposing to add affliction to my chains; but the latter out of love...' but he was able to declare: '...Whether in pretence or in truth, Christ is preached; and in this I rejoice, yes, and will rejoice' (Philippians 1:15-18).

Paul's few sentences are quite astounding – as long as Christ is being preached, he can rejoice, but for those who have been part of a STM team where you have one or two people who are not truly committed to Christ then they can become quite a problem and the team ultimately suffers.

Rev. Roger Peterson, chairman of the Alliance for Excellence in Short-Term Mission said, "If [STMs] are only about ourselves, then we're doing nothing more than using another culture...to get some benefit at their expense. I don't care what verse of the Bible you read, it's wrong, it's wrong, it's wrong."[1]

> 'All a man's ways seem innocent to him, but motives are weighed by the Lord' Proverbs 16:2, NIV.

Wise Counsel

Godly sound biblical advice alongside wise counsel can be sought from a mature Christian, (your pastor, youth leader, church elder), but well meaning people (who are not in tune with the Spirit of God) can give wrong advice (see Job 12:12 and Job 32:6-10). It reminds me of a young man who turned down an opportunity to join the Royal Navy because his girlfriend did not want him to join – within six months, the relationship had ended and the young man had no career.

- 'Every purpose is established by counsel...' (Proverbs 20:18).
- 'Where there is no counsel, the people fall, but in the multitude of counsellors there is safety' (Proverbs 11:14).
- 'The first one to plead his cause seems right until his neighbour comes and examines him' (Proverbs 18:17).

Why am I Going?

It is important and I cannot overstate the fact, that each individual should know WHY they are considering going on a STM. If you know why you are going and what you will be doing, then your mind will be made up to see the mission through to the end (regardless of the ups and downs and bumps that you may encounter along the way), and your expectations and realisations should be closely matched.

- 'We make a living by what we get, but we make a life by what we give' – Winston Churchill, Prime Minister of Britain.
- 'Changes in my own heart occur as I work to see changes in others. For me, missions teaches me that it's never all about me' – Jill Hekman.

Do Not Fear

Fear is a normal part of life, however some fear is rational and some is unrational. In regards to STMs, worst than fear of the unknown, is the fear of being paralysed into doing nothing and then spending the rest of your life with, "What if?" being run through your mind from one week to the next on a perpetual loop. If you do not go, you will never know, but you will always regret the fact that you allowed the opportunity to pass you by, and the opportunity of a lifetime must be seized during the lifetime of the opportunity. If you don't go – you'll never know!

> 'God has chosen the foolish things of the world to put to shame the wise, and God has chosen the weak things of the world to put to shame the things which are mighty; and the base things of the world and the things which are despised God has chosen and the things which are not, to bring to nothing the things that are, that no flesh should glory in His presence' 1 Corinthians 1:27-29.

The Bottom Line

STMs are life-changing experiences (as well as character building), because not only the hearer or receiver is blessed, but the giver as well. A STM will broaden one's horizons, will open our eyes to see how the other half live and how well-off we really are. A STM can be an adventure or time out between studies (or a job) and hopefully those that go, will go with the right motives and the right heart. It is always better to do something for the Lord than to spend your holiday time (and or money) on a two week beach vacation, which could have been better invested (for all concerned) towards a STM.

The person concerned, may only ever go on one STM, but they will never forget the experience. Who is to say that they will not be more active in home evangelism, raising mission support for those on the field (both financially and in prayer), encouraging other members of their church to 'go,' and become intercessors for the nations?

A missionary wrote: 'Today Christ stands before us and says to you and me, "Lovest thou Me?" What shall be our answer? Let us answer Him truly, for love is the condition of service, and service is the evidence of love. How much do you love Him? As much as you serve Him, as much as you give of yourself, your substance, and your service, no more.'

David Livingstone in the first few years of his ministry in Africa, (1840s), wrote: 'I feel the necessity more than ever of active devotedness to the Redeemer's cause. I don't feel anything we usually call sacrifices at home to be such. There is so much to counter balance them that they really don't deserve the name, and I am in a great deal more danger from levity [an inappropriate lack of seriousness] than from melancholy [a constitutional tendency to be gloomy and depressed]; indeed it sometimes makes me blame myself severely. When contemplating the mission field before I left England, I used to think my spirits would flag, but I feel no difference from what I felt at home. It is therefore no virtue in me to endure privations; it is only in those who feel them as such. I wish my mind were deeply affected by the conditions of those who are perishing in the heathen land. I am sorry to say that I don't feel half concerned for them as I ought.'[2]

I went on a two week STM because the lecturer of my missions class encouraged me to go. I was in my last year of college and he knew that it was now or never. I am so glad I went. Cheng-hee – Korea.

The RIGHT reasons to GO: A prayer of King Asa, "…O Lord our God, for *we rest on You*, and *in Your name we go* against this multitude. O Lord, You are our God; do not let man prevail against You!" (2 Chronicles 14:11). 'Let us hear the conclusion of the matter: Fear God and keep His commandments, for this is the whole duty of man' (Ecclesiastes 12:13) and Jesus said, "Go into all the world and preach the Gospel to every creature" (Mark 16:15).

Chapter Seven

Types of Mission Work
Preaching and Humanitarian

Jesus said, "Go into all the world and preach the Gospel to every creature..." "That repentance and remission of sins should be preached in His name to all nations..." Mark 16:15 and Luke 24:47.

Jesus said, "In as much as you did it to one of the least of these My brethren you did it to Me" Matthew 25:35-46.

The Length, Breadth and Depth of STMs

The world of short-term missions (STMs) is as long as it is wide and deep, with hundreds of organisations offering thousands of opportunities in a multitude of destinations in a large variety of capacities. You could go to the cold Siberian outback, a Middle East inferno, a mosquito infested valley in Africa, to the poor of South East Asia, into an European polluted back alley, an Islamic stronghold (or Communist nation); ministering amongst the multitudes in South America (or the materialistic masses of affluent North America); the high altitudes of the Himalayas' (in India or Tibet) or on a tropical island in the Pacific Islands of Oceania.[1] So, what can I do on a STM?

- Preach the Gospel – sharing the Good News about Jesus Christ.
- Humanitarian Aid – helping people with their immediate needs.
- Development Aid – assisting humankind in areas of development.
- Prayer Team – praying around locations and with individuals.
- Any combination of the above four.

Preach the Gospel

The primary concern of the Great Commission is to proclaim the Good News, which can split into many directions as part of evangelism, church planting and building up the body of Christ (teaching) etc. It is based on the commands of Jesus Christ:

- "Go therefore and make disciples of all nations...teaching them to observe all things I have commanded you..." (Matthew 28:18-20).
- "Go into all the world and preach the Gospel to every creature..." (Mark 16:15).
- "That repentance and remission of sins should be preached in His name to all nations..." (Luke 24:47).
- "As the Father has sent Me, I also send you..." (John 20:21-23).
- "You shall receive power when the Holy Spirit has come upon you and you shall be witnesses to Me in Jerusalem and in all Judea and Samaria and to the end of the earth" (Acts 1:8).

Humanitarian Aid

Humanitarian aid is concerned with the interests and welfare of humans – helping those who are in immediate need. It is material or logistical assistance provided for humanitarian purposes, typically in response to a humanitarian crisis. The primary objective of humanitarian aid is to save lives, alleviate suffering and maintain human dignity. Christians should support Christian humanitarian organisations that honour the Lord Jesus Christ; not secular organisation that reject His Word and His complete healing of mind, soul and body. See Chapter Forty-Four, The Love of Christ in Action. Humanitarian aid in a Christian context can consist of feeding the poor, clothing the naked, housing people, visiting those in prison, looking after widows and orphans (food, clothes and other support), giving education etc. It is based on Jesus' teaching of:

- Feeding the poor, giving water to those that thirst, clothing the naked and visiting those in prison. "In as much as you did it to one of the least of these My brethren you did it to Me" (Matthew 25:35-46).
- Medical missions became popular in the beginning of the nineteenth century. Often it is the only way into sensitive countries or into closed hearts and in many places still is. "They will lay hands on the sick and they will recover" (Mark 16:18).
- Education and feeding programmes. Jesus taught the people and fed the five and four thousand. In the case of

the five thousand, Jesus, upon being told by His disciples to send the people away (to get provisions) said, "You give them something to eat" (Luke 9:12-17).

- Visiting and assisting others. 'Pure and undefiled religion before God and the Father is this: to visit orphans and widows in their trouble, and to keep oneself unspotted from the world' (James 1:27).
- Love in action. 'But whoever has this world's goods and sees his brother in need, and shuts up his heart from him; how does the love of God abide in him? ...Let us not love in word or in tongue, but in deed and in truth' (1 John 3:17-18). This last verse is directed towards the family of God, assisting the brethren in their time of need, but still reiterates the biblical principle of love in action, which is universal to anyone. 'If your enemy is hungry, give him bread to eat and if he is thirsty, give him water to drink' (Proverbs 25:21). See also Matthew 5:44 and Matthew 19:19.

I help feed orphan children in one of the most closed countries of the world. Even though we are a humanitarian organisation, there are so many places that we are not permitted to visit. At an orphanage, one boy who looked five years old was actually nine. He was suffering from third degree malnutrition. Anonymous – North Korea.

Major Types of Humanitarian and Development Aid
- Education – teaching English (or other subjects) at a school.
- Working with children – orphanages or those with disabilities.
- Building Programmes – homes, community centres and school projects.
- Feeding Programmes – feeding (and clothing) the poor and needy.
- Hydration – sinking boreholes and making water wells.
- Medical Work – health clinics, dentists, surgery and family advice etc.
- Agricultural – improved farming techniques (training and equipment), better tools, seeds, poultry or cattle etc. which empowers citizens to become self-sustaining and can even grow into a local business employing people.

- Mechanical Maintenance – maintenance of vehicles, boats, ships and buildings etc.
- Sport Programmes – training, coaching and providing sports equipment to poor nations.
- Prison Ministry – visiting prisoners, friendship, helping to rehabilitate them and assisting their reintegration back into the community.

Development Aid

Jesus' words have also been used to inspire development aid (also known as development or technical assistance, international aid or foreign aid), which can include (building programmes, education, agricultural techniques etc.), and is a long-term solution. It addresses the underlying socio-economic factors (the study of the relationship between economic activity and social life), which may have led to a crisis or emergency. Jesus said, "In as much as you did it to one of the least of these... you did it to Me" (Matthew 25:40).

- Nehemiah led a large group of Jews back to Jerusalem where they rebuilt the city walls and the city itself. It was a massive project to undertake, but like Moses and the building of the tabernacle, it involved teamwork, where everybody sacrificed something, resources, materials and time to complete the job. 'So we built the wall, and the entire wall was joined together up to half its height, for the people had a mind to work' (Nehemiah 4:5).

Hand-Up Versus Hand-Outs

Humanitarian or development aid should involve giving someone a hand-up, rather than just a hand-out, though in times of famine and war, a hand-out is the only way. Lao Tzu said, "Give a man a fish and you feed him for a day, teach a man how to fish and you feed him for a lifetime." A hand-up could include: sheep, cattle, chickens, agricultural implements, seeds, or improved farming techniques, so that livestock can be raised, the land can be tilled effectively and families (or even communities) will become self-sustaining.

- 'Much food is in the fallow ground of the poor...' (Proverbs 13:23a).

Both Isaiah 2:4 and Micah 4:3 are in the context of the millennial reign of Christ, and speaks about people beating their swords into ploughshares and their spears into pruning hooks and that nations will not learn the art of warfare. Civil wars, armed conflict, alongside poor government policies, often reveal the desperate straits of citizens when these events ravage a nation. Government finances are spent on armaments and it is always the citizens that suffer; due to lack of agriculture implements, no seeds, bombed fields and fear of the enemy that drives them into hiding, resulting in little to no harvest and great distress, turmoil and extreme desperation.

See also Chapters Forty-Four and Forty-Five, The Love of Christ in Action and Giving to the Poor and Needy.

'Now may He who supplies seed to the sower, and bread for food, supply and multiply the seed you have sown and increase the fruits of your righteousness' 2 Corinthians 9:10.

Anne-Geri´ Fann and Greg Taylor in *How to Get Ready for Short-Term Missions* wrote: 'You must seriously consider that humanitarian work is not necessarily mission work. A hungry child with hollow eyes is evidence of Satan's hold on the world. Why? Because sin set into motion many selfish, corrupt systems that contribute to that hunger. The fact that this child's belly is full does not necessarily loosen Satan's grip. And although "seeds are being sown," you must consider whether you are truly *planting something substantial* or just tossing seeds on the ground and waiting for them to produce.'[2]

A Cooperative or a Lending Bank

Development aid can be in the form of a cooperative or a lending bank, though this is generally not associated with STMs as these forms of aid or assistance continue over years or decades, giving small loans or "gifts" to those who wish to start up a small business to assist them or their community.

- 'He who has pity on the poor lends to the Lord and He will pay back what he has given' (Proverbs 19:17).
- 'The righteous considers the cause of the poor...' (Proverbs 29:7a).

Widows and Orphans

Christian aid and love for mankind also incorporates God's love and concern for widows and orphans (see Exodus 22:22 and Psalm 68:5). In some cultures, it is the man's responsibility (or the only person who is permitted), to provide for his household and when he is absent, economic problems and hardships can exist for the remainder of the family.

- 'Defend the poor and the fatherless; do justice to the afflicted and needy. Deliver the poor and needy; free them from the hand of the wicked' (Psalm 83:3-4).
- 'Pure and undefiled religion before God and the Father is this: to visit orphans and widows in their trouble...' (James 1:27).
- 1 Timothy 5:3-16 relates how the Church, the body of Christ should look after and care for widows. 'Honour widows who are really widows' (v3), 'and do not let the Church be burdened, that it may relieve those who are really widows' (v16).

Prayer Team

A prayer team or an intercessory prayer team is a group of Christians, often from the same church, who go to specific places to pray and intercede. Sometimes they work alongside missionaries whilst at other times, they go and 'spy-out the land' praying on stony and hard soil to try and soften the ground before a STM team arrives. This ministry of prayer and intercession can either be an underrated or an overrated ministry with some team members knowing what they are doing, whilst others have not got a clue, yet think they do! This ministry is based on the principles of intercession and of pulling down spiritual strongholds with our spiritual weapons – doing spiritual warfare is Holy Spirit led prayer, which is known as intercession, standing in the gap. Biblical characters such as Abraham, Moses, Jeremiah, Isaiah, Ezekiel, Daniel, Hosea, Jesus and the apostle Paul were all intercessors alongside many others. See Appendix D for Scriptures and principles on prayer and intercession.

When I was in China on a mission, I felt led to go onto the 'Roof of the World' and intercede as directed by the Lord. I came under intense spiritual attack from the demonic spiritual forces (who knew I was no tourist) as I prayed round the Buddhist shrines as directed by the Holy Spirit. I had diarrhoea (diarrhea) for the next three days, but my mission was accomplished. Qday – Tibet.

Chapter Eight

Duration, Destination and Timing

Jesus said, "You shall receive power when the Holy Spirit has come upon you; and you shall be witnesses to Me in Jerusalem, and in Judea and Samaria, and to the end of the earth" Acts 1:8.

'...So it was that for a whole year they assembled with the church and taught a great many people. And the disciples were first called Christians at Antioch' Acts 11:26.

Right Place – Right Time
You may have heard the call to go on your short-term mission (STM), but you also need to be in the right place at the right time. Like Isaiah, you may be able to say, "Here I am! Send me" (Isaiah 6:8) – but may not have the faintest idea where to go, with whom, or know the duration of the STM, but with some basic research and waiting upon God in prayer, the will of the Lord will be revealed and He can give you perfect peace about the entire situation. Some factors to consider are:

Go with Whom?
- Mission Organisation – a specialist in STMs.
- Part of a church mission – youth group or a team of varied ages.
- Independent STM – with friend(s) or church associate(s).

Work in Association and Have Objectives
With all of the above options, you may work in association with a local church or ministry, orphanage, school, building programme or a missionary. If you are a leader then your team can either go on a STM with some defined objectives of: preaching the Good News, distribution of Christian literature, some form of humanitarian or development aid or any combination. You may work with a host church or missionary from within the country you are going to.

If there is just two or more of you on your STM (who are not part of a mission organisation) then you may have no fixed-in-concrete plans and be entirely led of the Holy Spirit as an independent STM team. As you travel, you pray for Divine appointments and see what happens as you move from one place to the next, moving across a district, country (like Jesus and His disciples) or countries.

In sensitive countries where evangelising is illegal then it is unwise to associate with a "missionary" as you may blow their cover and more often than not, they will want no contact with independent STM-ers. Some teams take in Christian literature and discreetly distribute them or act as an unofficial postal service!

Style of Your Mission
- One fixed location.
- Several locations within one country.
- Multiple towns across one country.
- From country to country.
- Multiple countries – even across a continent.

Duration of Your Mission and the Timing
- Weeks, months or a year or more.
- The time of year to go, there is big difference between summer and winter and the dry and rainy seasons. These factors are irrelevant if you are spending a year in one place, but if it is from weeks to just a few months then it can be a large contributing factor to help hone the decision and to eliminate certain places or times of the year.
- If you are going to sensitive areas, (especially for independent STM-ers) be aware that different religions celebrate their own feasts, festivals and holidays with their various rituals, which can heighten their emotional excitements and possibly be a threat to you.

Characters from the Holy Bible
If you are joining a mission organisation for your STM then all the above factors will have already been considered, noted and worked into their programme. The duration of your mission can vary widely, but let's look at some of the characters from the Bible and the length of their missions. The prophet Jonah's actual ministry at Nineveh (in Assyria) lasted just a few days, though he waited forty days to see God's judgment fall. It did not

and the mission was a success, though not in Jonah's eyes! (Jonah chapters 3-4).

Jesus' ministry lasted three years, but his legacy will last through eternity. The apostle Paul 'spent some time' (perhaps weeks) in Antioch (Acts 18:23), he stayed three months in Greece (Acts 20:2-3), eighteen months in Corinth (Acts 18:11), more than two years in Asia Minor (Acts 19:8-10) – which included three months in Ephesus (Acts 19:1-8) and two years at the School of Tyrannus (Acts 19:9-10). Due to a shipwreck Paul spent three months on the Island of Malta (Acts 28:1-11) and for two years he was under house arrest at Rome, and so people came to him for teaching (Acts 28:30).

See also Chapters Eleven and Twelve, The Short-Term Mission Team and Picking a Mission Team.

The Time of Your Mission

For many American Christians, two weeks is a good slot for their STM because of their vacation time and this often increases by a week for Christians within the UK. If you are a student, in between college or university then this period is extended and for some, can be a gap year.

With many mission organisations the length of their missions vary, but one, three or six months is quite standard as is the longer STM of one or two years, though many organisation have STMs of just two to three weeks; whilst your local church (or you and your friends) can tailor-make a mission. Staying in one fixed location for a fixed period is easier than moving from place to place during the same amount of time. Being away from home during a special season, depending on your family ties and traditions can be very hard and unsettling such as Christmas, Thanksgiving and special anniversary dates or birthdays.

The length and time of your mission can be determined by many factors:
- Holiday / vacation – How long is my time off from work?
- Term-time – school / college / university, when are they closed and for how long?
- National holidays – the locals go away, shops shut, for some locals it is family time and not a time for strangers, or a time for attending meetings or discussing spiritual matters which are unrelated to their own beliefs.

- High or low season – costs increase in the high season (at peak demand) and accommodation costs varies with supply and demand.
- Weather and climate – (summer, winter, dry or wet season?). Problems arise when the ministry is outside or during the agricultural seasons in rural areas when people work from dawn to dusk and beyond! Poor or hard weather will keep people off the streets (or public places) and away from special Christian meetings.
- The invitation – when (or if) you are invited to work with the local host church, mission or missionary. They may want your assistance in the summer months, but if you are not accustomed to extreme heat, you will fatigue quickly.
- Family considerations – will you, your parents, spouse or child need certain medical help at designated times of the year? Is it available or too expensive as compared with the British free NHS treatment? The quality and training of dentists, doctors and nurses etc. are not the same the world over and the levels of hygiene and equipment in hospitals or even doctors surgeries vary greatly.
- Special seasons – Christmas, Thanksgiving, Easter, Ramadan, Yom Kippur (though only one day), other religious festivals, special anniversary dates and national holidays – from your own country or to where you are going can hinder, disrupt, or enhance your mission plans. Flights are booked well in advance.

The World's Calendars

The world does not have a unified calendar which means that the calendar date, the time of day and year can all be measured differently depending on the country you are in.

I was in Ethiopia in 2008, where they were just celebrating the millennium – the year 2000! This is because they still use the Julian Calendar and not the Gregorian Calendar (the solar calendar), which was introduced by Gregory XIII in 1582 to correct an error in the Julian calendar by suppressing 10 days (and alterations in leap years) and was adopted by Great Britain and the American colonies in 1752. For Ethiopia, it also meant that their months were out of alignment with the rest of Europe, the Americas and many other countries.

The Islamic year differs from that of the Western world – ours begin from the birth of Christ Anno Domini (the year of our Lord) whilst the Islamic Calendar began in AD 622, (the year of the Hegira); the beginning of the Muslim year retrogresses through the solar year completing the cycle every 32 years. Jewish and Islamic dates begin at sunset and the dates of Islamic festivals and fasts are determined by an actual sighting of the appropriate new moon, thus they vary from one year to the next.

By October 2016, (from 1 January to 3 October) the calendars of the world were as follows: Roman (AUC), 2769; Nabonassar, 2765; Japanese, 2676; Grecian (Seleucidæ), 2328; Indian (Saka), 1938; Diocletian, 1733. The Jewish New Year (Rosh Hashanaha) was on 3 October 5777, with the Islamic New Year on 3 October 1438.

Time and Months

Crossing from one country to the next (or between states or districts) can change time zones. Greenwich Mean Time (GMT) is the standardised world time zone which is calculated as a plus (+) or minus (–) 1 hour from London, England.

British Summer Time (BST) starts on the last Sunday in March and ends on the last Sunday in October, at 1:00am GMT. In spring, the clocks go forward, losing an hour at 1:00am GMT, the UK moves to 2:00am BST. In autumn, the clocks go back, giving an extra hour at 2:00am BST, the UK moves to 1:00am GMT.[1]

In some countries, the day begins at sunrise and not at one second past midnight as in the West. In Ethiopia, there is a six-hour time difference so that five o'clock is eleven o'clock and if your bus departs at 12:00am (not midnight) it is actually 6:00am in the morning, which is the normal departure time for Ethiopian buses!

Beware of booking accommodation by using only numerals 6/08/16 as it could mean the sixth of August 2016 or the eighth of June 2016 as there is a difference between the day and the month between some countries – notably the UK and the USA. Always write the month in letters and not numerals to avoid confusion and an embarrassing situation as you may turn up at your booked accommodation late (and lose your deposit) or early (and find no rooms available)!

Questions to Ask Yourself

To aid discernment, in prayerfully choosing where to go, whilst narrowing down the options ask yourself the following questions:

- What languages can I speak? Do I need to speak a certain language if I am to go to —? It is not always necessary (though very helpful) to know the language, but if you speak English, Spanish or French then there are many countries open for you. See Appendix E.
- What can I do and what specific skills do I have? There is no point in trying to do medical work if you are not trained in this area and could not take the time to do a First Aid course!
- What is the neediest place? The world is needy, but where would you best be suited?
- Where can I go and be effective – where is the harvest? Jesus said we should pray for more labourers to be sent out into the harvest and that the fields are white unto harvest (see Matthew 9:37-38 and John 4:35-38).
- What time commitment are you able to give for your mission? Two weeks, a month, three months, six months or a year or two?
- Can I cope with the climate? Most countries are seasonal. Will I cope in the tropics or freeze in snow clad areas? What about altitude or if I am based near volcanic ash – asthmatics beware!
- Do I have poor health? It can be dangerous to go to some countries where medical aid is much to be desired and the hospital could be several days drive away.
- Finances – how much savings do I have – can I use them? Or can I get enough money for the STM?

The Cost

It is not fair to consider a STM which costs *£13,000 ($20,800) for a year if you expect your small church to finance you (when not even the pastor gets a wage), and especially if you have no savings of your own. However, faith should determine your venture and not your finances as God does not discriminate, He pays His own bills and where He guides He does provide! *This is the most expensive STM of one year's duration I have come across. Most STMs of one year will be less than half that amount (depending on the location), though there is one UK STM which only costs £3,000 ($4,800) per annum (2009/10). See also Chapters Sixteen and Seventeen, How much Money will I need? And The Independent STM-er Budget.

Chapter Nine

Mission Organisation, Church or Independent STM-er?

'I planted, Apollos watered, but God gave the increase. So neither he who plants is anything, nor he who waters, but God who gives the increase. Now he who plants and he who waters are one, and each one will receive his own reward according to his own labour' 1 Corinthians 3:6-8.

'The fruit of the righteous is a tree of life and he who wins souls is wise' Proverbs 11:30.

Choosing a Mission Organisation / Agency

If you are going on a short-term mission (STM), you are going as a helper to serve others. Regardless of whom you go with (a mission organisation, your church, or an independent STM – with two or more of you), the mission must not be confused with an all-inclusive holiday – or a vacation, because you are going to work for the Lord.

Most STM organisations, where each mission exceeds several months will have an orientation programme, a week or two of training (or even longer) where you can meet other members of your team and receive some basic training before you depart. The more you learn before you depart, the easier it will be when you arrive. For other organisations, there may be a brief programme on your arrival, perhaps just a few hours.

Mission organisations serve in different countries and each has its weak and strong points. Some are more experienced than others and the costs vary considerably; especially in regard to duration and location. All of these factors need to be taken into consideration. MissionsNow.co.uk under its 'Mission Links' page has numerous mission organisations and their opportunities and lists agencies which fit people (of varying ages and giftings / talents / skills) with various organisations working across the world with STMs ranging from two weeks to two years.

One mission organisation that I looked at listed more than one hundred opportunities in twenty-three countries on four different continents.[1] Another mission agency in their 2009 short-term service directory listed their STMs, gap year placements and career breaks under the headings of: Church related, communication / media, development, education, medical, practical and technical, social action, support ministries and others, with hundreds of positions waiting to be filled.[2]

'The steps of a good man are ordered by the Lord, and He delights in his way' Psalm 37:23.

A Common Vision and Beliefs

It is important that you share the same vision as the organisation that you intend to work with – what is their mission statement? You (or they) may hold a particular theological bias which will cause contentions and some things which you believe in (and experienced), they may deny – i.e. gifts of the Holy Spirit for today (1 Corinthians 12). They may not permit a woman to preach and you want to, though in some cultures, it is not permissible for a woman to preach to a mixed congregation. On the other hand, you may not want to preach (or share your testimony) and it may be required!

If you have an evangelistic gift and frown on the social gospel (where only good deeds are performed without sharing the Good News), then some organisations are not for you. On the other hand, most organisations will not be holding evangelistic meetings night after night to thousands or even hundreds (be realistic in your expectations of your mission), whereas some will expect everyone, on at least one occasion to share their testimony at a church or other meeting and this is nothing to be afraid of.

Other issues may evolve around: what you can or cannot wear (revealing clothing or no trousers {pants} for women), the time you begin in the morning, lights out (bed time!), relationships with the opposite sex, your general appearance (hair length, piercing, tattoos etc.) or headscarves for women (often in Islamic countries); things you need to bring (or are not permitted to); no mixed swimming, modest bathing costumes (men and women) and being accountable to the leadership team. There are many other rules that may apply to the mission organisation / agency you are considering.

Will the mission organisations look after you – what is their code of practice / conduct? Any company or organisation with a product will not downplay what is on offer, but mission agencies should show integrity in how they publish their opportunities and in what they offer. Inevitably, any organisation will make mistakes, but ideally, they will learn from them, improve or correct certain features for future STM-ers, otherwise the organisation will get a bad name and it will not survive. At other times, there are circumstances beyond their control, which affect STMs such as natural disasters, wars and terrorist attacks. There is also equipment failure (break down of vehicles or the boiler) and all these events, alter the best of plans, which may delay departure from one place to another, close a door to certain areas of a country, or keep you out of the shower!

'Your Word is a lamp to my feet and a light to my path' Psalm 119:105.

Gail C. Bennett in relating how to link with a mission agency wrote: 'Mission agencies with short-term programmes want to locate personnel as much as you want to find an appropriate agency.' Bennett correctly stated that well-thought-through questions should be put to the agencies, under the four headings: Theology (what do they believe?), Ministry Philosophy (what is their emphasis?), Goals and Objectives (what will they have you to do and how do they expect you to benefit from them?), and Ministry Environment (where do they work?).

Under Ministry Philosophy, Bennett wrote: 'What's their emphasis: evangelism, nurture or service? Does their approach to ministry emphasise flexibility and spontaneity, or stability and structured objectives? Are they people-orientated (evangelising, nurturing, or serving people through a variety of programmes) or task-oriented (specialists in radio broadcasting, literature production etc.)? How do they view the role of men and women in ministry? Could you see yourself fitting into an agency with their philosophy?'[3]

The Small Print

Do thorough research before you decide to join any mission organisation on a STM and pray for wisdom, discernment and guidance: that God will show you where He wants you in whatever country or district, with what organisation and when. Look at their website and read all their pages if you are serious about joining a STM team; especially the frequently asked questions (FAQ) page. Ask them to send you some literature. Do they have an open day near you? Ask questions via email or phone (have your questions written down). Do you know of anyone else who has been with them – what was their experience like?

If you are going with a mission organisation or church then they will tell you the exact price of the mission and what it covers, and just as importantly, what it does not cover. Often excursions for days off are optional and some organisations do allow their "workers" weekends off in which they may not be permitted to leave the area. As with all things, it is always better to find out what is expected and what is not permitted before you sign on the dotted line and pay your deposit. Read the small print!

Whatever you feel called of God to do, you must have a high level of confidence in the mission organisation that you are going to join for your STM. Pray for God's guidance and perfect will for your STM.

> Before I signed up with a mission organisation I was assured that many people of my own age would be there. When I arrived, everybody apart from myself was just out of school and because of the age gap, it was difficult to connect. We had to ask permission every time we left the compound; the leaders were younger than me and we were not permitted to go out on our own. James – Africa.

Going with your Church

Many larger churches (especially in the States) have regular STMs to various parts of the world where they link up with local churches or organisations and annually or biannually renew friendships, and minister within another country, state or county.

There are many advantages of going on a STM with your church; you know the people you are travelling with, you hold common beliefs and you trust the ones you are going with. On the other hand, it might be your church's first STM, so expect the unexpected and your 'leader' may not know what he or she is doing, but life is a learning curve and we do learn from our mistakes and those of others. Sometimes the pastor or youth leader will join the STM team but another person is the designated leader, simply because he or she has the experience in this area.

Maybe you are considering taking a team on a STM and have never been yourself. If so, start small and embrace the opportunity to help enrich the lives of others – those to whom you will serve, and for every member of the team (including yourself) as you learn in the college of life.

I spent a year in an African country teaching English, but I was the one who received an education! The culture, customs, accommodation, the people and the food was all an experience for me. The usual staple diet of matooke, rice, beans, posho, cassava, chapattis, tomatoes, onions, green peppers, grasshoppers and ants were common. Those who had a little more money could afford beef, but chicken, turkey and pork can be quite expensive. You usually have to kill it yourself though!
Russell – Uganda.

Independent STMs

Jesus led independent STMs as He and His disciples travelled from one town to the next proclaiming the Kingdom of God, calling people to repent, healing people of physical and spiritual infirmities (deliverance from demons), and teaching them about the things of God. 'Jesus went through all the cities and villages, teaching in their synagogues, preaching the Gospel of the Kingdom and healing every sickness and every disease among the people' (Matthew 9:35). Jesus was not the first independent STM-er as the Old Testament prophets went from place to place declaring the Word of the Lord and Jonah reluctantly went on a cross-cultural mission to Nineveh, to a people group from another nation.

The apostle Paul (also known as Saul) was another great example of an independent STM-er who travelled to multiple destinations on his mission trips, with different helpers, staying varying lengths of time in one place to the next, depending on the reception he got. He did receive death threats and was let down in a basket from the wall of Damascus so he could escape (Acts 9:25 and 2 Corinthians 11:13). His preaching and that of his friends and associates often caused riots and he was also arrested, expelled from a region or stoned for disturbing the peace (Acts 13:50, Acts 14:5, Acts 14:19 and Acts 17:13). It is very unlikely that your STM will be as extreme as Paul's!

At other times, Paul was generally unhindered for periods of time and stayed in one place (3 months – Acts 20:3), or for more than a year (18 months, Acts 18:11, and 2 years, Acts 19:10), and taught particular groups or built up a local church which he had founded. In some locations, he 'spent some time' (perhaps weeks – Acts 18:23). When he was a prisoner and shipwrecked on the Island of Malta by Divine providence, he spent three months doing the work of the Lord (Acts 28:1-11).

A large number of the STMs I have been involved with have consisted of travelling to multiple locations within a country or across several countries. The exception has been in mainland Europe, where to minimise costs, I have stayed in the same city or town and the duration of the STMs have always been shorter.

Most organised mission agencies and ministries will generally stay in one location or will move to a different town or city just once or twice within the year. The latter approach will broaden the STM-er's horizon, bring added experience and will reveal the different needs amongst those to whom they are serving. The former helps people to concentrate all their efforts in a singular place, making it easier to see the 'fruit' of one's labour. In the free enrolment in the college of life, we should all be students, ready and eager to learn from others.

The independent STM-er will encounter many more incidences that are varied and encounter more problems than one who only stays in a single location. The Christian centre, mission compound or the local hotel may be great; but the monotony of an isolated location can also bring about its own problems, especially when team members have fallen out or if there is no place for privacy.

'Deliver those who are drawn towards death, and hold back those stumbling to the slaughter. If you say, "Surely we did not know this," does not He who weighs the heart consider it? He who keeps your soul, does He not know it? And will He not render to each man according to his deeds?' Proverbs 24:11-12.

Sir Henry Edwards said, "He who has to act on his own responsibility is a slave if he does not act on his own judgment." William G. Blaikie noted: 'Acting on this maxim, he must set aside the views of others as to his duty, provided his own judgment was clear regarding it. He must even set aside the feelings and apparent interests of those dearest to him, because duty was above everything else. His faith in God convinced him that, in the long run, it could never be worse for him and that he had firmly done his duty.'[4]

Chapter Ten

The Will of the Lord / God's Guidance

'Trust in the Lord with all your heart and lean not on your own understanding; in all your ways acknowledge Him and He will direct your paths' Proverbs 3:5-6.

'The entrance of Your Words gives light; it gives understanding to the simple' Psalm 119:130.

What is the Will of God?

From a human perspective, we have looked at various things to consider in the previous chapters and whilst we can whittle out certain destinations or times of the year, eliminate some mission organisations or agencies and weigh certain factors into the equation, we have to be in the will of the Lord. If we go outside of the will of the Lord then we will not be able to get the maximum benefit for our limited time on our STM.

The world is a needy place and the fields are white unto harvest, but most people can only work in one field (Matthew 9:38 and John 4:35). The question is, "What is the field of labour for my STM?" The need of an area does not constitute a call for you to go there and minister, though it may be a deciding factor, as Cyrano De Words-u-lac noted: 'If two roads from one unravel take the one less travelled.'

We can do many things for God without Him, and He may even bless it, but when we do what He says, then He will anoint us for the task to bear fruit for His glory (see John 15:7-8). There is a big difference between God's blessing and God's anointing, which was seen, in Chapter Four, My Call or God's Call? Compare Acts 16:6-10 with Acts 19:10.

God can speak to you in many ways: He may directly say, "Go to ——," the Lord may burden your heart, or open your eyes to the needs of a certain people group or ministry job. God may impress upon you a certain mission organisation or your church may invite you to join the team (they may ask you to lead it) and you have the peace of God that it is His will. You may have the skills that fill a gap in a team or a natural disaster occurs and

- 57 -

you want to go and assist in immediate humanitarian or development aid.

God's Guidance

In *Discipleship For Everyday Living* I dedicate four chapters to finding God's will and knowing the way to fulfil it, in answer to the call of God to service and the following (within this chapter), is a brief summary of the main points.

God has promised to guide the believer, but there are conditions that need to be met (see Psalm 25:9, Psalm 32:8-9, Proverbs 28:9, Isaiah 42:6 and John 16:13), but they always revolve around obedience to God! If you are already in a job or studies, do not leave or quit unless you know it to be the will of God and it probably isn't. Take godly advice from your family, pastor and friends; sometimes a desire can be wishful thinking, or the devil, trying to confuse you over the timing and destination of your STM. Pray for God's perfect and pleasing will to be revealed.

My parents wanted to go on a STM within the UK. They are both in their late 50s, have many practical giftings and their English is OK. I emailed a Christian worker and asked him if he knew of any Christian organisation that wanted a 'handyman' and a 'general helper.' He referred me to a website, which listed numerous agencies and mission organisation, and three months later my parents found the right place for them. Els – Netherlands.

How God May Speak to You

- Through the Scriptures, His Word the Holy Bible.
- The Holy Spirit's still small voice (1 Kings 19:9-18, John 14:26, Acts 10:19, Acts 13:2 and Romans 8:16).
- Your inner witness (conscience) (Acts 15:28 and 1 John 3:20-21).
- Through nature and inanimate objects, e.g. the television, magazine, a book etc., something just sticks out (and it witnesses to your spirit). It captures your complete attention – a word, picture or verse of Scripture.
- Through Christians, by means of the gifts of the Holy Spirit, a word of wisdom, a word of knowledge or a prophecy (Jeremiah chapter 42 and 1 Corinthians chapters 12-14). If you receive a word from God via

another believer then weigh it and pray it. Test the spirits whether they are of God or not (1 Thessalonians 5:19-21 and 1 John 4:1-3). If you are not sure then ask God for confirmation (1 Corinthians 14:26 and 2 Corinthians 13:1b).

- By a dream, vision or trance (Genesis 41:8, 15-16 and Acts 10:16).
- Audibly like another person speaks (Exodus 3:4 and Exodus 33:11), this is not common.
- Through non-Christians, being rebuked, "Christians shouldn't do that!" Hopefully this is uncommon!

Abiding in God – Listening

Hearing God is sometimes only possible when you have taken, or are forced to take times of quietness, though we should all have a quiet time before God, when after our Bible reading and prayer, we stay quiet and focus on God and allow Him to speak to us. If you continually seek God's presence you will understand His will for your life and the how and where of your STM will also be revealed. Prayer and abiding in the Father's will is essential for discerning what He wants to reveal to you (see John 15:1-11, Acts 2:42 and 1 John 2:3-6). It is not just being able to hear God's voice that is important – so is obedience! See James 1:22.[1]

The Holy Spirit speaks lovingly, reassuringly and encourages. He will guide you into all truth (John 16:13), whilst the devil accuses, nags and speaks in a mocking manner. The devil will try to confuse you with regard to God's will by sowing doubt, fear and discouragement into your mind, "Has indeed God said?" (Genesis 3:1) – after all, he does not want you to go on your STM, as you will be invading his territory!

Checks from God

- The Holy Spirit may forbid you (Acts 16:5-10 and 19:10).
- Lack of opportunity (doors open or close) – the steps and stops of the Lord (1 Corinthians 16:8-9, Colossians 4:3 and Revelation 3:8, but in 2 Corinthians 2:12-13), even though a door had opened for Paul in Troas, he had no peace.
- Lack of peace (Colossians 3:15).
- Lack of a direct word from God (a rhema word) (Psalm 119:105 and Isaiah 30:1-2, 21).

- If you have the mind of Christ then the correct fruit and attitude will be manifested within your spirit (1 Corinthians 2:16 and Galatians 5:22-23). Do you have joy or peace about a given decision or will? (Psalm 16:11, Isaiah 55:12, 2 Corinthians 5:7 and Philippians 4:7). Is there doubt or faith, love or fear, joy or unhappiness, patience or impatience?[2]

'...We also...do not cease to pray for you, and to ask that you may be filled with the knowledge of His will in all wisdom and spiritual understanding' Colossians 1:9.

In September 1838, the London Mission Society (LMS), provisionally accepted David Livingstone to become a missionary under their auspices. They initially wanted him to go to the West Indies (Jamaica etc.), but he told them that his two years of medical study would merely be wasted as the West Indies had many practitioners. Livingstone proposed the East Indies (India), but the directors of the LMS deemed his giftings unsuitable for that destination. Livingstone's heart was then set on the needs of China, with its tens of millions, who had never heard the Good News, but the Opium War in China put an end to that possibility and so off to Africa he went! Common sense, coupled with the directors decisions and Divine providence opened the door, which no man could shut.

Two Right Paths

A choice between right or wrong is not difficult for a disciple to make, but when the choice is between two right things then we need some extra help, but as Hilys Jasper said, "God will always reveal His will to one who is willing to do it." Pray.

Under a sense of duty, David Livingstone in Southern Africa, had to make some hard decisions as he explored unknown territory looking for a new mission station for his family. His biographer wrote: 'It was his inviolable sense of duty and his indefeasible conviction that His Father in heaven would not forsake him whilst pursuing a course in obedience to His will, and designed to advance the welfare of His children.'[3]

Timing – the timing of a STM is as important as all the other factors. You could be with the right mission organisation at the right place, but at the wrong time. Don't run ahead of God or lag behind in His call for your participation on your STM.

Chapter Eleven

The Short-Term Mission Team

Jesus said to the disciples, "Let us go into the next towns, that I may preach there also, because for this purpose I have come forth" Mark 1:38.

After Jesus' resurrection He appeared to the disciples and said, "Peace to you! As the Father has sent Me, I also send you" John 20:21.

Short-Term Missions in the Holy Bible

Not every parent, sibling or spouse is thrilled with the prospect of the one they love, going away on a short-term mission (STM), taking a year out, or being away from them for just a few weeks. There may be many concerns, including financial and emotional.

Abraham must have been pestered and perhaps even cross-examined by his family when God called him to go on his mission, leaving as men would say, 'a certain for an uncertain good.' I am sure his friends told him it would be foolish to leave behind the good pastures, familiar surroundings and the warm home life. Undoubtedly they told him not to heed his wild imaginations of the call of God. Abraham grew up in Ur of the Chaldeans and in Mesopotamia God met with him (Genesis 11:31 and Acts 7:2), but what if he never set out on his long trek from modern day Iraq to Israel? Thankfully, he was obedient to the call of God and embarked on a mission that not only changed his life, but the course of history and in him all the families of the earth have been blessed (Genesis 12:1-4).

A large number of the characters of the Bible went on STMs, though, back then, it was known as a mission from God, a directive to go here, do that, or speak to such and such a person the Word of the Lord. Moses, Elijah, Isaiah, Jeremiah, Ezekiel & Jonah are perhaps the best known within the Old Testament.

Within the New Testament, we have several more characters of which Jesus was the greatest. Jesus the Son of God was the greatest missionary who ever walked this earth, because He left His familiar surroundings of heaven and came to earth. He identified with the people He lived with and moved amongst, and spent just over three years on His STM which changed the world forever.

> Selwyn Hughes, founder of Crusade for World Revival (CWR) wrote: 'Christ's call we must note, overrides convention and custom, family obligations and business commitments. The sons of Zebedee left their father, their boats and their business and, together with Simon and Andrew, set out to follow Jesus. His call upset their fishing careers but they went with Him to fish in larger waters and for a more important catch – people.'

New Testament STMs

Jesus led independent STMs – the Bible also mentions the first four disciples who went with Jesus on a STM (Mark 1:16-20), followed by the twelve disciples (Mark 3:13-19), and then the seventy disciples (Luke 10:1-17).

- 'Jesus went through all the cities and villages, teaching in their synagogues, preaching the Gospel of the Kingdom and healing every sickness and every disease among the people' (Matthew 9:35).
- Jesus said to the disciples, "Let us go into the next towns, that I may preach there also..." (Mark 1:38).
- Jesus said, "For I have come down from heaven, not to do My will, but the will of Him who sent Me" (John 6:38).

Paul's STMs, Fellow Labourers and Assistants

The apostle Paul was another great example of an independent STM-er, though he was called of the Holy Spirit and sent out by the church. He travelled to multiple destinations on his mission trips, staying varying lengths of time in one place to the next, depending on the reception he got! Paul travelled to many locations on three main missionary trips, had assistance and many helpers, travellers, companions and fellow labourers. Once, Paul was part of a group of eight on a STM, though, they all met up at the final location – Troas (see Acts 20:5). So who were some of Paul's fellow STM-ers?

- Sopater of Berea, Aristarchus and Secundus of the Thessalonians, Gaius of Derbe, Timothy, and Tychius and Trophimus of Asia, and Luke (Acts 20:4-6).
- Titus, a STM partner and fellow worker (2 Cor. 8:23).
- Epaphroditus, my brother, fellow worker and fellow soldier (Philippians 2:25).

- Various women who laboured alongside Paul in the Gospel, and Clement (Philippians 4:3).
- Tychius, a beloved brother and fellow servant in the Gospel, Onesimus (the former slave, see Philemon v10), a faithful and beloved brother, Aristarchus a fellow prisoner, Mark the cousin of Barnabas, Jesus (who was called Justus) and Epaphras, a servant of Christ and a prayer warrior, Luke the physician and Demas (Colossians 4:7-14).
- Silvanus and Timothy (1 Thessalonians 1:1).
- Demas deserted Paul and went to Thessalonica, Crescens went to Galatia and Titus went to Dalmatia. Luke stayed with Paul and Paul sent Tychicus to Ephesus. Erastus stayed in Corinth and Trophimus was left in Miletus because he was unwell (1 Tim. 4:9-12, 20).
- Paul teamed up with *Priscilla and Aquila (*wife and husband) in Corinth, and stayed with them, as both Paul and Aquila were tentmakers (Acts 18:1-3).
- Paul left Titus in Crete, to tie up the loose ends and to appoint elders in every city (Titus 1:5).
- Paul was going to send Artemas or Tychius to Titus, but wanted to meet him at Nicopolis, where he would spend the winter. He also asked for Zenas the lawyer and Apollos to be sent to him with haste and provisions (Titus 3:12-13).
- Epaphras a fellow prisoner with Paul; Mark, Aristarchus, Demas and Luke, Paul's fellow labourers (Philemon verses 22-24).

Logistics – an Essential Role

Within a large STM team, there needs to be someone in charge of the logistics, which is practical preparation of: transportation, accommodation, how to feed the team (self catering or eating out), purchasing supplies / materials for projects etc. This is often the team leader's responsibility, the host or shared responsibility, but some duties are delegated to responsible or veteran members of the team.

Sometimes logistic leaders are largely stuck at base camp (especially if you are cooking for a large team), while the team goes off and evangelises or does humanitarian work. From day-to-day, a certain member of the team may have to remain at base camp (on a rotational basis) to assist the logistics member or host member. Their work is no less important than the ones on the "front line" as each member has his or her duty to do. If a regiment was not fed and supplied then it would fail in its mission. The person(s) at base camp may be cooking, doing the laundry, chauffeuring, buying supplies, confirming the meetings and perform many other duties and double-check all details.

David, who later became King of Israel, had six hundred fighting men. On one occasion, two hundred men were so exhausted that they could not go on in pursuit of the enemy, but stayed with the supplies. On his return, David announced as a statute and ordinance, "As his part is who goes down to battle, so shall his part be who stays by the supplies; they shall share alike" (1 Samuel 30:9-25), and in eternity, we shall equally share of the rewards from the fruit and labour of the success of the STM team. This principle was first mentioned by Moses after the destruction of the Midianites, where half the spoil went to the warriors and the other half went to the congregation of Israel (Numbers 31:25-27).

The Optimum Number

Jesus began His extensive ministry of training with twelve handpicked disciples. These core men were with Him from the beginning. When Jesus sent the twelve disciples out on their first STM, He sent them in pairs, "He began to send them out two by two and gave them power over unclean spirits" (Mark 6:7). Jesus also sent the seventy out on a STM; they were close to Him, but not intimate as the twelve disciples, or very close as were the inner three, Peter, James and John (see Matthew 17:1), as only they were invited onto the mountain where they witnessed the transfiguration.

If you go with a church or organisation on your STM, then it is their responsibility as to how many people can participate. Often there are a set number of places for practical reasons, whilst at other times, especially for churches, they are happy to take along as many as can come, as long as they pay their own way and are committed to the work. Whilst a large team can do more work than just a handful, they can be difficult to manage, especially if there are a few (or just one!) who are prone to rebel and do not desire to pull their own weight. Accommodation, transport and eating arrangements can also be problematic for large groups.

The Bible declares that, 'A man who isolates himself seeks his own desire; he rages against all wise judgment' (Proverbs 18:1).

Therefore, it is advisable not to go on a mission on your own; though if you are being sent to work in a specific location alongside others then you will only being flying alone, but will join up with a STM team. Anybody on their own is prone to more difficulties than those who go in pairs or with a larger group. You are an easier target to rob, more prone to get lonely, frequently will have to pay a single supplement (or surcharge) at hotels and if you become unwell or even lost (it does happen on occasions in big unfamiliar cities), you only have yourself to rely on; though the Lord will never leave you.

In the past, lone missionaries have gone alone to do pioneering works in obedience to the call of God, simply because no one else was forthcoming or others dropped out. These pioneers had set their face like a flint to be obedient to the call of God on their life; but two or more STM-ers are always the better option.

Two's Company, Three's a Crowd

The old saying goes, 'two's company but three's a crowd,' and if there is a third leg in your mission partnership, there will be additional problems encountered in which just two people will not come across. Between any STM of three people, there will always be a stronger bond between two of them and the third person will feel isolated on occasions. I have known less than a handful of STMs as a team of three and none were ideal.

I was the third member of an independent STM team but always felt left out, as the bond between the other two was impenetrable. I could only put up with so much and without any discussion (which was unwise), I booked my ticket, told the guys, and flew home the next day. Joseph – Ethiopia.

Biblically, when three people go on a mission it is a case of two seniors, those who are experienced taking an 'apprentice' with them and showing them the ropes. The apprentice will always look to the two seniors for advice and help, and the two seniors will always look out for the one they are training. Paul and Barnabas went on their first missionary journey (around the area of Antioch, in modern day Turkey, not to be confused with the city and the mission sending Church called Antioch in modern day Syria), and took John Mark with them (Acts 12:25 and Acts chapters 13-14). It was the case of the two senior Christians taking an inexperienced team member with them. Less than half way through the mission at Pergia in Pamphylia, (the third city they visited), Mark quit the mission and went home (Acts 13:13 and Acts 15:37-38), whilst Paul and Barnabas completed the entire trip of all seven cities and were congratulated by the Antioch church, and gave their report (Acts 14:26-28).

The Church Council after reaching an important conclusion, sent 'chosen men,' Paul and Barnabas, Judas (also known as Barsabas), Silas and other leading men to disseminate what the council had agreed (Acts 15:22-29). At Antioch, after the mission was completed, Silas felt led to stay on, whereas Judas was sent back to the home Church at Jerusalem (Acts 15:32-34).

I joined a team in Asia with two men who had worked together for years. I realised that one of the guys found it very hard to accept me and treated me like 'a threat' to his place in the team. It took several months before he accepted me. Peter – Thailand.

Be Prepared
We all have gifts and talents and on your STM they can come to the fore and be a blessing to many, whilst love is a universal language. Long before your STM commences make sure you are prepared spiritually & physically, and with a good mentality:

- Spiritually – am I a real Christian, truly converted / saved, and a disciple of the Lord Jesus Christ? Do I read my Bible and pray daily? Am I faithful in attending church meetings and do I participate? Do I desire to share the Good News with others?
- Physically – do I have health problems or a medical condition, which may exacerbate on the STM or endanger my own life? Am I unhealthy, over or under weight? Am I addicted to junk food or dependant on my fix of coffee, chocolate, medicine, cigarettes or alcohol? If you have issues with the last two then it is best that you get them dealt with before you join a STM team.
- Mentality – do I know why I want to go and why I should go? What is expected of me? Do I realise it is not a holiday or a vacation and I will encounter some discomforts. There will be difficulties as I may be working with a group who are relatively unknown to me, and stresses and strains are inevitable with possible personality clashes.

Chapter Twelve

Picking a Mission Team

'He who rules over men must be just, ruling in the fear of God' 2 Samuel 23:3b.

'He [Jesus] went up on the mountain and called to Him those that He Himself wanted...' Mark 3:13.

Leadership and Leaders

To state the obvious, the person who leads a team on a short-term mission (STM) has a lot more responsibilities, trials, problems and burdens than those who are part of the team. As the saying goes, 'the buck stops here,' and if you're the leader, then it stops with you! If you belong to a mission organisation you should know what you're doing, but for a first time leader of a mission trip, it can be a daunting task.

Leading a mission team in one's own country is quite easy, but being responsible abroad is quite another matter and the stakes get higher, and problems can be more difficult to solve. In many different countries in Africa, I found out the mistake or faults may not have been mine, but the cost always was!

Jesus saw Simon and Andrew, two brothers who were fishing and said, "Come after Me [follow Me] and I will make you fishers of men" – and they immediately left their nets and followed Jesus. A little further on, Jesus saw two brothers, James and John, the sons of Zebedee, who were also fishermen, He called them and they too followed Jesus (Mark 1:14-18). Jesus saw Levi (Matthew), the son of Alphaeus sitting in his tax office and said to him, "Follow Me" and he arose and followed Him! (Mark 2:12-13).

The primary designation of the twelve disciples was to extend the Kingdom of God – to be trained by Jesus, (by word and example) and to go and minister in Word and power in Jesus' mighty name. 'Then He appointed twelve, that they might be with Him and that He might send them out to preach, and to have power to heal sicknesses and to cast out demons' (Mark 3:13-19).

For several consecutive years, I was part of a team that went to a North African country. One year, I knew that our leader, who often had gone twice a year, was not able to go. For many months the Lord was trying to get my attention about leading a team, and as much as I tried to put the inevitable off, I knew it was what God wanted me to do. Whilst I had led teams for evangelistic mission in the United Kingdom, to work with different churches, this undertaking far surpassed them all.

When I first went out as part of a team to North Africa (alongside ten or so other new recruits), I knew that the numbers had to be in single figures and wisdom dictated that I should only take men on this first leadership mission to a Muslim country. From observations, I saw that the financial burden of the team rested on the leader and I was new on the path of 'financial' faith. I did not want to open up the trip to just anyone, as I had observed on previous STMs that this had been abused by those who had little or no money for the mission, yet they did not seem to lack in other areas of their own need! As I sought the Lord, He spoke to me through Mark 3:13 'He [Jesus] went up on the mountain and *called to Him those that He Himself wanted...*' Thus I approached certain men, told them what I was going to do, the estimated cost, and told them to pray whether the Lord would have them come or not.

The mission itself was as much a learning curve for me as to the one man who came with me and valuable lessons were learnt.

Picking the Team – The Options
- Open to anyone and everyone (of all ages from different churches or your youth groups).
- Open only for those within your church or youth group.
- For members of your youth group or cell group.
- Selectively ask those with whom you would be happy to take along (and be responsible for – if they are from your church or youth group).
- Allow God to guide you as Jesus hand-picked His disciples after a night of prayer.

Reasons for Going on a STM
There are many reasons why a person wants to be part (or does become a member) of a STM team but not all reasons and motives are honourable, whilst others are more understandable.

- Because my friend is going and I want to join her / him.
- Because I want to come for the free ride (not that they say that!).
- Because I can afford it (because I can!).
- Asked to join the team for the exposure to missions.
- For the adventure / experience.
- Gap year – a break before studies begin, it looks good on the C.V. or you have to do something over the next year and do not fancy getting a job.
- Trying to run away or avoid your responsibilities or duties.
- Time of trauma or tragedy and need to get away from familiar surroundings / bad memories etc.
- God has called me.
- I want to be obedient to the Great Commission.

Non-Christian Team Members

The Church in America is very big on STMs – especially humanitarian and development aid, building work, feeding the poor and medical help etc., which has led to a rise in allowing skilled non-Christians becoming part of the mission team. On occasions people of other faiths have gone along on some church mission trips (without realising the Christian content!), purely as humanitarian or development aid to use their skills, but this is just asking for trouble. The Bible warns: 'Do not be unequally yoked together with unbelievers. For what fellowship has righteousness with lawlessness? And what communion has light with darkness?' (2 Corinthians 6:14).

There may be exceptions to the rule – very few and far between, (a husband and wife as part of the church team). Only one spouse was converted after marriage and the other is not. An individual under consideration may be a faithful, helpful and a good natured member of your church youth group, who is not a Christian (as yet) and it may be this mission which tips the balance, or it may be this mission that they begin to play up and upset the entire team!

A choir from Europe came to work alongside our Christian institution. One evening, at a team meeting, I was told that one of the teenage girls had just given her heart to the Lord. I asked my European friend to explain what he meant, as I had assumed that all these members were Christians. The girl had given her

life to Christ and had become "born again" on the sofa of a
sitting room. Jeffrey – Wales.

Children, Youth and the Team Members

In recent years some churches have permitted children (as
young as ten or eleven) to be part of a STM team if
accompanied by a parent or relative. But is this wise? Whilst it
could birth an interest in missions, it could be problematic. There
may be no comforts as at home, perhaps no TV, bath, carpet or
wooden floors, fridge, and there may be mosquitoes, insects
and strange foods. The child may cry constantly and beg to go
home. Who will look after your child when you are busy and
what can a child of ten or eleven realistically contribute to the
team?

Some teenagers are more mature than others. Some are quiet
and shy, others are extroverts and some can be difficult. One
highly-strung character can disrupt a team and cause
embarrassments to all concerned (the team and the host), and
bring the name of Christ into disrepute. Many of us have had
zeal without knowledge and we have all made mistakes in the
past, so bear that in mind, before you decide to exclude (or
decline) someone from joining the STM team, though on
occasions, there is no option but to make that tough call for the
benefit of the majority.

We left the States to do practical work at a Christian institution in
Europe. Our two children cried all day long, as we scrubbed,
painted and cleaned. Never again! Mr and Mrs — USA.

Elderly and Disabled Team Members

There are some parts of the world where an elderly person
may not be able to cope; in a cramped bus, or where you have
to run for your seat or stand for five hours on public transport
over potholed dirt roads. This can be true of disabled team
members where the developing world has little to no wheelchair
access or the nearest hospital could be some distance away
(hundreds of miles) and ill equipped at best. Facilities in some
countries or districts are very poor with no health and safety
consideration.

Other elderly people put the youth to shame, in late May 2009,
65-year-old Sir Ranulph Fiennes, on his third attempt made it up
Mount Everest, beating many a person who is half his age!

There were more than twenty of us on our STM, from teens to retirement age. One couple on the team, did not preach, teach or give their testimony and the team were not involved in humanitarian work. One day, the husband, who had underlying health problems was rushed to hospital. We were all very worried. The entire team and leaders spent a day off from the mission. If you have health problems then think twice before you go. Ellie – Brazil.

Release of Liability
We live in an age where health and safety and risk assessment are at an all-time peak. Whilst all travel involves some measure of risk – you don't want to be sued by some zealous parent or individual who has had an accident whilst under your care or supervision on their STM.

Chris Eaton and Kim Hurst in *Vacations with a Purpose – A Planning Handbook for Your Short-Term Missions Team* recommend that a 'Release of Liability' form should be filled out by all participants, so that leaders, the church or mission and all concerned will not be liable and cannot be sued if an accident occurs or anything unfortunate happens. They state: 'It's an unhappy thing to consider, but all travel presents some risk of injury to the participants. We strongly urge you to choose destinations with team safety in mind, and encourage your team members to use good sense and caution at all times. Nonetheless, injury may occur. Some mission agencies have found it wise to ask each participant to sign a release.'[1]

To save money, my friend and I hired a motorbike which we shared for a few days. He was much bigger than myself and when we drove on a dirt road, I lost control and we crashed. I was OK, but my friend hurt his knee. We saved money but risked our health! Papulos – Cambodia.

Warnings and Considerations
Beware of freeloaders and spongers – if the church is paying for the mission trip, you will get a lot more applicants than if each individual is responsible for raising their own finances! Some people only come for the "free holiday / vacation," whilst those who have not contributed have nothing to lose if they drop out or fly home early. On the other hand, you do not want to limit the trip only to those who 'have' and decline the 'have-nots,'

discriminating against those who do not have disposable income, who may not have a circle of friends, or relatives who can help them, is also wrong.

I am reminded of the Israelites who collected manna in the wilderness where '...he who gathered much had nothing over, and he who gathered little had no lack...' (Exodus 16:18). There is enough money within Christian wallets to take the Gospel to the ends of the earth; it just needs to be distributed correctly, instead of being spent on pleasures and self. '...Let him labour, working with his hands what is good, that *he may have something to give him who has need*' (Ephesians 4:28), and we 'must support the weak' remembering Jesus' words, "It is more better to give than to receive" (Acts 20:35).

After announcing that a church is going on a STM, some have asked for an initial deposit of £50 ($80) as a refundable token payment, before the team has been picked. This separates the 'serious ones' from those who are 'just looking' because having half your 'proposed team' fall away after a month of preliminary meetings (to discuss the STM) is disheartening for everyone.

Once you know who is going, then a period of payments needs to be worked out. A non-refundable deposit (often to buy the plane ticket or to pay a deposit on the accommodation) is essential and then three to five instalments over the next 2-8 months. If you are the mission treasurer, keep a log of each payment received and issue receipts. A separate bank account should be opened for the mission money in the names of two unrelated people.

Some applicants may be unable to attend different church meetings or outreaches because of essential prior commitments – family or job responsibilities and so should not be excluded from the team application due to an apparent lack of commitment. At times, unexpected things do happen. Many years ago, to apply for a visa to India, I had to give my flight details and my ticket number. That is, I had to buy my plane ticket *before* I could receive permission to enter the country!

My church bought the plane ticket for a young man to join us on our mission. He had been before in a previous year and we knew his worth and value to the team. Unfortunately, his visa application took too long in processing and he was unable to join us – the flight ticket to South America was lost – there was no refund and we were not amused. A church in Wales.

The Leader Decides

Allow God to guide you in whom to take and also whom not to take; whether the trip should be open to all or selective ages (youth groups or 20-30s) to a limited number (4 to 12 persons etc.) or a larger group (20 to 40 persons). Remember that the larger the group the greater the logistics of plane seats, accommodation, transport, eating out, purchasing supplies in a small village etc.

As the team leader your job is to do the will of the Lord and by ignoring the small still voice of the Holy Spirit or obvious signs of someone's immaturity or lack of commitment, you are setting yourself up for trouble, disharmony within the team and a possible lack of blessing on the STM.

The Leader and the Team

Members of any STM team can greatly assist the leader by being submissive to them and taking their advice; whilst a great leader will know the strengths and weaknesses of their team. There is also the problem when older STM members refuse to submit to a younger leader. A leader should bring out the best in each member, and know (or soon discover) their qualities and strengths and utilise them. If your STM consists of development aid where specialised skills (or giftings) are needed, *do not assume* the builder wants to build, the chef wants to cook or the bus driver wants to drive the hired mini-bus. Ask them.

Team Covenant

Each member of the STM team should sign a team covenant, a basic written agreement that each member will cooperate with the team leader and all the other members of the mission. To do their duties as unto the Lord, that they will be Christ-like, considerate towards others and stay clear of the use of improper language, coarse joking, discrimination, racism, tobacco, drugs, alcohol and improper sexual conduct.

The team covenant should be signed (and dated) in the presence of the leader and the other members of the team. Each member should receive a duplicate copy of the covenant. The team covenant is something to fall back on if a team member begins to cause concern; the leader can pull out the covenant and remind the person concerned of their pledge.

Norman Grubb wrote: 'A single-handed ministry is not God's way. Even the Saviour quickly called twelve round Him. ...While having in a general spirit of fellowship towards our brethren, we can be extremely individualistic in our work for the Lord; indeed, we can become real isolationists. Against this we must guard.... Real teamwork leaves room for mutual challenge, and on its highest level encourages it. We need each other. When there was a shade of disunion in the Philippian church, Paul urged them to watch their minds, not their hearts (Philippians 1:2-7, 2:2-5 and Philippians 4:2). He took the mutual love of their hearts for granted.... Unity is an obligation...and when there is unity, there is team work, and when there is team work, there 'the Lord commands the blessing' (Psalm 133).'[2]

Expectation and Realisation

For leaders: Sometimes expectation and realisation is interlinked with the preparation (or lack of it), long before you arrive at your STM destination. This is also coupled with what your host thinks you're going to do, what you have planned to do and whether or not this has been communicated clearly (leader to leader) and then passed onto your team.

Not everybody has the gifting and anointing of Billy Graham and Reinhard Bonnke, or the heart of compassion of Mother Teresa, Elizabeth Fry or Heidi Baker.

In 1807, Robert Morrison, the pioneer Protestant missionary to China, was standing in the office of the ship owners at the docks at New York; ready to embark on his missionary career. The merchant, turned from his desk and with a sardonic (scornful or mocking) grin said, "And so Mr Morrison, you really expect that you will make an impression on the idolatry of the great Chinese Empire?" "No sir," said Morrison with more than usual sternness, "I expect GOD will."[3]

We were part of a large mixed team in a Muslim country and a group of us girls were invited by the bride to a three-day wedding feast! It was so exciting and we were the only foreigners there. Each day we would come back and report to the team about the day's events and on the last day of the feast we presented our presents, (both spiritual and practical) to the bride and groom. We will never forget that mission. Keumhee – North Africa.

Chapter Thirteen

Dangers and Concerns

'Those who are wise shall shine like the brightness of the firmament, and those who turn many to righteousness like the stars forever and ever' Daniel 12:3.

'…The people who know their God shall be strong and carry out great exploits' Daniel 11:32b.

The Dangers and Concerns of Missions

There are many dangers involved in short-term missions (STM), as there are dangers in doing anything, in any place, at any time. The person who decides to stay at home to be safe has forgotten about earthquakes, typhoons, hurricanes, toxic spills, fires, floods and many other dangers. But, to allow fear of "what might happen" is to be paralysed into doing nothing and then you will live with nagging regret – "What if?"

From my doctor's surgery I picked up their quarterly newsletter and read about all the dangers and statistics from British people who had accidents at home. These statistics are published annually. 220,000 went to hospital because of DIY accidents as compared with 290,000 injured (including fatalities) on the roads! Each year in the UK there are approximately: 87,000 injuries whilst working in the garden, including 5,300 accidents caused by flowerpots; 14,000 people injured whilst preparing vegetables (sharp knives and boiling water); 11,800 accidents involving socks, tights and stocking; 5,300 went to Accident and Emergency owing to mishaps whilst putting on a pair of trousers (pants); 760 were injured caused by washing-up liquid and there were 400 bra-related accidents! Need I say any more about dangers and why we should not be afraid of going on a STM?

Gap Year Preparations

More than 250,000 Britons (most of whom are non-Christian) annually take a gap year before or after university. Insurance data statistics reveal that one in three people who go on a gap year find that their trip is spoiled by a serious accident, illness or crime, whilst many of these are bad enough to cut the trip short.

In 2008, a coach crash in Ecuador, killed four British gap year students and a tour guide, whilst in May 2009, it emerged that Princess Eugenie (of the British royal Family) suffered a traumatic brush with muggers in Cambodia during her year out.

Peter Slowe, director of the gap year company Projects Abroad, noted it was important to keep the figures in perspective. "People are very concerned about safety and while we can never provide absolute safety, we can provide a certain level of reassurance," he said. "...We need to work out how to prepare people effectively. ...The second thing is they need to do some research, for example how much money they will need and what inoculations to have. If you do the basic research, which does not take long, you increase your chances of finishing your project safe and sound by 300 per cent."[1]

> I stayed in a place that had not been occupied for months except by the creatures that live in empty places in the tropics. I experienced a little of what pharaoh and his people experienced in the third and fourth plagues of Egypt. There was no sleep the first night, from fightings without and fears within! Rees – Madeira.

Finances to Thought

Things to consider as to why I should go on a STM and not let fear get in the way.

- Finances – God will provide for all my needs.
- Faith – God is faithful.
- Fun – it will be fun and enjoyable working for the Lord as well as hard work!
- Fear – do not allow fear of the unknown to paralyse you.
- Thought – should I go, versus, do I want to go?

Concerns and Dangers

- Having members of your team who are uncommitted or half-hearted.
- Those with an unteachable spirit.
- Those who come with ulterior motives – especially if the financial liability or responsibility is not theirs.
- Those who have come to see the sights and to shop till they drop.
- Those who think they are superior to others and look down on those to whom they have been sent (to serve).

- The isolationist who wants to work alone.
- Hygiene freaks and those who are allergic to everything!
- The moaners and complainers, about anything and everything.
- The 'If I had done this' personality, I would have done it this way!
- Those who choose not to have personal contact with the locals.
- Those who think their STM ends when they leave their hosts' church or community and refuse to keep in contact when the hosts have been so kind, warm and considerate.

> For $3 (£1.90) a day, we hired a 100cc scooter. I have a driving licence, but have no experience on two wheeled motorised forms of transport. The man at the hotel handed me the scooter, I got on it and test rode it around the courtyard. As I pulled the brake lever, my wrist pulled back on the throttle and I ended up driving up the hotel steps! It was embarrassing. Stuart – Cambodia.

Epidemics and Pandemics

From time to time, there are outbreaks of diseases, fears of epidemics, scare-mongering, actual epidemics and occasional pandemics. In the past we have had SARS, Bird Flu and Swine Flu, the latter of which began in Mexico and grabbed the world's headlines in 2009.[2] Ebola in 2014 and the Zika virus in 2016!

Other preventable diseases such as Cholera, TB, Yellow Fever, Chicken Pox, Measles, Mumps etc. do break-out in parts of the world, though some in isolated towns or districts, and can cause myriads of deaths amongst those who are too poor to aid preventions by inoculation, vaccination or immunisation.

> Before I went to Africa, *I felt* the Lord telling me not to take anti-malarial tablets, but to trust Him and that to take them would be a lack of faith. I came home with the worst form of malaria, which came back every few months. We should be practical, not super spiritual. Dave – Malawi.

Life-altering Consequences

It would be unwise to go on a STM to an infected area and expose your team to life-altering consequences – that is unless you are the medical team! Sometimes these hot spots of infection only last a few months or can continue for years, whilst at other times, the whole scenario can rapidly change and a town, which could be in a state of "lock-down," can be open for business as usual within weeks.

Border controls can sometimes be tricky when these diseases are prevalent and in 2003, because of the threat of SARS, the Vietnamese border guards were very nervous about tourists spreading the disease. We had to fill out additional paperwork, including the state of our health, with questions such as, 'Have you had a temperature or headache in the past week?' We had to pay on top of our visa fees for a man who wore a facemask to read our answers, tick and stamp our paper and then we were allowed to enter the country!

This event is minor compared to what has happened in the past. It reminded me of an American minister travelling through the Holy Lands in 1849, where everybody coming from Egypt was quarantined in Gaza for five days as a safeguard against the introduction of the plague! The minister wrote: 'So strict is the regulation, that if one going out of the lazarette [the quarantine building which is divided into small buildings], after completing his time, should unfortunately touch another coming in, or anything belong to him, the former would have to return, and be subjected to new quarantine [a further 5 days].'[3]

George Verwer, founder of Operation Mobilization wrote: 'Short-term mission is a serious ministry and must be done in a way that will honour God and bless the people we serve. There needs to be serious orientation, interviewing and training before people go. There should at least be some life, action and godly reality before a lot of money is spent to travel and serve among people in a different country and culture.'[4]

Ten Short-Termers we Don't Want

George Verwer, has been involved for fifty years with both short and long-term missions, which has given him some very strong convictions about who should go and who should not go on a STM. The following are ones who should stay at home:

- Mr Selfish – the person who mainly cares about them self and how much they can get out of the trip.
- Mr Lazy – they will have many reasons each day as to why they cannot get out into the work.

- Mr Tourist – the person who just wants to see the sights and hear the sounds. Not interested in hard work, serving or presenting the Gospel.
- Mr Big-Spender – they bring a lot of money / travellers cheques and want to spend much of their time shopping.
- Mr Insensitive – people who push their own country or culture and are insensitive to other people's culture. They often leave behind a very bad testimony.
- Mr Critical – these people see everything that is wrong in the church and country, even among their co-workers. It is contrary to the basic message of 1 Corinthians 13.
- Mr Unteachable – they are often very prejudiced and stubborn and bring hurt and confusion.
- Mr Prayerless – to me, it is unthinkable to have prayerless people in ministry or service. We are in spiritual warfare and we must use the weapons that God has given us to use.
- Mr Addicted – people, especially with sexual addictions, should not go. They can so quickly bring huge offence and even scandal. People with alcohol and other drug addictions need to get that sorted out beforehand.
- Mr Proud – pride is such a deadly sin and often leads to division and broken relationships. People with heavy national pride easily insult and hurt the very people they are trying to serve.

One member of our STM team wrote on her postcards about our work amongst the Muslim population. Upon being told of the dangers this could cause, she acknowledged the error, but still chose not to place the postcards in envelopes! Jeanette – North Africa.

More Harm than Good
On any mission trip, an individual or an unprepared team can do more harm than good. Some negative and harmful traits as well as oversights are:
- Little to no preparation – not understanding the culture or lack of resources etc.
- No vaccinations or personal medical supplies.
- Refusal to interact with the locals.
- Selfishness – do it my way.
- Arrogance – I know best.

- Pride – superior attitude and I have all the answers, can't teach me anything.
- Flaunting your wealth – money, clothes, gadgets and bling.
- Acting like a cash-cow – giving money and gifts to anyone who asks without thinking of the consequences.
- Stubborn – we do it like this or not at all!
- Lack of communication – this is what they want (without asking the host church!).
- Leaving things undone – unfinished jobs, that which cannot be accomplished without further financial aid.
- Lack of foresight – if the water pump breaks down can the locals replace the parts? Do they have the money?

> I was doing ministry in Europe with some other Americans. Around the breakfast table these people belittled the country and its people; declaring why it was all a mess. I was so embarrassed. Alex – Germany.

More Effective than Defective

To be more effective than defective we need to lay aside our culture, our mindset and become servants, ready to serve; being clothed in humility and wrapped up in the love of Christ.

- Go prepared – spiritually, financially, physically and with a good mentality.
- Be flexible – change happens, the best of plans can fall through.
- Be considerate to others.
- Have a willingness to learn and to be taught.
- Ask the right questions in the right way – inquire rather than condemn.
- Try to fit in – assimilate, mingle and interact (appropriately) with the locals.
- Be humble, gentle, kind and courteous and have a servant heart.
- Be wise in all you do and say.
- Look after yourself, physically, spiritually, mentally, and financially. It is easy to throw money into bottomless pits.
- Listen and obey your leaders – they will probably know best and do not have to give the reason for their actions, requests or statements.

- Wear the right clothing and be sensible.

> I heard about the local swimming pool and as I had some free time from my STM I paid it a visit. It was only about 20oC and I was only in the sun for a few hours, but being so close to the equator, and the fact that I did not wear my sunhat, I got badly sunburnt. Mark – Zimbabwe.

Government Warnings

Many governments of the world issue travel warnings to its citizens – places to avoid because of civil, political or other forms of unrest; as well as dangers because of terrorist activity and recent natural disasters. Some countries that are listed as dangerous are quite safe apart from isolated areas or certain regions in which the local government may have no control over rebel forces; especially in mountainous or disputed border areas.

> I was in a hotel in Jerusalem, looking out over a beautiful view. When I put on the BBC news, it showed riots in Jerusalem. I did not see them or hear them, yet I was there! Just because there is a problem in one area, does not mean the entire country is affected. Just because a forest fire rages across parts of California does not mean that the USA is going up in flames! Donald – Israel.

Natural Disasters

Natural disasters can occur at any time. Being a Christian (and on a STM) does not make you (or your team) untouchable or immune from disasters and dangers. In January 2010, a 7.0-magnitude earthquake hit Haiti, which left 3 million homeless and more than 230,000 dead. Haiti is the poorest nation in the Western hemisphere and a popular STM destination. The BBC news interviewed one STM-er who was part of a large STM group. She recalled, that as the quake hit, she ran out of the building when a large piece of masonry fell right in front of her (narrowly missing her), and that the whole ordeal was quite frightening. The team had finally been able to fly out of the nation while most of the country's infrastructure was in ruins, including the airport's control tower.

Every mission team leader would be wise to consider having an emergency evacuation plan for the team (or a team member), not only for medical emergencies, but in cases of terrorism and natural disasters etc. In mid-April 2010, a volcano erupted in Iceland and volcanic ash closed the airspace over parts of Europe for six days. Thousands of flights (in and out of Europe) were grounded. This stranded 100,000+ passengers across the globe, on both sides of the Atlantic and the Middle East. Some policies have 'Industrial Action' and 'Volcanic Disruption' options. Finding out what your travel insurance covers (before you purchase it) and what it DOES NOT COVER is essential. 'Acts of God' are an exemption clause where you are not covered!

Valid Passport and Visa

If you do not have a passport then you had better get one soon! They cost money and take time to process. For those who already have a passport, make sure that it will not expire whilst you are on your STM. Some countries will expect you to have at least six months outstanding (sometimes a year), before they even allow you to enter their country or before they will issue you with a visa. Visa requirements change from one nationality to the next as do their costs.

If you join a mission organisation, they will advise you on the type of visa needed for the country of your mission, and what you should fill in under 'nature of your visit.' If you are an independent STM-er then it is advisable NOT to tick the Business visa box. Whilst you are participating in your "Father's business" to use Jesus' words, you are not going as a businessperson to make money, to buy or sell or to trade in wares – and so the Tourist or Pleasure box can be ticked. Under the nature of your visit, it is advisable NOT to write 'missionary' or 'preacher of the Good News' as you may be turned back at the airport or border and refused entry – even if you write humanitarian or development work. With most countries, you will have to fill out an Arrivals Card and these are issued on the plane or at immigration. Sometimes you have to return your half of the Arrivals Card on your departure, so don't lose it!

> I saw fishermen using cormorants to catch fish (in Bangladesh they use ferrets). This ingenious method of catching fish in China has been carried on for nearly three centuries, but I thought it was cruel. The birds had rings on their necks to restrict their gullet. Thus, only small fish can pass through their gullet whilst the larger ones are collect in their distensible pouch for the fishermen. Merton – China.

Chapter Fourteen

Financing your Short-Term Mission

'My God shall supply all your need according to His riches in glory by Christ Jesus' Philippians 4:19.

'And God is able to make all grace abound towards you, that you, always having all sufficiency in all things, may have an abundance for every good work' 2 Corinthians 9:8.

Raising Support and Financing STMs

There are many ways and methods of raising support and obtaining your financial needs for your short-term mission (STM); some of which you may feel led to do, some of which you may feel prompted not to do and some of which you may disdain. What is right for one person may not be right for others, and if you are an older person going on a STM there are some options, which a younger person would not hesitate to do, which are not fitting for an older person. There are many and varied views in regards to raising support and financing STMs, with good arguments for, and against, some of these methods. I will give the options and it is for you to be led from God for how *you* should finance your STM. However, DO NOT go into debt, by taking out a loan, putting it on the credit card or borrowing, as this is not an option to finance your STM.

'*Owe no one anything* except to love one another, for he loves another has fulfilled the law' Romans 13:8.

Financial Options

1. Praying to God to move people to send you money. You can either keep quiet and tell only God your needs or pray and inform others at the same time. See Chapter Fifteen, Finances – Trusting God.
2. Raid your bank account. However, this does hinder others from being a financial blessing towards your STM.
3. Ask your church for some (or all of the money). For some, asking a church to entirely finance their mission is

unethical, if they support the church little and / or are well-off themselves.

4. Ask your parents / family for a contribution. They may not be impressed by your decision to go on a STM or could greatly surprise you by their delight that you are doing something you believe in. They may be glad to see the back of you for a few weeks or months!
5. Carry out various sponsored events to help raise support – sponsored walk, cycle ride or swimming etc.
6. Make items to sell, baking cakes, bread or bird boxes etc.
7. Sell items which you no longer need – your car, sports equipment, jewellery, computer games, books etc.
8. Get a part time job or do some overtime.
9. Offer your services to clean cars, dig the garden, sweep the yard or baby-sit etc.
10. Any combination of the above, though you should always try to get your local church onboard, as you are part of the local family of God and your endeavours can stir others to be obedient to the Great Commission and raise prayer support.

Whatever you feel led to do, wrap it up in much prayer and ask God's blessing on the endeavour, and do it with all your might as unto the Lord.

Methods to Support Missions

- The apostle Paul had a 'tent makers' job for a time (Acts 18:1-3 and 2 Thessalonians 3:7-9). Paul tried to provide for his own necessities and for those that were with him (Acts 20:34-35).
- On occasions, Paul asked various churches to 'help him on his way,' or 'send him on his journey' (Romans 15:24, 1 Corinthians 16:6 and 2 Cor. 1:15-16 – financially etc.).
- Paul asked the church to assist others such as Phoebe, a fellow labourer, 'in whatever business she has need of' (Romans 16:1-2).
- When Paul was in prison, Philemon's runaway slave, Onesimus, assisted him. Paul wrote: '…That on your behalf he might minister to me in my chains for the Gospel' (Philemon 13). Onesiphorus also 'ministered' – 'in many ways he helped me' (2 Timothy 1:18), NIV, to the incarcerated Paul in Ephesus as one who 'often refreshed me' which implies food and clothing (2

Timothy 1:16-18). The gift of ministering or service from Romans 12:6-7 is a general ministry of helpfulness to others in an unobtrusive way, which could include giving of your time e.g. 'serving tables' and helping to distribute food as demonstrated in Acts 6:1-6.

- Romans 10:15 says, 'How shall they preach unless they are sent?' When a church sends someone out on a STM then it is their duty to financially (and prayerfully) look after them, unless they have forewarned the STM-er that they are unable to, due to financial restraints.
- The Philippian Church sent aid for Paul's necessities by the hand of Epaphroditus (Philippians 4:15-16), which was 'a sweet smelling aroma, an acceptable sacrifice, well pleasing to God.'

Asking for Money

The unnamed writer for the *Short-term Service Directory 2009* wrote: 'How do I go about raising support? A good place to start is by telling people about your plans. If you don't talk about it then others may miss out on the opportunity to bless you. Think creatively about sponsored events. It's a great way to get your friends involved. Wherever possible, your church should be involved in your plans and there may be funds available to help you. And don't forget to pray. Amazingly, this is often the last thing people do. In my past experience of sending teams to Africa, I have been amazed to see how the funds come in for team members. God stuns me every time! Largely, it's because they've prayed and had others praying with them. We have a great provider and should never underestimate His generosity.'[1]

Jesus was teaching a huge crowd of people and having compassion on them, He wanted to feed them. He delegated this duty to the disciples. They found a lad who had five barley loaves and two small fish, which was miraculously multiplied to feed more than five thousand men, besides women and children (Matthew 14:13-21 and John 6:1-14). On another occasion, four thousand men were fed, besides women and children with seven loaves and some fishes (Matthew 15:32-39). In other words, God can provide for your needs. In the case of the feeding of the five thousand, the disciples asked a young lad if they could have his large 'lunch' so that Jesus could use it. What is in your hands that Jesus can use to help finance your STM?

I was given a large some of money and 'knew' it was in answer to prayer so that I could go on a two week STM. The team leader booked my plane ticket, but my church was not enthusiastic when I told them what I had done with *their* gift. I was informed that the money was for next terms college fees! Veronica – America.

The Church and Finances

If your local church sends you out on a STM then it is generally their duty and responsibility to pay for the mission, though not all churches have the resources (Romans 10:15 and 1 Timothy 5:8, 18). The apostle Paul received money from some churches in order to minister to others because he did not want to be a financial burden (2 Corinthians 11:7-9 and 2 Thessalonians 3:8) – so don't be a burden to your local church! However, many churches would be delighted to assist any of their *committed* members to go on a STM; those who have proved faithful at home. The Philippian church sent aid for Paul's necessities by the hand of Epaphroditus (Philippians 4:15-16) which was 'a sweet smelling aroma, an acceptable sacrifice, well pleasing to God.' On occasions, Paul asked various churches to 'help him on his way' or 'send him on his journey' (Romans 15:24, 1 Corinthians 16:6 and 2 Corinthians 1:15-16). Paul also asked the church to assist other fellow labourers (Romans 16:1-2 and 1 Corinthians 16:10-11).

If you have been a receiver of spiritual things, it is your duty to help minister in material things, to continue the spread of the Good News (Romans 15:26-29, 2 Timothy 1:16-18 and 3 John 5-8). If you have more than enough, it is your duty to share (Luke 3:8-11 and 1 John 3:17-18). The disciples sent aid to the brethren living in Judea (Acts 11:29-30 and Romans 15:26-28). The phrase, 'Send them forward on their journey' (3 John 6), means to provide aid for travelling preachers. These helps can be: accommodation, recommendations, food and money etc., and inhospitality is condemned (3 John 9-11).

In the Bible, there is a spiritual principle of sowing and reaping – if you help others, God will help you. Nearly a decade ago, I gave £1,000 ($1,600) to help send a STM-er around the world. Little did I know that the Lord would send me to many countries of the world on my own STMs, and He paid all the bills! John – England.

Chapter Fifteen

Finances – Trusting God

'As the eyes of servants look to the hand of their masters, as the eyes of a maid to the hand of her mistress, so our eyes look to the Lord our God...' Psalm 123:2.

Jesus said, "Seek first the Kingdom of God and His righteousness, and all these things shall be added unto you" Matthew 6:33.

Not Asking for Money

In the previous chapter, we looked at raising support and financing short-term missions (STMs), the different financial options and asking for money, but in this chapter, we look at different aspects of raising support as we trust God to provide for all our needs for the STM (outside of the influence of others).

Most people who go on STMs are happy to ask people for their financial support, but this may not be you. Some may not feel able to ask for money towards their STM or like Abraham, after rescuing Lot, he refused the spoils of war from the King of Sodom, thus not allowing the king any opportunity to boast that he had made Abraham rich (Genesis 14:12-24). You'll be surprised how many individuals or churches give small amounts towards STMs (or nothing at all) and then boast as if they entirely supported the mission team!

> The small mission team stood before the church as the pastor prayed a blessing on the mission; insinuating that the church was sending us out. Little did the congregation know that the church never financially supported us in any of our missions, and it was the Holy Spirit who told us to Go! Lucardo – Italy.

Your Own Provision

You may be praying for money for your STM and you may be the answer to your own needs! The apostle Paul worked as a tentmaker for a time (Acts 18:1-3 and 2 Thessalonians 3:7-9) which allowed him to pay his way whilst participating in the

Great Commission. The term 'tentmaker' is now synonymous with Christians who work on the mission field to support themselves and / or who have an occupation, which permits them to stay within a country. Paul tried to provide for his own necessities and for those that were with him (Acts 20:34-35).

Nehemiah was the governor of Jerusalem, yet he refused to tax the people or to take what was rightfully his, because the people were already very poor. He even provided out of his own means for all his servants and administrators (Nehemiah 5:16-19). Thus, if your church is hard-up and you are not, don't expect them to pay for your STM. Could you get yourself a Saturday job? Work hard and save as much as you can towards the cost of your STM.

It is wrong to expect others to make sacrifices to send you on your STM, if you have wasted you own resources on 'good living.'

I was reading about the life and sacrifices of J. Hudson Taylor who founded the China Inland Mission in the second half of the nineteenth century; the phrase economise to evangelise[1] came to mind as he lived a very frugal life in order to be better equipped in his part in the Great Commission. Hudson bought cheaper food, less coal for the fire and walked more frequently rather than take public transport. He economised so he could be an extra blessing as he visited the slums of London, England, distributing tracts, preaching and relieving the poor. His sacrifices also helped him pay his college fees as he was training to be a medical missionary, which later opened many doors for him in the hard land of China.

David Livingstone in the first few years of his ministry in Africa, wrote: 'I feel the necessity more than ever of active devotedness to the Redeemer's cause. I don't feel anything we usually call sacrifices at home to be such. There is so much to counter balance them that they really don't deserve the name...'[2]

Asking for Goods

Whilst some people do not feel comfortable to ask for money for their STM, they may wish to ask for financial support for supplies, such as for the construction of a building, a water pump, medical supplies, Bibles or other Christian materials. But, whatever they decide, it is between them and God. At other times, there may be no other option, but to look to God to supply all your money for your STM as all other avenues have failed.

Bible teacher, F.B. Meyer said, "You do not test the resources of God until you attempt the impossible."

Looking to God by Faith

God may call you to look to Him by faith for your needs (Hebrews 11:1), and if He has, you need to be guided by Him very meticulously (see Proverbs 16:3, Proverbs 16:9, Psalm 32:8, Psalm 123:2 and Psalm 127:1). Don't play with sin because sin separates us from God. The psalmist wrote: 'No good thing will He [God] withhold from them that walk uprightly' (Psalm 84:11). Are you walking uprightly / living a godly life?

You may wish to make your needs known only to God or you may feel at liberty to share your prayer needs with a faithful friend, so that he or she can pray specifically and intelligently. Beware, they may feel that you are dropping hints; this can also be true of prayer letters. Only God knows the heart and the motives, but we can so easily deceive ourselves; do not despise gifts from family or friends, or the widow's mite.

Jesus said, "He who is faithful in what is least is faithful also in much; and he who is unjust in what is least is unjust also in much. Therefore if you have not been faithful in the unrighteous mammon, who will commit to your trust the true riches? And if you have not been faithful in what is another man's, who will give you what is your own?" Luke 16:10-12.

George Müller

Prussian-born, George Müller was based in Bristol, England, and 'prayed in' £1.5 million, from 1833 until his death in 1898. In 2014, the money would be in excess of £90,000,000 ($144 million)! At the height of his ministry he supported 2,100 orphans, 75 day schools and 29 Sunday schools, having nearly 10,000 pupils, and assisted a little under 200 missionaries from the China Inland Mission, so he not only looked to his own ministry needs but that of others.

In 1834, George Müller founded The Scriptural Knowledge Institution for Home and Abroad. Some of the rules were: 'We never intend to ask unconverted persons of rank or wealth to countenance this institution...in the name of God we set up our banners. We do not mean to ask unbelievers for money. We never intend to enlarge the field of labour by contracting debt...but in secret prayer...we shall carry the wants of the Institution to the Lord, and act according to the means that God shall give us.'

A year before his death, George Müller stated that he had established 117 schools scattered across the globe, and through the Scriptural Knowledge Institution, 279,000 Bibles in various languages, 1,440,000 New Testaments along with 109,000,000 books, pamphlets and tracts had been distributed!

George Müller had five main Scriptures, which were conditional for his needs and those of his ministry. First, he had to ask God (Matthew 7:7-8). Second, he had to be assured that what he was praying was God's will (1 John 5:14). Third, he asked in Jesus' name, so that God would be glorified (John 14:13-14). Fourth, he prayed in faith and with faith, believing that he would receive (Mark 11:24). Fifth, he knew that if he had sin in his heart his prayers would not be heard (Psalm 66:18).

J. Hudson Taylor, founder of the China Inland Mission said, "God's work, done God's way, will not lack God's resources."

God's Miraculous Provision
- Clothes did not wear out (Deuteronomy 8:4).
- The widow's oil and flour multiplied (1 Kings 17:9, 14-16).
- Oil was miraculously multiplied (2 Kings 4:1-7).
- Money in the mouth of a fish (Matthew 17:24-27).
- The feeding of the five and four thousand (Matt. 16:8-10).
- Turning water into wine (John 2:1-11).

There were only two of us going on a STM – we were praying and trusting God to financially provide for our mission. Within 24 hours of our departure, the remaining fifteen or so percent of our budget was supplied, in three gifts, from three people whom had never supported us before and no solicitation was made. We were very impressed and we rejoiced in the Lord for His provision, though we would have liked to have been delivered sooner! Matthias – Tunisia.

Rees Howells was a missionary to Gazaland, Africa, during 1915-1920. In 1924, he founded the Bible College of Wales, without a committee, council or denomination backing him. He lived by faith, trusting God to provide his everyday needs as he walked in obedience to Him. In reference to founding the College, he wrote: 'God wanted to prove that faith and prayer are efficient agents, along with implicit trust in His Word for meeting all needs. He wanted to raise up a college to be a testimony to the world that God's work, carried on by the Holy Ghost, needs not the patronage of the world and that God's work, carried on in God's way, will never lack finances, because God is the owner of all the silver and gold.'[3]

Mary Slessor, missionary to West Africa, said, "Lord, the task is impossible for me but not for Thee. Lead the way and I will follow. Why should I fear? I am on a Royal Mission. I am in the service of the King of kings."

God's Provision

We may tend to believe that God's provision will always come by means of a stranger handing us large sums of money. This was not the experience of the apostle Paul; it is not mine (though I am ready to receive!). Paul received support from churches and friends. I've received the same, alongside "blessed handshakes" (in which money appears), anonymous cheques (checks) have been posted to me (but they are signed!), and hand delivered envelopes with money inside have been posted through my letter box. Other Christians have received wads of notes / bills! Don't be disappointed if your parents, church, friends or work colleagues give you money towards your STM – this is God's provision. To scorn them as donors is to scorn God's means of support. God is practical! Be thankful for the widow's mite as well as the businessman's bonus!

Trust God

Whatever you do, trust God to lead and guide you as He has promised to provide for your needs as long as we seek His Kingdom first (Matthew 6:33 and Philippians 4:19). We are also informed: 'Be anxious for nothing, but in everything by prayer and supplication, with thanksgiving, let your requests be made known to God and the peace of God, which surpasses all understanding will guard your hearts and minds through Christ Jesus' (Philippians 4:6-7). In the parable of the labourers, Jesus said, "You also go into the vineyard and whatever is right I will give you" (Matthew 20:4). 'God's man [or woman] in God's place at God's work done in God's way will never lack God's supply' – Mrs Charles E. Cowman, President of the Oriental Missionary Society who founded World Gospel Crusades in 1949.

> My church promised to support me on my STM, but they NEVER sent me any money! However, the Lord sent me money by other means – the message was clear, put your trust in the Lord, not in man! Paul – USA.

Prayer Support – It's Vital

Prayer support for your STM is essential and your local church should know all about it and you. Long before you depart on your STM, you should ask your church to pray for you, and speak to whoever leads the weekly prayer and / or mission meetings. Send them a copy of your itinerary (if you have one, but not if it is confidential), and keep them up to date. If possible, send regular emails back to your supporters and encourage them and remind them that you value their prayers. Some church members will be very diligent in lifting you up to God in prayer and other members of your team.

> Before we left on our STM we prayed every week as a group. Our leader encouraged us to contact our churches and friends to ask them to pray for us. There were at least ten different churches praying for us, potentially thousands of people! Chenghee – Korea.

On your return home, remember to report back to your prayer supporters and tell them how things went – good or bad, but don't dwell on the negative. You may be given a five or ten minute slot to briefly summarise your mission and to share answer to those prayers.

Experience has taught me, that just a handful of very committed people (genuine intercessors) praying regularly and persistently for the STM team is more effective than hundreds who have no real concern, and no burden.

> 'The apostle Paul wrote to the church at Rome: 'For God is my witness, whom I serve with my spirit in the Gospel of His Son, that without ceasing I make mention of you always in my prayers...' Romans 1:9.

Chapter Sixteen

How much Money will I need?

'Nor was there anyone among them who lacked; for all who were possessors of lands or houses sold them and brought the proceeds of the things that were sold and laid them at the apostles' feet and they distributed to each as anyone had need' Acts 4:34-35.

Jesus said to the disciples, "When I sent you without money bag, sack and sandals, did you lack anything?" So they said, "Nothing" Luke 22:35.

The Budget

On any short-term mission (STM) there are lots of things to budget for and you do not want to cut corners or make a financial mistake as it will cost you in more ways than one. For those who are joining a mission organisation, all the costs will have been worked out and they will be able to inform you of any other money you may need, or what is not included in the price. If you have a Student Card you may be able to get a discount on your plane ticket or other items.

If you are travelling with your church, (you may be the leader who is organising the trip) or a group of friends are making up the mission team, then the smaller your budget, the more strains and tensions that will arise. If your daily budget is tight you may find yourself haggling over pennies and cents; a fraction of the cost of a chocolate bar – and in that situation you lose sight of the purpose of the mission.

If you are financially exploited, (and you can expect it at least once), on any independent mission exceeding a month, then it may take weeks to recover from your loss or overspend in the only overpriced hotel in town. Some towns and countries are more expensive than others, and whilst you may overspend in one, you can make savings in others.

An extra £3 ($5) per person a day in a developing country can make all the difference between a flee pit of a room and one that is adequate, whilst in Europe, the difference between adequate and nice can be an additional £25 ($40) per person. Your church may have arranged your stay with the locals and whilst they may not charge you rent, you cannot be a burden to them, financially or otherwise. If you are the leader of a young inexperienced STM team then you don't want to be taking them to flee pit accommodation!

If you are based in one location for weeks or months, then it is easier to work out the cost of living. If you will be in several locations, even across countries you will need to take an average costing of the entire trip.

Daily Living Expenses – Cost per Day

If you are going on your STM independently of a mission organisation, you will need to work out your daily living expenses, the cost per day – how much can I live on? This must include: accommodation, food and transport. As you will be going in pairs (or more) you must include your budget and the other STM-er budget (your friend) to get the total daily budget. It is cheaper for two people to share the same room than if you both had single rooms in the same hotel. Some rooms can accommodate three or four people and therefore you pay a lot less than if you had two rooms. You will probably be eating together at the same restaurant, fast-food outlet, roadside food stall or self-catering, so a common pot with all things shared is the best financial solution. But disagreements can arise if your friend eats twice as much as you or only buys the expensive meals or branded fizzy drinks instead of the cheaper local ones.

For example, if the cost per day is £24 ($38) for two of you (you and your mission buddy), this means a personal budget of £12 ($19) per day. £12 ($19) per person per day (going in pairs) might be OK for South East Asia, but in parts of Africa would be a stretch and would be nigh impossible in some African countries, such as Zambia or South Africa, where £18+ ($29+) per person a day is more realistic. Though you can live and eat as cheap as you want to, but flee pit, cockroach and rat infested hostels and rooms will get you down after a while, and can be damaging to your health. It is also false economy and can dampen your mood, making your STM less effective.

Some STM-ers say you can live on $8 (£5) a day in Asia. That's only possible if you sleep in flee pit accommodation (where bedbugs, cockroaches and possibly other vermin rule); you eat from roadside food stalls, stay in one location and never take public transport. Be realistic, get a real budget and prepare for additional costs. Joe – USA.

The Extra Ten Percent

The leader of a church who is estimating the cost of the STM should always add the extras just in case – ten percent. A mixed group of eight to ten people will often need better accommodation / better food than just two people participating on their own STM who are more happy to go with the flow. Within any large group, there will be greater needs and by budgeting in additional finances it will make it easier for the group, and hopefully reduce the chances of illness, bedbug bites and grumblers! See also Chapter Seventeen, The Independent STM-er Budget.

My missions have taught me that you always need 10% more money for your STM. I had $40 (£25) stolen and because I had no reserve funds I suffered trying to budget that loss. Michael – India.

Plane Ticket

Shop around for your plane ticket as there are bargains to be had, search on the internet and use budget airlines if possible. Some non-European countries do not like permitting people into their country if they only have a one-way ticket. They are suspicious and think you may be a burden on their society or are up to no good. Make sure that the correct spelling of your name in on the ticket and keep the return / roundtrip ticket safe! Confirm the time of your departure three days in advance. See also Booking a Plane Ticket in Chapter 17.

Travel to and from the Airport

Do not forget the cost of your travel to and from the airport. This may be by train, coach (minibus for a group) or by car and if it's the latter, you will need to budget the additional cost of a long stay car park (parking lot) if you're going for less than three weeks. Long stay car parks (parking lots) are always cheaper offsite in locked compounds than at the airport. If your plane arrives back home after 11pm, or sometimes as early as 9pm (depending on where you live) you may not be able to get a train or coach back home and will be stuck at the airport until morning! Bear this in mind when you are looking for a flight and remember that midweek flights are generally cheaper (Tuesday-Thursday) than at weekends, and book well in advance.

The Cost of a Visa

Visas – prices vary between countries and for different nationalities. Most consulates charge in U.S. dollars; the standard visa fee ranges from being free to $200 (£125), though most are around $50 (£31) for a single entry visa. Multi-entry visas can cost considerably more and your visa may state by which method you can enter or leave the country – by land or by air or state at which entry or exit. Unless your mission organisation states otherwise you do not need a business visa (but a tourist one) as you are not going to trade, to make money. The cost of a visa can change from one month to the next, depending on diplomatic relationships and how hard-up the country is! In Asia and Africa, you *only* pay in U.S. dollars.

In Kathmandu, Nepal, we got our visa for the next country and took the bus. When we got to Dhaka, we realised that we could not leave the country by airplane unless we got our visas amended. This took half a day of travel and bureaucracy, to fill in the right forms, to get the correct stamps and the signature of the correct civil servant! Edward – Bangladesh.

Inoculations and Jabs

Prevention is better than cure so have all the jabs and inoculations you need before you depart. Tetanus and Hepatitis jabs are free in the UK – see your local doctor. Prices do vary between health centres for other non-NHS jabs and only designated centres can give certain inoculations such as yellow fever. You must always take the accompanying yellow fever certificates with you when you travel abroad as the border guards may ask to see it. Without it, you will not be permitted to enter certain countries or be issued with a visa! The jab costs from £40-60 ($60-100).

Jabs x3 against the rabies virus are around £100 ($160) but are only really needed if you are going into remote jungle-like areas. The choice is yours. Dogs, monkeys, skunks, bats and other creature can be carrying the rabies virus and are found in many places of the world. Even if you are bitten or scratched by these animals you still need another course of treatment which is equally expensive, but potentially life saving.

> I skipped some jabs at home and bought a non-effective treatment in a developing country – though I did not know it at the time! I got really sick. I saved time and money at home, but it cost me in the long run. George – Laos.

Medication

Some anti-malarial tablets are taken daily, others are taken weekly and you may have to take them two weeks (or longer) before departure and two weeks after your return. There can be side affects; but you DO NOT want to catch malaria. It is reported that fifty percent of local medicines (especially anti-malarial brands) in some developing countries are ineffective. You may save a little, but it could cost you your life! Expect to pay from £50-100 ($80-160) for a six-month supply in a Western nation, plus the cost of a private prescription.

If you are on the pill, some medicines can make this form of contraception less effective, so married couples beware; on your one year STM you may return home with an extra mouth to feed!

> In the 1870s, Rev. Dr. Robb, of the Calabar Mission (West Africa – Niger region), in relation to missionaries wrote: 'The Church should select the fittest men and women for such a climate and the best means known should be used to preserve them. The laws of health should be ascertained and obeyed.'[1]

Travel Insurance

Travel Insurance is from £50-200 ($80-320) for three months to a year. You will probably have to get a backpackers type travel insurance as the majority of insurance companies do not extend cover for lengthy periods of time – though if you're only doing your STM in one country it should be cheaper than if you will be passing through several. If you are part of a mission organisation they will be able to advise you.

I do not advise travelling abroad on a STM without travel insurance and be very diligent in filling out the application form. Always put in the correct details and double-check. In late July 2009, a national newspaper covered the story of Andrea Salkeld from Newton, Chester, UK, who became critically ill whilst on holiday in Barcelona, Spain. The thirty-five year old mother of two, collapsed with a heart attack and fell into a coma and may now have brain damage. She had booked her travel insurance online, but because the wrong dates were filled in, her insurers say she isn't covered. The family now face medical bills of thousands of pounds and must also pay £18,000 ($28,800) for an air ambulance home to England.[2]

Shop around online for good insurance deals and remember that if you participate in extreme sports (on your day off – even skiing) you may not be covered. 'Acts of God' are not covered. Always read the small print (however tedious) and remember that most policies do not cover expensive electrical goods, laptops, digital cameras and only a limited amount of cash. Always keep the details of your travel insurance emergency telephone number and policy details handy. In some countries, you can have two broken legs and be lying in a hospital corridor, but you will not be treated unless you have the means to pay!

In mid-April 2010, volcanic ash from Iceland closed the skies of parts of Europe for six days. Tens of thousands of passengers were stranded at airports worldwide, whilst ferries and trains in and out of parts of Europe were booked solid for days with bedlam ensuing! Many people ran out of money and some could not obtain a return flight for a further two weeks! Some airlines by law are responsible for their stranded passengers and 'reasonable compensation' can be claimed, e.g. the hotel bill.

David Livingstone was the famed missionary explorer of the mid nineteenth century who opened up central Africa to the world. In 1856, he returned to England, having spent seventeen years in Africa. He had travelled over 11,000 miles; caught fever thirty times and had been endangered by seven attempts on his life. Thankfully, your STM will not be so extreme! Livingstone wrote: 'I have also found the art of successful travel consisted in taking as few impedimenta as possible, and not forgetting to carry my wits about me, the outfit was rather spare [sparse], and intended to be still more so when we should come to the canoe. Some would consider it injudicious [unwise] to adopt this plan, but I had a secret conviction that if I did not succeed it would not be for lack of 'knicknacks' advertised as indispensable for travellers, but from want of 'pluck,' [courage] or because a large array of baggage excited the cupidity [extreme greed for material wealth] of the tribes through whose country we passed.'[3]

So whilst there are some items you may need to acquire for your STM, you do not need to go over-the-top. See chapters Twenty-Two and Twenty-Three, Items to Buy and What may be Practical, and Gadgets and Bling – Do I pack it?

Chapter Seventeen

The Independent STM-er Budget

Jesus said, "The time is fulfilled and the Kingdom of God is at hand. Repent and believe in the Gospel" Mark 1:15.

Jesus said, "Go into all the world and preach the Gospel to every creature" Mark 16:15.

Independent Short-Term Missions (STMs)
If you go on an independent STM you may be led of the Lord to stay in a single location or move to different towns or cities or even across countries. The latter approach will broaden the STM-er's horizon and bring added experience in the college of life, to reveal the different needs amongst those to whom they are serving. The former helps one to concentrate all their efforts in one place. Your STM may be in your own country as you work with a church or Christian ministry in another state or county for any period of time. You may even travel from one church or town to the next, preaching, evangelising and looking for opportunities to share the Good News.

The independent STM-er will encounter many more incidences that are varied and run into more problems than one who only stays in one location. A Christian centre, mission compound or the local hotel or youth hostel may be great; but the monotony of an isolated location can also bring about its own problems, especially when team members have fallen out or if there is no place for privacy.

What to Budget For – The Independent STM-er:
- Plane ticket and travel to and from the airport. Possible long-term car park (parking lot) fees for the car.
- Visas – prices vary between countries, from nothing to $200 (£125), though most are around $50 (£31). In Asia and Africa, you *only* pay in dollars.
- Inoculations and jabs – within the UK many are free; others range from £40-60 ($60-100). Jabs x3 against the rabies virus are around £100 ($160).

- Medication – anti-malarial tablets from £50-100 ($80-160) for a six-month supply, plus a private prescription.
- Cost per day – which must include accommodation, food and transport.
- Emergency money (10%+).
- Gift money to help others and to bless them.
- Money for an interpreter, guide or vehicle hire.

See also Chapter Sixteen, How much Money will I need?

Add the Extra

As a good rule, whatever you have estimated your STM to cost, add a minimum of ten percent and throw in some extra just in case, as the unexpected can happen. Visa prices can double overnight without warning and some countries will not issue you with a visa until they have a letter from your embassy and these do not come cheap (UK embassies charge £45 ($72) per letter in 2015). The cost of oil can rapidly increase and I have known fixed taxi prices to rise twenty-five percent within two days.

Some STM-ers recommend an extra twenty percent on top of your estimated bill, but from personal experience, this is excessive and perhaps goes down to bad planning in the first place; ten percent is a more reasonable amount. If you do not spend all the allocated money, you have lost nothing. If the church has largely supported the STM then it is best (unless you are directed otherwise) to return the remaining amount back to the church (or support others who are going on a STM, or support indigenous evangelists) and inform the church treasurer / leaders – you do not want bad reports to circulate that you and the STM team have fleeced the church! The church may give you the additional ten percent float / emergency money on the understanding that if it is not used, it is returned.

On several occasions a two week ministry trip as part of an organised team to North Africa has cost me £500 ($800) a head (the rest of the body comes free!), but that same amount of money can last months in Eastern Africa or Asia. However, when I did the same North Africa STM with friends, I was able to reduce the cost, knowing where savings could be made without lowering the standards or the itinerary of the mission trip.

I took a team of students to North Africa on a STM and we had prayed in all the finances. I made the STM-ers responsible for their own money. However, when some of the students saw they would not need the entire amount that had been allocated to them, they began spending it in on unnecessary things – squandering it, much of what had been given sacrificially. Now, I give each STM-er "pocket money" so that they can buy a snack or drink without having to ask me. Fortuanto – Morocco.

Buying a Plane Ticket

The plane ticket is always the heftiest part of any STM budget and unless you are flying on a budget airline (the no frills airlines) you could pay more than £1,000 ($1,600) for a return (roundtrip) trip to Australia, whereas the Orient (China, Korea or Japan can cost up to £800 ($1,300) and these prices are for economy class. Naturally during holiday and festivals (the peak season) prices increase and will decrease during low season or as supply and demand dictates.

Look to see what time your proposed flight departs and arrives before you purchase. It may depart at 10am, which is not a bad time, but can you drive the 3 hrs to the airport (or catch the coach) and arrive within the two-hour check-in period? This means you will have to leave your home by 5am! But you still need to allow extra time for a flat tyre. Some evening flights mean that you arrive in the dark and will have to check straight into a hotel, which means an extra night without having seen any of the country, and unless you have pre-booked, you may pay more for your accommodation than you would like to. If your plane lands at 9pm, it can take up to 1 hour for baggage retrieval and then you have to take public transport (but often a taxi) to take you to your destination. Nighttime taxis have a higher rate than daytime ones.

Weekend flights are more expensive as is Friday and Monday. International airport departure taxes can be as high as £85 ($136) each way. Fuel duty can add an extra cost to your ticket even after you have bought it! If you use your credit card then a handling fee is often applied, from £3-9 ($5-14), but can be 1.5-3% of the ticket. Therefore, if your plane ticket cost £400 ($640), a 3% handling fee will be £12 ($19).

My evening flight into Cairo was delayed by three hours. I arrived in at 3am just as the airport was closing and there were no taxis. I had to negotiate with some of the airport workers for a lift into the city centre. I was in no hurry as finding a hotel at that time of the morning can be tricky. Newton – Egypt.

Budget Airlines

Budget airlines (the no frills carriers) are notorious for cancelling their flights when not enough seats have been sold and whilst you will get a refund, and a slim possibility of getting on the next flight, the problem is yours, not theirs. You may get a refund of the cost of the £30 ($48) flight, but to book another flight (to the same destination) could cost you £120+ ($190+) and all the inconvenience that entails.

With budget airlines, real bargains can be had but you must always read the small print. Prices do not include taxes and duty, (air passenger duty) which in Britain is £13 ($21) each way for economy class. The cheapest budget airline seats are sold well in advance. When the seat is "free," the taxes, duty and check-in luggage is not, nor is the handling fee and if you book over the phone the cost is also more expensive.

Additional budget airlines fees can include: Online payment handling fee, check-ins if not done online, priority boarding fee (optional), check-in baggage per flight, as well as an additional fee for each bag. A fee for sport or musical equipment, flight change fee and a name change fee, which is always the most expensive.

I have thankfully never had any problems flying with any budget airline, but their charges can considerably add up; and their 'add-on fees' alter frequently. Airport taxes have to be added onto the price of the flight which are set by the airport / government and are beyond the control of any carrier. There are no complimentary refreshments on budget airlines, but food or drink can be purchased in-flight at a good mark-up.

In essence, read the small print and the more you can do online, the cheaper it will be. Budget airlines are designed for those who travel light and who do not check-in luggage. If you can fit all your items in one bag, take it as hand luggage – it cannot get lost!

Paul Hattaway, Director of Asia Harvest wrote: 'Often during my travels in the West I feel a bit weird. We meet many sincere Christians who spend all their time and energy "reaching" towns in their country, which already have churches on every street corner. Then we travel thousands of miles through areas of Tibet or Central Asia where not a single church building can be seen. There are no Christian workers, and few people have ever heard the name of Jesus. Such things must look strange in heaven.'[1]

Chapter Eighteen

Spend Wisely

'The fear of the Lord is the beginning of wisdom; a good understanding have all those who do His commandments. His praise endures forever' Psalm 111:10.

'His lord said to him, "Well done, good and faithful servant; you were faithful over a few things, I will make you ruler over many things. Enter into the joy of your lord" ' Matthew 25:21.

Spend Wisely

You have been saving for months, working hard and praying for finances to come in – and they have. You know where you are going to, the mission team has been prayerfully chosen (even if it is just you and your friend) and hopefully, most things will go to plan. But wouldn't it be a shame if you spent your short-term mission (STM) money unwisely and so had to come home early, or had to ask for more funds to be sent on to you?

Whilst the majority of this chapter is not relevant to those who are going with a mission organisation, there are still helpful truths that will allow your money to go further, and for you to be, hopefully, reducing the number of times you pay over the odds for items or services.

I met two Asian girls in Africa who did not know how to budget their money and it soon ran out. On one occasion, they were at a campsite and could only afford a bed in the open air! They phoned home and their parents wired them the money to fly back to Japan. Chuck – Sudan.

Pre-Booking

I rarely pre-book accommodation. On three occasions, it was a disappointment. In Ireland, the hotel was over-booked so we got turned away! When we flew into Switzerland, I had incorrectly written down the name of the road by missing out just one letter, yet a road of that name existed! Our hotel was on the other side of town and this mistake cost us nearly 2 ½ hours! On another occasion, we pre-booked inside the country of our STM for the next town and when we arrived, the accommodation was filthy and grotty. Our only condition when we booked was that the room had to be clean and even the tour guide worker was embarrassed at the hotel he had to take us to, as it was the worst in town! We phoned the tour owner who told us it was our problem! For many people in poor or developing countries, the philosophy is that as you're rich, it's your problem and even though it's not your fault, you have to pay for it!

Pre-booking tours or trains through an agent is more expensive than doing it yourself, but it does save time, though problems can be encountered. In India, the agent informed us that the train that we will be travelling on arrives and departs from the same city, but at two different train stations. What he failed to inform us was that the distance between these two stations was greater than the span across the English Channel; from England to France! It was a two-hour bus ride, but it took us three hours to find the correct pickup point as the bus did not stop at either of the two bus stations in town!

On occasions, I have taken a taxi to the booking office for the train or coach, only later to find out, it was an agent who charged me four times the actual cost of the ticket on public transport! Some drivers will take you to the agent or ticket office of *their* choice as they get a cut. Some agents sell tickets for transport that does not even exist! Whilst others will try to sell you a ticket to anywhere; even if it is in the opposite direction to where you are going! Have a map handy.

> The team got a lift on the back of a 4x4 pickup. Our other passenger was a large bristly pig. It was tied by its legs and squealed all the way as we bounced along the mud road. Rodney – Laos.

Hotels and Accommodation

The advantage of an independent group is often purchasing power – you can go to a more upmarket hotel (say 2 or 3 stars) during low season and pay the same as you would in one of a lesser quality of 1 or 2 stars. Frequently, when I travel with my brother, we ask the receptionist or manager if they have any cheaper rooms or if they can do a better deal. The worst they can say is no, and the best is a discount or an upgrade. If you don't ask you don't get! You can rent an apartment or large house for two weeks, a month or longer. Often this is easier with a person on the ground making the arrangements.

High season is holiday season or at times of religious festivals and occasionally the demand can outstrip the supply and that is when room prices / house rentals can be greatly inflated. You spend the same amount of money, but for less quality, you get to share your room with cockroaches and other vermin!

An independent STM-er may stay in many different types of accommodation, such as a hotel, motel, youth hostel, inn, B&B, guesthouse, campsite or university accommodation (outside of term time, often in the summer). I do not recommend campsites on STMs because you have to take additional gear with you (tent and sleeping bag) and security is not great. For those frequently on the move, you may wish to purchase some address labels, instead of having to write your name and address every time you check-in.

The receptionist was able to give us a discount on four rooms for three nights but it was still beyond the reach of our mission team. Our leader then spoke to the manager and asked if the hotel could be more flexible, and they were! The manager, after gentle persuasion was even kind enough to fill up the swimming pool where we relaxed in the evenings! Keumhee – Tunisia.

The bus arrived in the dark halfway through our two-day journey. A non-governmental organisation (NGO) worker who was on the bus suggested that we got a fixer to find us a place to stay (one who fixes problems for a fee). It was not necessary; we looked out of the window as we drove into town and knew where the accommodation was! The next morning, before sunrise, we boarded the bus by 6am and saw the NGO who had been there since 5am. His fixer had given him the wrong departure time, whereas we just asked the bus driver! Jason – Kenya.

What's the Cost and Haggling

When shopping, always ask the price before agreeing to buy something; otherwise you may pay more than you need to. Many people automatically inflate the prices for foreigners so haggling is often essential. Even the price of a tube of toothpaste in the marketplace can be cut in half if you haggle. This is not a case of taking advantage of the stall (or shop) owner, but the owner trying to take advantage of you!

At other times, the cost of an item in the market or on the street may seem so reasonable that it is only fair to pay them what they ask without quibbling or haggling. Do not try to beat a market seller down by minute amounts when that extra will make all the difference to them and not to you. Some people quibble over pennies and cents yet think nothing of spending fifty pounds or eighty dollars on an adventure sport for just a few hours, which is more than what the market seller earns in a month. Have a conscience and use wisdom.

The price of a bottle of water and food can vary from one shop to another so look / shop around. The amount of money saved over a bottle of water (and items of food) may seem little, but over many months, it adds up! It is better to be generous giving money to Christians than to be inadvertently giving it to people of the world who are trying to take advantage. I have been in shops and the price is on the label yet, they still expect me to pay more, so I always point out the correct price. If they still disagree, just go to another shop and pay the correct price. Vote with your feet!

' "It is good for nothing," cries the buyer; but when he has gone his way, then he boasts' Proverbs 20:14.

If the seller begins to laugh once you have handed over the money and walked off with your item, you know that you have paid over the odds, but as long as you agreed on the price, then you're both winners! In essence, pay a fair price for a fair product. If you have been ripped off (by a guide, a tout or the cost of a service), put it down to experience and learn from it.

Jesus said, "Behold, I send you out as sheep in the midst of wolves. Therefore be wise as serpents and harmless as doves" Matthew 10:16.

Chartered Transport – A Vehicle and its Driver

Be very wary, if others jump aboard your chartered transport – a vehicle and its driver, which you have hired for the day, or just to a destination. Sometimes the driver brings his friends along for the ride, whilst at other times they are there to back him up or are dropped off along route. If you are female then you should never travel without being accompanied by another woman and should refuse to go anywhere, if men begin to pile in the back of the pickup or car which you have hired.

Always, pay on arrival, not before you depart, though sometimes petrol money may be needed to get you going. If so, you may (or may not) wish to give a percentage of the money before you drive off. I especially take a dim view of price renegotiations on arrival at a destination or at worst, half way through the journey when you are in the middle of nowhere! See Matthew 20:1-13, "Did you not agree with me for a denarius?"

I hired a pickup and its driver on the side of the road, to take me to an out-of-the-way location. After taking us to the middle of nowhere, the driver stopped and demanded additional money. Try to go with someone you trust. James – Malawi.

Taxis and Public Transport

If you take a taxi use the meter (if it works) or agree on a price beforehand, if this is possible, otherwise any crazy figure could be given at the end of the journey. The danger with the meter is that you may be taken the long route. Some rickshaw drivers on arrival at your destination will ask (or even demand) more money than what you agreed before departing! Pay what you have agreed unless the 'driver' has been exceptionally helpful (then give a good tip) or if they have had to go out of the way; thus the journey took longer than anticipated.

Some countries have 'skin tax' as one Asian pastor informed me whilst laughing profusely! On occasions, locals have arranged transport for us and bought the ticket on our behalf because they pay the going rate!

In Dhaka, we could not get off a rickshaw without the driver ALWAYS demanding much more money than what we had agreed. On our arrival in the capital, a local businessman told us, "Only pay what you have agreed, not a *Tak more." Mark – Bangladesh. *The local currency.

Some taxis pick up people enroute and in many African countries, this is common. Your agreed price may only include your seat (not the entire taxi) to your destination and a five-seat car may take six or seven! It is common to be charged more than the locals. Taxi drivers (which may be a minibus taxi) upon arriving in town will either drop people off at set stops or along a route. The driver may take you to a hotel, or a selection of hotels, but naturally, you will have to pay extra if this is out of the way.

Taxi drivers often have the best local knowledge for cheap accommodation and you can save a small fortune. However, some taxi drivers or rickshaw drivers (notably in India) will take you to their preferred hotel (or shop) because they are paid to bring tourists there.

In Calcutta, we took a taxi with a local pastor and at the end of the journey, we had to pay double the meter price. The rate on the meter was set a long time ago and prices had increased since then. I am glad we were with a local; otherwise, we would have only paid the amount on the meter and accidentally short-changed the driver! Mark – India.

Borders and Hidden Taxes

If you make purchases on borders, you need to clarify not only the price, but possibly the currency as well. For example, on the Nepalese border, the hotel manager and the rickshaw drivers wanted to be paid in Indian Rupees rather than Nepalese Rupees because the rate was higher – but they only told you that when you went to pay! It is always best to find out the cost of a hotel, food, or drink, *before* you place your order, or use the establishments services as you may be in for a shock.

We went to the local cafe and ordered a drink. The cafe worker got a bottle of coke and took the top off. He told me it was two dinnars. I do not read Arabic, but I could see that the highest price on the drinks board was 0.50 dinnars. A fellow team member expostulated with the waiter, and pointed to the menu; the waiter shook his head and I had to give in. Always ask, "How much?" before you order! Nicholas – Tunisia.

Most guidebooks give approximate prices for various services and foreigners generally pay more than the locals. In India, I was taken aback at the entrance fee for tourists at the Taj Mahal. It seemed very high but then I realised that compared to Western prices it was about the same. Rarely do hotels specify their rates for nationals and non-nationals (but some do) and this policy, however official or unofficial can even apply for plane tickets.

Chapter Nineteen

Stretching Your Budget

'A little that the righteous man has is better than the riches of many wicked' Psalm 37:16.

'Wealth gained by dishonesty will be diminished, but he who gathers by labour will increase' Proverbs 13:11.

Making Savings on the Mission Field

Economising whilst on your STM can come in many shapes, sizes and varying ways and if you have learnt to economise at home then on your mission it will be just as easy, if not more. One of the best tips is to always ask the price before you buy and shop around. Shop around to save a pound (or a dollar) and as the old saying goes, if you look after the pennies (or cents) the pounds (or dollars) will take care of themselves. Once again, if you are part of a mission organisation then much of the content within this chapter will not apply to you and your situation, unless you are the leader.

The cost of accommodation varies greatly and most towns have several hotels or guesthouses, whereas some streets are full of them. In Ho Ch Minn City (Saigon), Vietnam, there were ten hotels within a one minute walk and by looking at all of them (no kidding), we got the very best deal with quality amenities. Hotels, lodges and guesthouses often have star ratings and more often than not, the lower the star, the lower the price, though it's not always the case.

If you come from the West, you will find the cost of living whilst on your STM in the vast majority of countries in Africa, large portions of Asia and South America, cheaper than at home. Sadly though, on the other hand, if you live in a developing nation and go on your STM to the West, then it will be harder as the prices and cost of living is generally higher.

Tourist Sights and Attractions

Going on a short-term mission is not a holiday and should not be regarded as one. You are going there to work, to minister and to serve others. However, it would seem strange to go to a country on a STM without seeing at least one of the sights *if* it be enroute and *if* time permits. I have travelled as part of a team on several STMs and the leader(s) have always taken the team to some sights of historical interest – including early cradles of Christianity; martyrs sites, famous mosques, a synagogue, Roman monuments and mission stations etc. At these sights, whilst we may have just a few hours to ourselves (or go round as a team) before we met back, we have always been able to do the work of the Lord, witnessing to individuals or distributing Christian materials in the local languages.

There are some countries that you may only visit once in your life and perhaps a detour of a few days over a several month trip is quite acceptable, but only possible if you are a independent STM-er. Mission organisations do not have such flexibility unless it has been pre-planned into the mission and there is a big difference between a STM of two weeks and three months.

Not everybody would agree with the previous two paragraphs, but as someone who appreciates history (and who films STMs for Christian television), I believe that each mission should be rewarding; not only spiritual, but also educational, which is character building and stimulating to the brain. I believe it adds to the experience and seeing important sights can help us understand the people and culture to whom we are ministering to, or at least understand to a small degree, civilisations from the past.

The authors of *Mack & Leeann's Guide to Short-Term Missions* wrote: 'We focus on people, not places. The Lord says taste and see that the Lord is good (Psalm 34:8), not taste the world to see the Lord. A long-term mindset encourages ongoing personal relationships rather than wanderlust. It puts tasks secondary to relationships. When you are in one place for a long time, the lure of the exotic wears off. We gently but firmly resist short-term missions that are cleverly disguised vacations. Take a vacation if you wish, but to mix vacationing with missions sends a mixed message to the people to whom you go. Drink in the sites when they happen, do not seek them out.'[1]

I took a team of teenagers to Brazil on a STM and the work went very well. But their parents had given them too much spending money and it became a problem. The teenagers wanted to go shopping all the time. Now, I stipulate an amount for STM-ers to bring (and no more), so no one will have more money than others, which also eliminates jealousy. Frederick – Brazil.

How to Save Money

When it comes to your STM, there are many ways to save money, to stretch the team's budget – shop around for the best deals. The following are suggestions to consider.

Transport Possibilities

- Look into taking two flights instead of the non-stop one, however it takes longer and is more tiring. You may be able to fly one leg of the journey via a budget airline, and as a team, you could make a good saving.
- Take the bus instead of a taxi around town.
- Rent or buy a local bicycle when you have arrived.
- Take a coach for longer distances instead of the train.
- Travel overland across borders instead of flying.

In East Asia we took an overland route to cross the border which saved us $100 (£63) each. It was great travelling with the locals and the experience was more real, rather than a sanitised airport. Henry – Asia.

Accommodation

- The cost between hotels, inns, guesthouses, lodges, B&Bs, motels, hostels and rented apartments do vary.
- It is considerably cheaper to have two rooms with four people in each rather than to have four rooms with two people in each. Is it cheaper to rent an apartment?
- As a team, negotiate a discount.
- Shop around for the best deals.
- Do I really need air-conditioning (AC), a heater or a TV in my room? Some come as standard or AC is needed!

Food and Supplies

- Avoid the expensive hotel restaurant.
- Go to the local restaurant, cafe or street vendor.
- Buy bread and fruit from the local market.

We checked-in late at night and found that the hotel menu had one set price (expensive) for a buffet meal, which did not even look appetising. We took a taxi to a fast-food joint, had a great meal, took a taxi back to our hotel and all this was cheaper than the hotel buffet! John – Swaziland.

Souvenirs and Presents

- Do you really need to buy it?
- Haggle and do not pay more than what you want to.
- If you are buying a gift for your host, make sure the item has a function, and not a mantelpiece object.
- If you are buying gifts for your supporters back home, then make sure that they will fit into your rucksack or suitcase and travel well. Who wants to bring back a broken vase?
- Do not bring back false gods, tribal facemasks, items connected with other religions or objects that are used in witchcraft / occult rituals – they are accursed objects. See Exodus 20:3-6, Deuteronomy 7:26, 13:7, Joshua 6:18, chapter 7 and Isaiah 54:11. See Appendix F.

I went to the market to buy some boxes of dates for friends and supporters back home. A local whom I had become friends with, refused the pre-packed boxes and told the seller that I wanted *fresh* dates. My new friend observed the market seller as he packed each box and threw out all the bad ones. I bought eight boxes at 1 kg each and the weight took its toll on my backpack and my body! Next time I'll buy letter openers! Gillé – Tunisia.

Scams and Warnings

Additional food that you did not order can appear on your table and you will be charged for it, though in some places in North Africa minted tea is freely served after the meal. Ask before you sip, otherwise it is too late and it goes on the bill! On rare occasions, bottled water can be delivered to your table and the seal may be broken. Always reject it, as it is but tap water at best or stream water at worse and could make you unwell. Watermelons are also sometimes pricked and left in the stream for a while to make them more juicy!

Students who desire to practise their English may also approach you. A good opportunity to evangelise but be cautious if they invite you to a cafe or restaurant, as it may be their job to drum up customers into expensive establishments – such as happens in China. On the other hand, I have been in a restaurant having a meal with a group of local students and when the bill arrived, the locals vehemently complained to the owner over the inflated foreigner's bill!

Not everything that is labelled or touted as handmade is handmade, whereas those goods that are will be more expensive than mass produced merchandise. Just because someone puts a 'present' in your hand and tells you it's free does not mean that it will cost you nothing! At other times, sellers will put items in your hand and refuse to take it back, yet expect money for it. If you don't want the item and they refuse to take it from you then place it on the ground or somewhere safe, where they can see it and just walk away. Don't be emotionally manipulated into buying items that you don't want or parting with more money than you have decided to spend.

A common swindle in Kathmandu, Nepal, is for mothers (with babies in their arms), ask you to buy powdered milk for their baby. The mother is in collusion with the shopkeeper and once you have disappeared, she returns the goods to the shop, both seller and mother get a percentage, and the cycle continues. Some beggars also work for pimps who pay them a wage whilst the pimp gets the larger proportion.

False Economy

There is a time when economising to stretch your budget is a false economy. Eating street food can be one of the best culinary experiences on a STM; it is frequently very cheap and fulfilling, but on occasions can make you unwell. Fresh fried food I have found to be the safest option, and I have always asked the vendor to put it back in the oil, or on the fire to burn off any germs as you don't know how long it has been sat around!

In the UK, I have never travelled first class on a train, but in developing countries, I have. In Egypt, for fear of tourists being injured, you can only travel on certain trains, which are very pleasant, though not as cheap as the local carriages. In India, on a very short trip with a local pastor we bought third class tickets, but were so squashed, standing bolt upright in the carriage, (and people were hanging out of the doors holding on) with sweaty armpits in your face; the experience whilst different, would rather not be repeated. The pastor told us to beware of pickpockets, which we did not need reminding of as it is a problem in public places worldwide, but as ByFaith travels with a film camera and various related items it would have cost us a small fortune if we had had our items stolen.

Sometimes it is worth paying more for peace of mind and added security whilst at other times it is merely foolish indulgence. You can travel on a night bus or train, thus saving the cost of a room, but you may not sleep much and could be unwell in the morning. In the case of train travel by night I have always paid the extra to have a bed and if possible a berth / compartment.

> Smith Wigglesworth believed in being reasonably comfortable when he travelled. His wise words were, "I'm not saving the Lord's money, I'm saving the Lord's servant."[2]

Travelling from a border town in Sudan into Khartoum was a two-day journey so we went first class. To our dismay, the carriage had no beds, the seats were hard and dusty, the fan did not work and the sliding door to our compartment fell off! The train carriage, so the Sudanese pastor informed us, came from the latter part of the nineteenth century, but we counted our blessings. We travelled with friends, thus we knew our belongings were safe, and third class had wooden slated benches; that would not have been a pleasant journey! At some ticket offices, it is assumed that you will have first class because you are a foreigner, so it pays to ask if there is a cheaper option.

In Ethiopia, the roads in the north of the country are mostly gravel and dirt and the buses are old; you get to feel all the stones in the road as you are rattled, rocked and rolled about in your seat and sometimes into the aisle! After an eight or twelve hour journey of just 150-250 km you are glad to arrive at your destination! One Korean traveller we met unwisely took a two day consecutive journey which made her unwell for two days and was incapacitated during that time. If time is money, and some say it is, then that was two days lost from her already short schedule, and if your mission is only two or three weeks then that is a big percentage of your schedule disrupted, so learn to be flexible, and take travel sickness pills.

Whilst God loves a generous giver; when you are travelling across a continent on public transport, or taking frequent journeys every few days for months on end, then these savings do add up and you are able to be an extra blessing to your interpreter, the local church or individual brethren etc.

Chapter Twenty

How to Travel with Money

'Owe no one anything, except to love one another' Romans 13:8.

'The rich rule over the poor and the borrower is servant to the lender' Proverbs 22:7.

Travelling with Money

Nobody wants to be robbed of their possessions or be stuck abroad on their short-term mission (STM) with no money. This chapter covers the methods of travelling with money; using ATMs (cash points), hard cash and other financial options. An independent STM may have additional financial concerns which an organised mission would not. If you are going on a mission across many nations for lengthy periods of time, then a selection of financial options are the best; hard cash and cash cards, so that if one option fails or is limited in one area, there is another method to fall back on.

Travellers Cheques and Travel Money Card

I have always travelled with hard cash (American dollars and British pound sterling, though euros are also good), alongside cash cards and credit cards. The first time I went abroad, I used travellers cheques and lost a lot of money due to the high rate of commission. In some developing countries, travellers cheques are not widely accepted or *only* certain brands can be cashed. I cannot recommend a prepaid Travel Money Card (TMC) because the Financial Services Compensation Scheme does not always apply; there are many restrictions on its use, and generally higher fees than a cash point (ATM) transaction.

Cash Points – Cash Cards and ATMs

Most capitals of the world have Automatic Teller Machines (ATMs), commonly referred to as cash points. Cash cards / debit cards are the greatest fiscal blessing to STM-ers or travellers. As the years tick by, cash points that accept VISA or MasterCard continue to grow and are located in more and more towns and even obscure villages. However, in some countries, one or the other is more dominant and widely accepted. Make sure you can withdraw funds (use an ATM) from abroad via your current account and you will be financially set up – that is unless your card is swallowed by the hungry hole in the wall monster! Getting a new card shipped out by courier is expensive.

Most financial institutions charge for cash withdrawals abroad when using their VISA or MasterCard debit card. This is generally a set fee of £1 ($1.50) or more, plus 2-5% of the transaction amount. The bank ATM from which you withdraw may also charge a fee. Take out the maximum amount in each transaction rather than use the ATM twice a week.

It is VERY important that you inform your bank / building society and credit card provider that you will be using your cards abroad (which country or continent and ask them to make a note on their records), as transactions out of the ordinary may be deemed as fraudulent and your card may be cancelled. Also, make sure that your cards will not expire when you are on your STM, as it is a great bother and an unnecessary hassle which can be avoided with a little preplanning.

Find out online or use a guidebook to discover if there are any cash points outside of the capital (or major cities). Make sure you take enough money to last you to the next cash point or beyond.

Credit Cards

Credit cards should be used responsibly and not to incur debt. If you are not paying your balance off IN FULL every month then you should not be using them. On the mission field, I use them to buy plane tickets and hire vehicles, and they also carry your insurance excess if you have an accident. I have known people to go on holiday and become incredibly ill and hospitalised. They have had to use their credit card to pay their hospital bills (in excess of £10,000 / $16,000) which was later reimbursed by their travel insurance.

You can withdraw money from cash points using your credit card (a Cash Advance) but I do not recommend it. You will get charged daily interest (at a VERY high rate) and some cards also charge a transaction fee. Some businesses add a handling fee when you pay by credit card, from £3-5 ($5-8), but can be 2 or 3% of the product purchase. Credit cards may be swiped through the machine twice (thus charging you twice). You may not realise this until you have checked your statement at home and weeks or months could have elapsed!

I was about to drive out of the parking lot in a hire / rental car when I received a phone call on my mobile / cell. It was my credit card provider. They had noted an unusually large transaction in Prague and were phoning to see if it was authorised. Thankfully it was. Wan-Jin – Czech Republic.

American Dollars
The American dollar is the number one currency; it is stable and is widely used across the world. In many countries in Asia, you can pay for your purchases (even at some restaurants) in dollars, whilst some establishments prefer it. Most embassies will expect you to pay for their visa in American dollars and you have to pay airport taxes in developing countries (in dollars) if this tax was not included in the price of your plane ticket. I got caught out once in Vietnam and had to rapidly exchange money before my flight departed!

I have never had denomination (bills) of higher than $50 and have travelled with mostly $20 bills. In South East Asia, they are very keen on $1 bills and as with most foreign notes / bills, they have to be clean and crisp. If they are marked or creased some Foreign Exchange Bureaux (FEB) or shops will not accept them. Some FEBs do not accept bills that are printed prior to the 2000 series (or even a more recent date). That is, if your dollar was printed before the year 2000 they will not take it. Smaller denomination of $1, $5 and $10 also occur a lesser exchange rate than larger bills. Always take a combination of bills and keep them in a waterproof belt hidden under your clothes.

In the fourth week of January 2009, the American dollar to British pound sterling rate changed to $1.35 to £1.00 (a 23-year low), rebounding a week later to $1.39. If a person in Britain exchanged £1,000 (as compared to Nov. 2008 rate, which was $2.00 to £1.00), you would have lost $650 (£403) worth of purchasing power – or 32 nights in a clean hotel in East Africa!

Foreign Exchange Bureaux
Be very careful when exchanging money, not only at a Foreign Exchange Bureaux (FEB), but also at border crossings. Make sure you do the calculations on your own calculator (that's why you have a pocket calculator) as some may be fixed and not in your favour! Looking at new money can be confusing. Take your time and count the money out, do not be hassled or rushed and

check each note / bill that it is the correct denomination with the right amount of zeros on it. Once I was handed 106,800 Tanzanian shillings when I should have received 163,800!

Always ask for mixed denominations as a wad of pre-counted money in single bills may lack one or two notes / bills. I was in India at a small FEB and some travellers exchanged their money. They asked for smaller denominations, but were told that they did not have any. I was intrigued as I had just exchanged the local currency of various denominations and knew that they had smaller bills. The travellers patiently counted out about 50 bills and told the worker that they were one short. He did not bat an eyelid and duly handed over the extra note without a word as he had been found out!

Look confident as you examine the notes / bills, as if you know what you are doing! It is always helpful to look on the internet to see what the countries bills look like – you do not want to be handed worthless out-of-circulation notes / bills. Whilst exchange rates vary by the minute, check online to see the general exchange rate.

Most major currencies can be purchased within your own country, but where and when you buy it, can vary greatly. Research has shown that it does depend on picking the right place and the right time, though the latter is not so easy to 'predict' but research in the former is easy – just shop around for the best deal! Difference between rates can seem deceptively slim, but if it is not in your favour, it can quickly push up the cost of your STM! The person who exchanges at the 'last minute' at the airport or an international train station will get the worst rate.

Research by Currency Direct in August 2009, revealed that travellers could end up with an average of seven percent fewer euros or dollars per pound if they do not shop around; with a whopping eleven percent difference between the best and worse exchange rates. This equates to a loss of more than £100 ($160) when applied to the weekly average British family of four, £1,046 ($1,674) per week overseas holiday spending money.[1]

In the Pacific, at the end of our STM, I changed all of the team's local currency into U.S. dollars and lost lots of money because of the poor exchange rate. Only afterwards did I notice that British pound sterling was a good rate, but by then it was too late. I could have saved loads and changed the British pound sterling back in the U.S. Tim – Papua New Guinea.

Money Transfers

If you are abroad and you need money quickly there are ways of obtaining it without selling any of your body parts or vital organs! There is Money Gram and Western Union, the latter having more branches where money can be sent and received. An instant transfer costs around £25 ($40), but if you can wait a day or two the service costs around £10 ($16).

You can also transfer money from one bank or building society account to one abroad. If the sending and receiving banks are of the same company then it is a generally a free service, but sending money between different banks can cost upwards of £20 ($32) and can take up to one week to clear. The receiving bank may charge for their service and exchange rates (which fluctuate), can drop significantly within a week.

Good planning is the best prevention of trying to eliminate needing extra cash by working out the correct costs, the total budget and cost per person. It is ESSENTIAL if you are the team leader, as you cannot expect your team members to pay for your oversights / mistakes, though unforeseen circumstances, 'Acts of God' occasionally occur (see pages 82 and 98).

We were planning an evangelistic campaign in South America. I spoke to the South American's involved in the campaign and delegated various duties. I told them not to spend too much money and be careful with the finances as we had a limited budget. When we arrived on our STM, they had overspent on the budget and did not know how they were going to pay the bills. I became very concerned for the treasurer of the campaign because his reputation within the community would have been damaged. I called the local group together, I told them how unwise they had been and after giving some practical advice, said that I would pay all the outstanding debt. Frank – Brazil.

Internet Banking and Internet Cafes

My advice is not to use your online bank account (even to check your funds) from an internet cafe (especially in developing countries) or cheap hotel. Try to avoid making purchases online. A programme could be collecting all your details. WiFi security is also vulnerable, however, do not get paranoid, just be aware of these things. If you are not using your own laptop, Tablet, iPad or smartphone, remember to 'log out' after all applications where you have had to enter a password to access information – even your email account and do not press, 'Remember Me' or, 'Keep me signed in all Day,' or unclick the button when it automatically defaults to that setting. After you have logged out of your account you should delete the computer's history – information that remains within the computer's memory such as websites visited and passwords. This takes from 5-10 minutes in developing countries. With your internet browser open, click on Tools > Internet Options > Delete; where you can delete your browsing history: Temporary Internet Files, Cookies, History, Form Data and Passwords.

Daily Budgeting, Journal and Receipts

I would encourage anybody who goes on a STM to keep a journal, however brief, even if just a short paragraph per day. In sensitive countries a detailed journal can be incriminating evidence! The weakest ink is better than the strongest memory. In my A5 spiral bound journals (a new one for each STM) I keep a daily record of all the places that I have been, what I have eaten or seen, observations, how I feel and the day's expenses.

Daily, I tally up the expenses (accommodation, food and drink, travel for the team) and then add them together to form the week's expenses and then add up the monthly budget. This way I can keep a tight tab of the mission budget and if we have overspent one week, we have to make cuts the following week. The monthly tallies are recorded at the back of my journal alongside all the money exchanged and withdrawals at cash points (ATMs), with a separate list for money, which is given to Christian workers (interpreter, evangelists, pastors) or love gifts to Christian ministries / organisations (schools, orphanages, money for Bibles or other Christian materials etc.). This helps to balance the books.

A journal is very interesting to read when you go through what you did each day, one year on from the mission and after several years, you can pick it up as a travel adventure and the memories will come flooding back.

Any mission leader should keep a tight tab on the team's budget and some will carry a notebook to write down all the costs of the team, which is very wise. Where possible keep receipts (especially in regards to accommodation, transport, food, materials as well as gifts) as you may have to submit them to the church treasurer. Many small cafes and restaurants do not issue receipts, but when they do, remember to calculate how much this costs in your home currency and write it on the receipt.

Chapter Twenty-One

Preparation Before You Depart

'Unless the Lord builds the house, they labour in vain who build it...' Psalm 127:1.

'Commit your works to the Lord and your thoughts will be established' Proverbs 16:3.

Prepare as a Team

If you are going on a short-term mission (STM) as a team then you should prepare as a team. The group, where possible should meet together once a week, for prayer, discussion, mission orientated Bible study etc., and things should be fully explained so that each individual knows what will be expected of them. If you are joining a mission organisation, then there will probably be some training within your own country before you fly off to the destination of your mission. This helps you bond with other team members to prepare you for the STM.

Worship as a STM Team

As a STM team, it is a good idea to take some worship songbooks or some photocopies (copyright permitted) of your favourite worship songs, hymns and choruses which can be sung unaccompanied. A member of the team may wish to take their guitar, flute or other musical instrument along. Some instruments are delicate, some are very expensive, others are bulky and there may be a surcharge at the airport as the instrument has to be processed through check-in as fragile and as a second bag.

'Sing to the Lord, all the earth; proclaim the Good News of His salvation from day to day. Declare His glory among the nations, His wonders amongst all peoples' 1 Chronicles 16:23-24.

The Correct Mindset

Your STM will be an amazing adventure, but if you go with the wrong attitude, you will miss the best that God has to offer. Go with a positive mindset, "I am going to have a life changing trip – an opportunity of a lifetime!" There will be difficulties and perhaps many things that you will not like (even about yourself), or disapprove of, but nonetheless, if you are going in obedience to the Great Commission, to serve others, you will get a lot out of it because you will put your all into it. Remind yourself, "I am going to go and embrace the experiences and allow the experience to embrace and change me, and this may reveal any character flaws or weak areas I may have."

Expect the unexpected and don't be phased by it, as the unexpected can happen! Situations may not seem fun at the time, but are all part of the experience and turn into great stories for others!

In 1812, Adoniram Judson and his wife sailed for India and by 1814 they were in Burma (modern day Myanmar). Judson was looked upon as obstinate and chimerical fanatic (wildly fanciful imagination) for labouring in such a place, but he was upheld by the faith that years afterwards inspired his famous reply, when asked of the prospects of the conversion of the heathen – "As bright as the promises of God." In June 1819, they baptised their first convert, Moung Nau and in the same year, they built their first chapel. Within five months, seven more Burmese were baptised including, Mah-men-la, the first Burmese Christian woman.[1]

The Gospel is:
- The Gospel of the grace of God (Acts 20:24).
- The Gospel of God (Romans 1:1).
- The Gospel of Christ (Romans 1:16).
- The Gospel of the glory of Christ (2 Corinthians 4:3-4).
- The Gospel of your salvation (Ephesians 1:13).
- The Gospel of peace (Ephesians 6:15).
- My Gospel said the apostle Paul came through the revelation of Jesus Christ (Romans 2:16 and Gal. 1:12).

Preparation Before Departure – Research

Long before you depart on your STM, do your research and do it well. If you joined a mission organisation they will fill you in on all that you need to do. Nevertheless, consider enrolling on an evening language course, especially if your destination speaks French, Spanish or Arabic. You can also buy language CDs, install them onto iTunes and put them onto your iPod for quick reference. These CDs and accompanying phrase books can be picked up for less than £5 ($8), second-hand. Whilst English is spoken widely, learning another language (or just essential phrases is a rewarding experience) and any language study is a worthy investment; by putting more in now, you will get more out during your STM. See Appendix E.

Consider enrolling on a First Aid course – a little bit of basic knowledge can be a lifesaver when you are a long way from help or at least read a First Aid book to know the basics! If you are an independent STM-er (or the leader of any team) then you should know the basics. If you are going to an extreme or isolated place (days from civilisation or in harsh weather conditions / terrain) then consider enrolling on a basic survival course, or at least read a survival book and try to take it in!

Preparation Before Departure – Physical and Spiritual

Make sure you are fit, your STM could be demanding and will probably not be a 9 till 5 day sat in the office like at work! Go out for a thirty-minute walk at least three to four times a week. You won't be expected to run a half marathon (nor the mile in under four minutes) but just do some exercise! I have known days on a STM where I have been on my feet all day, from 9am-7pm and on one, hopefully never to be repeated STM location, I had to walk 16 km (thankfully *down* a mountain) with my backpack to catch some public transport to the next town.

Pray for the mission: yourself, your leader, your team members (by name), your host, for Divine favour, protection, wisdom, discernment, confidence, boldness, health, for spiritual fruit, for favour, for Divine appointments, good interpreter, team cooperation, servant-heart and team dynamics etc. Read some biographies of famous missionaries (or just one), be inspired and learn from them. See Appendix G.

Spend additional time with God, in prayer, listening to Him and in study of the Holy Bible. Your STM may be your first and only opportunity (hopefully not) and you must go as prepared as you can, give as much as you can and get as much out of it as you can, learn, make new friends and build on your character.

Make sure all your electrical gadgets work. Are all your batteries charged? Do you know how to work your new digital camera, camcorder, Tablet, smartphone or iPod? Have you bought your plug converter? Do you have the right clothing?

A puppet frame was lent to a STM team who were ministering in South America. One person could assemble the plastic frame in less than three minutes. Unfortunately, during the STM the members of the team were unable to put the frame together as they had never attempted it before and thus it was never used. The puppeteers had also not practised their routine and the team leader was not amused as the puppets, uncoordinated, opened their mouths that faced the ceiling, and not the audience! Practise makes perfect.

Leadership Preparation

The leader may consider flying to the host country from one year to eight months before the mission begins, though this may depend on the prospective number of team members, as there is a great difference in logistical planning between six or sixty team members! The reconnaissance mission helps build up the relationship between the host leader, (local ministry or church fellowship) and the one who is planning the STM. They can see what resources are available, scout out prospective accommodation, transport and cooking facilities (or local places to eat) etc. and take some photos or video footage as these make recruiting for STMs easier.

If you are leading a STM team then make sure your team members know what is expected from them. Prepare any drama or mime sketches well. Those who are preaching or giving testimony, ensure they have ample notice to prepare. If you are involved in humanitarian work then be sure to pack what tools or equipment is needed. Distribute any tools or Christian materials throughout the team and remind them to pack it! Have all the team's passports with their visas arrived? Has every team member paid his or her money? Has the accommodation and the time of the plane's departure been confirmed? Is the church mini-bus and a driver still available to take you to the airport? Beware of double bookings!

A day before my church youth group set off for its weekend retreat (to our usual destination), I phoned up the Christian organisation to confirm that all preparation had been arranged (which in hindsight was too late). The person on the end of the line confirmed that he was expecting us. When I asked about the teaching session, I was informed that these had not been asked for. I was so busy with church affairs that the most important item I had overlooked! A pastor – Wales.

Research and Recommendations
The world is a big place, yet it is also small. Most countries in the West are multiethnic. In most major cities there are people of different ethnic and cultural backgrounds, from those from the Orient (Chinese, Japanese, and Koreans), to Arabs, Eastern Europeans, East and West Africans or Latinos and beyond. You may be able to begin your preparation by entering into some of these communities within your own city and meeting the type of people with whom you will be ministering to and working alongside.

Essential Research to the Country you will be Visiting
- Educate yourself about the country and people you will be going to. If language is permissible, read their online papers to see what is happening in their country.
- Buy a travel guide – and read it!
- Find out the country's history, religion, culture, geography, climate (to include seasons – hot, cold, wet, monsoon, humid), politics, cost of living, staple diet and types of accommodation if need be – each country has certain specific names and 'hotel' only means a restaurant in at least one country in East Africa.
- Learn some basic phrases in the local language, e.g. "Hello," "Thank you," "My name is —," and essential phrases, "Where is the toilet!?" "How much?" "Where is the…" "Hotel," Buy a pocket phrasebook if available.

Medical missionary Len Moules went to North India in 1936, where he spent two years in language study before ministering to the Bhotya Indian / Tibetan traders in the Himalayas, along their seasonal migratory routes, on the borders of Tibet and Nepal. He served twenty years in the WEC Himalayan missions (having been called up during WWII), before returning to Britain in 1953, when all foreigners had to leave the sensitive area.

In regards to language learning Len Moules wrote: 'Two fellows sat face to face. At first glance, you'd think they were spitting at each other! No – only a munshi [language teacher] and his missionary pupil, and the latter trying to imitate the new sound stuttered by his teacher; labials, aspirates, dental were tongue-twisting, lip-perverting exercise to give anyone pseudo-tonsillitis!'[2]

If and Where Possible

- Visit a church of a language group (or cultural group) similar to the country you will be visiting.
- Ask some of the Church leaders for their advice and tips.
- Invite some of them to your home for dinner.
- Go to a restaurant of the country to whom you will be going and order some 'local' cuisine. It is also a good excuse to try to Lebanese, Ethiopian, Mexican or Chinese food!
- Rent a DVD, download a travel programme or search the internet for film clips of the travel destinations you will be going to.
- With the advent of digital radio (or via the internet) you may be able to listen to some 'local' radio from the comfort of your own room prior to your departure.

In extremely cold weather, exposed skin (and especially your nose, toes and fingers), can freeze, giving rise to frostbite. If the temperature is in double digits below zero, metal watchstraps in direct contact with the skin can freeze to the skin. Cold weather with piercing winds or freezing / driving rain can also cut skin.

When There

There are lots of things to do when you are in the country of destination, but a few things to do when you have settled in are:

- Familiarise yourself with your local surroundings. Look for landmarks.
- Go out and meet the locals – a must do on any STM!
- Visit different churches (if permissible).
- Try the local cuisine and drinks (non-alcoholic).
- Watch the local TV programmes, but especially the news.
- Listen to the local radio.
- Having your hair cut is always an interesting time and is good for social interaction. But be aware that your words may get lost in translation!
- Haggle with a street seller. It is fun, educational and you will hopefully buy something that you like, need or will use as a gift or a present for another.

Chapter Twenty-Two

Items to Buy and What may be Practical

Jesus said, "Do not worry, saying, 'What shall we eat?' or…'What shall we wear?'… But seek first the Kingdom of God and His righteousness, and all these things shall be added unto you" Matthew 6:31, 33.

Jesus said to the disciples, "When I sent you without money bag, sack and sandals, did you lack anything?" So they said, "Nothing." Then He said to them, "But now, he who has a money bag, let him take it, and likewise a sack…" Luke 22:35-36.

Clothing and Considerations

You're going on a short-term mission (STM) and you need to take some essential items with you. At a minimum, you will need a set of clothes and a bag; but at worse you will try to take several suitcases packed with all your favourite clothes; electrical goods and items that you 'just cannot' do without. When it comes to STMs, less is best – travel light and it will be a delight. Though many STM teams take extra bags full of materials and supplies, which are used during the STM. It is often far easier to buy things along the way, or at your final destination than to take too much and struggle, than to know what to give away. See also Chapter Twenty-Four, Go Pack Your Bag.

Where you are going to and at what time of year dictates to you the type of clothing and items you will need. Where am I going to? What will the weather be like? If you know what the elements will be like (and you should know) then you can purchase items accordingly, however you probably have most items already. If it is hot then loose clothing is better, whereas if your location will be cold then multiple layers are more practical. Are you going in the rainy season? All these factors must be weighed and considered before you embark on your STM.

Once again, any mission organisation of which you are signed up with will be able to inform you of your needs and will provide a recommended checklist of items to take. If they have no list and are unable to give you any advice, then I would suggest the organisation should be avoided.

The Best Deal

The prices listed within this chapter are for 2016; whilst many non-electrical prices have been constant for several years, technology prices vary rapidly as newer items supersede the old.

When it comes to items of clothing and a rucksack, I have always gone to a shop in person to try on the garment and examine the bag. Some items if purchased online can appear compact and light, but in reality they are heavy and cumbersome. Like most things, if you need something in a hurry then you will probably pay over the odds for it. So be prepared, know what you want well in advance and wait until the price seems right or until the sales; often just as the season draws to a close, or if the weather takes a sudden turn and stays constant for a few weeks. Prices do vary significantly between shops and during different seasons. In essence, ask yourself, "Will my purchase accomplish the job for which I need it?" You may also wish to consider with electrical items: Is it lightweight, compact, reliable and do I really need it on my STM? See also Chapter Twenty-Three Gadgets and Bling – Do I pack it?

Essential or Practical:
- Rucksack (backpack) or suitcase £10-100 ($16-160). See Chapter Twenty-Four, Go Pack Your Bag that covers the various types of backpacks, bags & suitcases.
- Money belt £3-12 ($5-19) an essential safety feature to protect your excess amounts of money, your passport and cash cards. NOT a bum-bag (fanny pack / belt bag).
- Pocket Calculator £2-7 ($3-11).
- Waterproof Jacket (breathable are best as plastic raincoats make you sweat) £20-200 ($32-320). If you are going to a cold and windy environment then you should consider a windproof jacket.
- A sturdy pair of shoes or boots £15-60 ($24-100). If you are going into well below freezing temperatures, then specialist boots can cost around £150 ($240) for -50oC protection! Make sure you break any boots in before you depart; otherwise, you will REALLY suffer.
- Scented foot insoles (£3+ $5+) otherwise within a few weeks your footwear will stink!

- A quality pair of sports sandals £10+ ($16+) to give your feet breathing space.
- Trousers (pants with zip-off legs are better) or skirt with zipped or Velcro pockets (for security of your passport, wallet or purse) from any camping type shop £15-35 ($24-56). Camouflage trousers are not advisable as you may be mistaken for military personnel. In some African countries it is illegal for non-military to wear camouflage.
- First Aid kit £5-30 ($8-48). Often it is better to make your own First Aid kit rather than buy an off-the-shelf one; visit your local chemist. You should take plenty of plasters (Band Aid), two bandages, anti-septic cream, fungicidal cream, safety pins and some medicines at a minimum. Safety pins have multiple purposes like holding your bag together, keeping your trousers (pants) up (if you are not good at using a needle and thread) or have just lost your button or broken your flies (zip).
- Mini Sewing Kit (matchbox size) £1-7 ($2-11) which includes a few needles and various colours of thread.
- Small lightweight torch (flashlight) £3-20 ($5-32). LED lights are more powerful. Headlight type torches are more practical than handheld ones (ranging from £7-35 ($11-56), because of power cuts (early mornings and at night), just when you are trying to pack your bag! A windup LED key ring torch costs at little as £4 ($6).
- Digital watch with alarm, day and date, built in light and ideally waterproof £10-100 ($16-160). It is easy to lose track of time, and with early buses or trains to catch before the sun rises, I have found a digital watch indispensible on STMs. If it does not have a light, you will be constantly waking up on the day of your departure trying to find your torch (flashlight).
- Up-to-date Guidebook £14-30 ($22-48). Backpackers type (for independent STM-ers) I have found useful (cost of transport, accommodation, bus routes, food, scams to beware of, border crossings, visa costs etc.).
- Pocket-sized phrase book £3-10 ($5-16). Useful when you are only ministering in one location.
- Flip-flops (thongs) for the shower £2-10 ($3-16). Most budget accommodation have dirty concrete floors. You do not want to get a verruca (or other foot viruses) by being barefoot in the shower or your room.

- Journal – A5 spiral pad and a pen or an iPad or Tablet!

I have always been cautious of not taking too much or too few items on my STMs. Unfortunately, it is often whilst you are on your STM that you say, "I wish I had taken — and should have left — at home!" STMs are always a revaluation of one's possessions. James – Thailand.

Items to Consider:
- Travel towel (micro-fibre type) £6-20 ($10-32).
- Sun cream and sunhat £5+ ($8+).
- Moisturiser and lip balm £4+ ($6+).
- Compact Umbrella £3-15 ($5-24).
- Backpack cage £45-65 ($72-104) for added security for independent STM-ers, though can be weighty.
- Locks (key or combination) £3 ($5) each for your rucksack (2 small ones for your side pockets). One medium sized lock for a hotel cupboard or for your room's door (especially in cheap accommodation).
- Small pocket knife with scissors and tweezers £8-20 ($13-32) – which CANNOT be taken aboard a plane as hand luggage, or any sharp objects, liquids, creams and aerosols over 100ml.
- Neck wallet (a pouch that is hung round your neck) and hidden under your top for your passport or money £3-8 ($5-13), which is not as good as a money belt, but more practical for women when wearing a skirt or dress.
- Travel sickness pills £3-5 ($5-8). Travel sickness pills can also take the edge off a long journey to help you sleep.
- Small handheld mirror £2-5 ($3-8).
- Toiletries (deodorants, toothbrush etc., feminine hygiene products, razor, creams), and mosquito repellent?
- Prescription for medicines and a spare pair of glasses (they do break!). It would be unfortunate to go on a STM and have to wait till you return home to check your photos to see what your STM looked like in focus!
- A three-man tent is ideal for two people and their bags £30-150 ($48-240). The lighter and more compact a tent is the more expensive they are. If you both have individual tents then you will have to rent two pitches.

One or other of the following:

- Silk bag liner or a lightweight 750-gram sleeping bag £25-40 ($40-64) for basic or cold accommodation.
- Space / foil blanket £2-6 ($3-10) a pocket sized foil blanket that can be used in emergencies – or when cold!
- Sleeping bag £10-80 ($16-128) will you be camping? What rating do you need? The higher the rating the warmer (and heavier) the sleeping bag.

Electrical Items
Many of the items below are of personal preference, but a digital camera, charger, plug adaptors, a form of personal entertainment (or work on the go), mini laptop / iPad or Tablet and iPod are the most common items. Chapter 23, Gadgets and Bling – Do I pack it? Covers many of these items in detail.
- A digital camera. 10 million pixels from £40+ ($64+).
- Memory cards (standard SD type, non WiFi – not Eye-Fi) 2gb £3+ ($5+), 4gb £5+ ($8+), 8gb £8+ ($13+).
- Rechargeable batteries (if your camera has not got a lithium battery). 2900 mAh (nickel hydride) £5+ ($8+) for two, and take a spare set and fast charger £5-30 ($8-48).
- A wind-up re-charger for your iPod or mobile / cell phone £7 ($11) though I have never needed to use one.
- Plug adaptors for the country you are going to and a shaver (two-pinned plug) £2-6 ($3-10) each.
- Small cheap video camera and tapes £100+ ($160+) plus £3+ ($5+) per tape or SD cards.
- Personal Entertainment: iPod £40+ ($64+), MP3 player £15+ ($24+) or MP4, £40+ ($64+).
- Mini laptop (250gb, WiFi enabled, 10 inch screen, 1.6 kg) £220+ ($350+). Or an iPad, smartphone or Tablet.
- Travel kettle with a plug (and not a 6-volt car adaptor). They are supplied with two cups that fit inside the kettle. Great for tea, coffee, soups, boiling water and for instant noodles £7-20 ($11-32).
- Shaver, in developing countries, a fast rechargeable shaver is best with 3-10 days charge £40-200 ($64-320). A twin-head dynamo (windup) shaver with USB charging and plug £10-15 ($16-24). Wet shaves are cheaper!

Other items to Consider
- Plastic bowl for noodles, cereals or instant soup.
- Plastic spoon and fork or chopsticks.

- Plastic cup (if not included with your travel kettle).
- Six pegs (clothespins), for your washing and for holding curtains closed!
- Thin string (5-8 metres) – which can be used as a washing line (clothesline) or for holding things together.
- Spare pair of shoelaces – after several hard weeks or months they can break at any time. Nail clippers.
- Four A4 plastic wallets to keep documents safe and dry.
- Plastic or wooden doorstop, a great security device for when you are inside your cheap hotel room.
- A gift(s) for your host and small gifts for when you are invited to someone's home for a meal.
- Change, so that you can phone home on your return.

Prescription Medicines

It is important that you keep all prescription medicines in their original packaging with the accompanying pamphlet. These pamphlets also state the medical composition of the tablets or capsules, and so make it easier for the pharmacist abroad to issue you with what you need, as not all medicines are generic and your brand name may not exist in some places.

Some medicines require a letter from your doctor if you intend on passing through customs unhindered (ask your doctor); even some prescription medicines in the West are illegal in other countries. It was in 2005, that a British woman was stopped at Dubai immigration, because of a passport irregularity and had to give a urine sample. She had codeine in her bloodstream (that came from her painkillers) but codeine is illegal in Dubai. She was arrested, spent time in jail, though was later acquitted at her court case.

Does it all Fit?

Many items have been listed in this chapter and it sounds a lot, but the author is no magician and with careful packing, the vast majority of the items mentioned (excluding a tent, sleeping bag and video camera) can fit into a reasonably sized rucksack alongside a *small* carry on bag. You have to pack your bag intelligently and utilise your space. It is not uncommon to pack and unpack your rucksack or suitcase up to three times, as you juggle items and remove others. If you need two large bags to pack all your items then you have far too much! Remember, you may need space to pack team materials!

Chapter Twenty-Three

Gadgets and Bling – Do I pack it?

'For some thought, because Judas had the money box, that Jesus has said to him, "Buy those things we need for the feast," or that he should give something to the poor' John 13:29.

Jesus said, "Take heed and beware of covetousness, for one's life does not consist in the abundance of the things he possesses" Luke 12:15.

Can I Live Without it?

There are many items in the twenty-first century, which whilst we use daily, we often wonder, how would we live without them – mobile / cell phones and the internet, to name just two. Out on a short-term mission (STM), we can often feel dislocated from "normal" society as many of these items we have to leave behind or are advised to. However, it is relatively easy to live without these items, and sometimes it's nice to have an enforced break from them; whilst at other times, they do come in rather handy on a STM and people have been known to pine for their gadgets (as well as favourite foods) for weeks.

> For my first few months in Africa, I tried to avoid staying in accommodation that had a TV. I wanted to live life in Africa, and not see fictional life in the West on TV every evening. William – Zambia.

Gadgets and Electronics

There are many gadgets you can take on a STM, some will enhance your mission and help you remember the people you met and the places you went to, whilst others can be more of a distraction if abused, by isolating yourself from other members of the team and keeping you away from interacting with the locals. A mini laptop, WiFi enabled can be a handy asset as many cafes, restaurants and accommodation have free WiFi.

Just remember that any item you do not own and would like to take with you is an additional expense, and all items can be damaged, lost or stolen and so can their power sources. If you are with a mission organisation and are staying in one location then the contents of your bag can be heavier than if you have to carry it on your back and travel frequently.

Jesus said, "Do not lay up for yourselves treasures on earth where moth and rust destroy and where thieves break in and steal, but lay up for yourselves treasures in heaven..." Matthew 6:19-20.

Batteries, Electricity and Power Cuts

Whilst it may be helpful or essential to have some gadgets to take on your STM, you still have to power them and this can be problematic in some areas or in certain circumstances. It is always wise to have two sets of batteries for your gadgets – but this is extra weight. Rechargeable are the best option, but is there a power source where you can get them charged? Is your iPod or digital voice recorder only chargeable via a USB port? Remember to take a plug adaptor with you, as you can generally only find them in the more expensive hotel rooms in the capitals of developing countries.

In Asia, free WiFi in cafes and accommodation is quite common. A wind-up re-charger for your iPod or mobile / cell phone can be bought, though in many East African countries there are reputable street vendors where you can charge your phone from their electricity source or car battery – hopefully they won't run off with your Blackberry or iPhone!

I learnt from experience that when in poorer nations, write short emails and send them off as soon as you can. It is so frustrating having spent thirty minutes writing an email to find there is a power surge or a power cut! John – Ethiopia.

If you have a digital camera with 10 million pixels or higher then it is best to buy rechargeable batteries of 2900 mAh or greater (if you do not have a lithium battery), and take at least one additional set of batteries. A fast charger that can charge two batteries in under two hours is ideal. All equipment should be tried and tested before you depart for your STM; better to get a fault fixed now, than be disappointed at your destination.

Power cuts are a regular feature of developing countries (from 10 minutes to 12 hours) and at other times electricity is sporadic, sparse or is turned on and off at certain times of the day or night. From May into June 2008, Zanzibar (in Africa), was without electricity for over two weeks! Charge your equipment when you can as if you procrastinate, you may find that when you want to, you cannot!

> I found it refreshing on my STM being away from all my familiar means of communication. However, after a short while, the novelty wore off and I could not wait to use the local internet. George – Lesotho.

Memory Cards
Take enough memory cards for your digital camera so that you will not be limited – more is better and whilst memories will fade, pictures last a lifetime. 4gb set at Normal on a 10 million pixel camera will hold about 2,200 pictures; 1,400 at Fine or 860 at Superfine / Best. Memory cards in developing nations are very expensive; in Dar es Sallam, Tanzania, 2gb memory cards are nearly eight times more expensive than in the UK! You can purchase WiFi memory cards and send your photos from your digital camera direct to your computer but they are expensive.

Mobile / Cell Phones
Mobile / cell phones on the mission field can be a blessing but also a bane. They are great to have in an emergency but a bane to carry unless it's a phone watch! It is another item that needs charging (which could get damaged) or stolen and you may end up with a whopper of a phone bill. Most Pay as you Go phones do not work outside of their designated country and if you feel that a mobile is a necessity for your STM then use local SIM cards and email your number to your friends. On a STM of less than three weeks, I have generally taken a mobile / cell with me and the blessings have outweighed the disadvantages.

In many developing nations, there are telephone shops which consist of numerous phone booths for calling, whilst, budding entrepreneurs in marketplaces use their mobile / cell phones to make money. Or buy an international phone card.

On one STM, around midnight, my phone rang and the minister on the end of the line (whose local time was two hours earlier than us) wanted to speak to the team leader – this meant that I had to get out of bed, get dressed and walk outside across the courtyard and wake the leader up. I would add that on getting home, I received a bill for £15 ($24) as you pay a percentage of the cost of incoming calls when abroad. So beware.

On a positive note, in one country whilst aboard a busy train I was pick-pocketed (that's not the positive bit), but upon realising the situation was able to phone up my bank immediately and get my credit cards cancelled. I would add that if my trouser (pants) pockets were zipped or had Velcro on them this theft would have been avoidable. It was a foolish mistake to have trousers with wide pockets, but a lesson was learnt.

One evening, a large multinational STM team split into pairs for an evening's work of unofficial Christian postal deliveries in a sensitive country. When we came back to our hotel, we were alarmed to find the police in the lobby, not only chatting to the hotel workers, but waiting for us! The senior members of the team indulged the officer's questions whilst the other members of the team used the pay phone and asked their churches and friends to get the international prayer chains active. Prayer prevailed, glory to God, for what otherwise could have turned into a dire situation. Foolishly, most of us forgot to phone back the following day to tell our churches and friends that the crisis had been averted. So until we returned home (more than a week later), many were unnecessarily worried for the teams welfare. This was a grave error on our part, though we all appreciated the additional prayer!

> I was in a restaurant with a group of Muslims when my phone went. It was a church secretary confirming that I would be speaking at her church the following Sunday. All present were very adapt with the English language so I had to use wisdom and discretion in what I said, and explained to the secretary where I was, and that I would be speaking on the Sunday. David – Tunisia.

Bling – Do I Need It?

You are going on a STM, and whilst most people like to look good, it is advisable that you leave your bling at home. Chunky chains, gold watches, excessive jewellery, fancy handbags and designer labels are not practical and can alienate you from those you are trying to reach. They also make you standout as a target to rob. However, your bling may go down well if you are ministering in Monaco amongst the wealthy elite or to Shanghai millionaires!

Chapter Twenty-Four

Go Pack Your Bag

Jesus said to the disciples... "But now, he who has a money bag, let him take it, and likewise a sack..." Luke 22:36.

'Then he took his staff in his hand; and he chose for himself five smooth stones from the brook, and put them in a shepherds bag, in a pouch which he had...' 1 Samuel 17:40.

What to Take
When it comes to clothes, it is really up to you what you want to take on your short-term mission (STM), though if you are going with an organisation they will advise you of what you need and give a general ideal of how many of each items. However, before you decide what to take; you will need a good backpack (rucksack), bag or suitcase to put it all in. See also, Chapters Twenty-Two and Twenty-Three, Items to Buy and What may be Practical and Gadgets and Bling – Do I pack it?

Items to Consider with your Bag
The bag that you will take on your STM is a vital component and there are many factors involved, but with some simple logical questions and answers, it will help you get the right rucksack, bag (or suitcase) for you:
- Will it go as hand luggage? Not if it is too big or heavy!
- Will I be staying in one place or multiple locations?
- Will I be constantly travelling on public transport?
- Can I carry the bag when full?
- Will I be transporting heavy materials?

Your Bag
Rucksacks / backpacks are my preferred choice of bag for STMs, though when I had to take large quantities of Christian materials (Bibles, Videos, pamphlets etc.) I used a suitcase with wheels. I have never come across the perfect rucksack.
Rucksack capacities are measured in litres / liters (L):
- 20-30 L is a standard day-bag backpack.

- 35+10 L is what I first took to Asia (and it was small).
- 50+10 L is what I used in Africa for 6 ½ months and on my second STM to Asia. It is my personal preferred size.

Anything above 60+10 L may be too big to carry and a hindrance on public transport and anything above 80 L is just excessive. However, there is nothing wrong with having a bigger bag except you may be tempted to fill it to its brim. All too frequently I have seen young people struggle with their backpacks, some of which stood nearly as tall as they did, whilst some have a rucksack on their back and a large day-bag on their front and can just about waddle along. If you have a weak or bad back then a suitcase on wheels may be better, but it's no fun pulling them through the mud in the rainy season! Even the elephant carries but a small trunk on his journeys – David Thoreau.

Suitcase / Travel-case

If you think a suitcase is best for you then ask yourself, "Do I need wheels?" and "Does it need to be a hard case?" Hard cases are heavier than soft cases and offer more protection for fragile items, but they have no give in them when trying to store in an overhead bus rack or under the seat and weigh more, though they can be used as a seat! Does your bag need to be lockable? Do I need compartments? The more complex your bag, the more it will cost, and remember, more expensive luggage does not guarantee better or sturdier quality.

Weight of your Contents and Bag

Whatever rucksack, bag or suitcase you buy, make sure you can carry it when packed! If you cannot carry it up a flight of stairs then you have too many items. The general rule of travelling is, if you cannot carry your rucksack on your back for more than an hour or lift it above your head to stow it on your bus, then it's too heavy! In addition, just because you are strong does not mean that you should pack more items into your bag! The only exception is if you are going on a mission to one fixed location and leaving items behind, then the weight of your bag is not an issue (except the airlines baggage allowance). If you are part of a mission organisation, you may be asked to bring items, such as Christian: books, videos, DVDs, CDs, Bibles, pens, medical supplies, tools or clothes for the locals.[1]

A few years ago, Doug Lansky, author of *First-Time Around the World* spent a few days around Stockholm's central train station where he surveyed and weighed travellers and their backpacks. He found that the average weight was 20 kg whilst some of the heaviest packs (over 25 kg) belonged to women who weighed less than 55 kg. He wrote: 'It looked like they were going to be crushed at any second, Wile E. Coyotie style-like under their packs.'[2]

> On my first mission trip, I took fresh clothes for every day. My suitcase was hard to carry, awkward on public transport and too big. Now I use a rucksack with just two sets of clothes, plus extra underwear. If I need more, I buy local. Dirty clothes are normal in developing countries, it's just so unavoidable. Nick – South America.

Baggage Allowance

Airline baggage allowance varies between airlines (and between countries) though 15-23 kilograms (kg) for check-in items and 5-10 kg for hand luggage is a general rule. Obey the size guidelines for hand luggage, which change from time to time, and each airline has its own rules! If you exceed your baggage weight allowance, you will have to pay an excess baggage charge. This can vary considerably (from £4-34.50 ($6.50-55) per kg whilst some airlines charge a flat fee of £49.50 ($79) for up to 10 kg additional weight! Other airlines base their charges on a percentage of the one-way economy fare, which are typically 1-1.5% of the fare per extra kg. On a long-haul flight, this fee can be large.[3] Airlines can be flexible with charities and groups *if* you speak to them in advance.

All essential or valuable items should be taken on the plane as hand luggage (in a day-bag) because your rucksack or suitcase, which has been checked-in, may get lost at worst, or not be at baggage reclaim when you are! You can always wear your heavier or bulky items (jeans, big boots, and additional jumper (sweater), and jacket) with you on the plane instead of packing it.

Team Materials

If you are taking Christian materials with you (tracts, Bibles, pamphlets, videos, DVDs, CDs, medicines etc.) and other equipment (including work tools) then it is best to distribute these items throughout the members of the mission team. If not, you may be stopped at customs as a mobile library, *pharmacist (*bring correct paperwork – if needed) or a sales agent who is trying to avoid paying duty and taxes on the goods, which they believe you are going to sell. Some mission teams like to have team t-shirts – it may be cute; helps identify a group of strangers as one, but at times it is not practical and can be unwise. If you are passing through customs with all your material, if one of you is stopped, and the official is not happy with your Bibles or tools, then don't be surprised if you *all* get stopped and everybody's luggage is searched.

Practical Clothing – Not Problematic

Remember that you are going on a mission and not a fashion parade. What may be trendy or acceptable at home may not be practical or appropriate where you are going. It is possible to alienate the people you are trying to reach simply because your normal day-to-day clothes are too good or that you have a change of clothes for each day and others don't. Remember to bring something smart to wear to the local church and jeans are not a good option in most parts of the world. In some deprived areas, STM teams have found that their work clothes have been better than many of the locals' Sunday best.

The clothes you pack should reflect the type of climate you are going to. Take modest swimwear, as you never know when you may have the opportunity for a dip, use of a hot tub or a warm spring. Remember your wide rimmed sun hat if your ears are prone to burn (like mine), a long sleeved shirt to protect your arms from sunburn and by upturning your collars your neck is preserved from looking like a lobster after a day in the sun, though your team mates may call you Elvis!

Beware of having clothes that reveal too much. Even in some countries, it is frowned upon, or even forbidden for women to reveal their shoulders or upper arms in public. Muslim countries are not enthusiastic with men wearing shorts above the knee. There are always exceptions to the rule, especially in tourist towns, but a betrayal towards the feelings of others to whom we are trying to reach may cause them to reject not only us, but also our message.

Wrong colours such as light green and light brown can show up sweat marks (or become see-through) and thus reveal, in sweaty climates patches of dark material, which can be quite embarrassing especially when sweat has run down your back onto the seat of your trousers (pants) or dress! Zipped or pockets with Velcro are essential as a prevention from being pick-pocketed. Trousers with zip off legs are also very handy.

Patriotic clothing, such as Union Jack shirts or the Stars and Stripes are best avoided and military clothing is a no-no. If you wear desert camouflage (as the UK and US troops wore in Iraq and Afghanistan) and enter into some countries there may be retaliations against you. Be safe, use wisdom, be practical.[4]

Packing your Items

Before you pack, lay all your items out on your bed or on the floor, to see if you have got everything. Ideally, take two of each items: t-shirt, trousers (pants) / skirts, (more for underwear), but only one jacket and one pair of flip-flops (thongs) and sandals. Remember, you will be wearing one set of clothes with you and can buy additional items whilst on your STM.

DON'T pack revealing items or those that you *really* cannot live without (they may get damaged) and any other forms of impractical clothing. Do you need to buy some small presents / gifts for your host or if you are invited round someone's house for a meal? In many cultures, if they invite you into their home, a gift is expected and those from home, mean more than locally bought items. Small trinkets / souvenirs are appreciated.

Clothes List

The clothes on this list are a general guide and the quantity includes what you may wear on the plane, one set of clothes, your jacket and sturdy pair of boots. Extra items that you deem most practical should be packed, but leave some space in your bag for items you purchase whilst on your STM. As a good rule of STMs – pack less, wash your clothes frequently and take items that are relevant to your destination's weather conditions.

- Trousers (pants) or skirts x2
- T-shirt x2
- Smart shirt / blouse x1
- Zipped fleece jumper (sweater) x1
- Waterproof jacket x1
- Underwear x4+
- Socks x4+
- Hat, scarf and gloves x1
- Sturdy pair of boots x1
- Sports Sandals x1
- Flip-flops (thongs) x1
- Shorts x1 and nightwear x1
- Swimwear x1

I was in North Africa as part of a STM team. It was summer, so real hot, yet my British roommate insisted on wearing his dressing gown and slippers after each shower! I found it very humorous and it was a constant source of laughter and banter between us. Jake – Tunisia.

Documents and Hand luggage

Do not forget to pack photocopies of important documents (valid passport with visa, medical insurance, plane tickets in clear A4 plastic wallets), your guide book (if needed), Bible, medicines and some passport size photos as they may be required for new visas or given to your new friends! All of your valuables, journal, pens, charged electronic items. and essentials should go as hand luggage whilst some people recommend a change of clothes as well – just in case!

We were in the mini-bus ready to depart on our STM and one of the team members strolled over. The leader asked her, "Where is your bag?" "In my room," the STM-er casually said, "When are we going?" – "NOW!" said the team leader and the woman, in a panic, ran off to her room to pack and ten minutes later emerged! Sarah – USA.

Departure

Three days before departure, phone up the airline to confirm the time of the flight (sometimes they change) and make sure you know how you are getting to the airport! Do you need a map? If you are joining a mission organisation, arrive on time or be early. Most airline check-ins are open two hours before the flight departs, though many airlines allow you to check-in online 24hrs before the plane departs; so you can pick your seat and order any specialised meals. Do not be late to the airport (take an earlier coach or train) and have your passport and plane ticket handy. Some airlines are not sympathetic if you have missed your flight and if you are flying with a budget airline you will probably have to buy a new ticket!

Do not try and take sharp objects on the plane e.g. scissors, nail file, penknife, or uncharged batteries. Airlines have many other restrictions and prohibited items (which change from time to time) but liquids, creams and deodorants of more than 100ml each are forbidden, though you can purchase the latter items once you have passed through the secure area of the airport.

Chapter Twenty-Five

I've Arrived – Settling In

'May the Lord watch between you and me when we are absent from another' Genesis 31:49.

'Go in peace. May the presence of the Lord be with you on your way' Judges 18:6.

The Arrival

Arriving at your final destination on your short-term mission (STM) can be ever so exciting, but also a major letdown, as reality may not be as good as expectations, and your journey can upset your senses and emotional well-being. You may not have rested on your night flight; especially if your ten-hour flight consisted of a rugby team who only believe in drinking and not sleeping! I was on one flight where a senior passenger (not part of our mission) sat near a student South African rugby team and finally snapped! It took real diplomacy for the air stewards to calm him down!

> The first day on a STM in a different continent has always been difficult for me. The jet lag, the cold (or heat), the noise, dirt and troubles. I often ask myself, "What have I done coming here!?" However, it all works itself through within a couple of days and I embrace the mission. Derek – various places.

However much you prepare (and the more the better) you can be easily caught unaware as expectation and reality can be far apart. In 1871, Henry Stanley, a reporter, was sent out by the *New York Herald* to Africa to find Dr. David Livingstone, who had not been heard from in three years. On his first day in Africa, Stanley wrote: 'One day's life at Zanzibar made me thoroughly conscious of my ignorance respecting African people and things in general. I had imagined I had read Burton and Speke [explorers of Africa] through fairly well, and that consequently I had penetrated the meaning, the full importance and grandeur of the work I was about to be engaged upon. But my estimates for instance, based upon book information, were simply ridiculous, fanciful images of African attractions were soon dissipated, anticipated pleasure vanished, and all crude ideas began to dissolve themselves into some shape.'[1]

On the journey to your "new home" there are new sights, sounds or smells and even stirred emotions, which may be hard to take in, thoughts of those you left behind and possible jetlag. Like everything, it does take time to settle in and to recover from a journey, especially if you have crossed time zones, but after a few days your body will readjust and everything will get back to normal.

You may not be initially too impressed with your new dwelling place, which is yours for a considerable amount of time, but count your blessings, you have a roof over your head, you will get fed at regular intervals and you have a job to do.

I would also encourage you to read a chapter of Proverbs and Ephesians everyday whilst you are on your STM, and don't neglect your quiet times with God (Bible reading and prayer).

We arrived in the capital of Botswana having the night before slept in a cockroach-infested room on the Zambian side. We killed at least twenty of the vermin! Jack – Botswana.

If you are with a mission organisation, your arrival will be much easier than if you 'go it alone' with a friend (independent STM) as everything is prearranged, from transport to accommodation. For everyone else, there may be problems with the language, money exchange (for some countries you can only buy currency within the country), airport taxi drivers (always a few who try to take advantage), the unfamiliar surroundings and the primary object of finding a place to stay, a hotel, motel, youth hostel, guesthouse, lodge or B&B. You will also meet touts, some are very helpful, others are a pain, whilst a minority are like leeches – they don't want to let you go and try to get anything and everything from you!

Homesickness can also set in after several months, but can be after just a few weeks. You are more prone to being homesick if you have never spent time away from your family.

Types of Toilets
Toilets the world over are not the same. They may be Western type (the bowl and seat – though the seat is not always there), a

bucket which you empty (like in old prisons!) or the squat types (a hole in the ground) which are also known as long-drops. If you remember doing squats thrusts in your physical education class at school (and I hope this does not recall bad memories) then this is how you use squat toilets – you squat down, but without bouncing back up every few seconds. There is great pressure on your thighs, (impossible to read your magazine) and the stench in outside squat toilets is frequently nauseating – quite literally, with flies buzzing everywhere. The floors can be very slippery and often there is no light and never any toilet paper; with the idea being that you wipe yourself with the left hand (or you provide your own paper), pour water down the hole and then wash your hands without soap – simply because there will be no soap present. There is often a tap or a bowl of water where you pour some water down the hole and let water displacement take care of the rest.

When I was in Sudan, I urged and urged in a squat toilet and had to stuff toilet paper up my nostrils and tell myself to get over it and get used to it. If you're wearing trousers (pants), be careful that you pull them down low enough; otherwise you can make a mess in them! I could tell you a story about that – but I won't bore you! With your trousers being inverted, your coins and other items in your pockets are liable to fall out – another reason why you should have zipped or Velcro pockets! Incidentally, months before I went of to Africa, I began practicing squats to strengthen my thigh muscles and to aid balance – it paid dividends. Not all is bad though, if you make it to Japan, you may have the pleasure of sitting on an all-singing, all-dancing (not literally) electronic throne of thrones!

I needed to go to number two and found directions to the toilet. All that was there was a hole in the ground. I looked at it and pondered how it should be used, as there was no porcelain throne or toilet seat. I quickly sussed it out and pulled my trousers (pants) down and sat over the hole. Nobody told me that it was designed for squatting over! Jack – Thailand.

Some toilets are in the bush and it is customary to dig a little hole and cover up after yourself. On one STM that consisted of a night in the desert, one person could not be bothered to dig a hole or cover their waste and another trod in it! She was very annoyed and threw away her trainers. It was a funny event, but not for the unfortunate person and the guilty party never owned up – we had our suspicions though!

If the bus stops after a few hours on a dirt road, with no building in sight, then the men go to one side of the road and the women to the other side, and aftertime you will feel quite at home in the wilds of Africa or Asia, blending in with the locals on day long journeys. If you are going to spend a day on a bus, do not eat and drink too much for breakfast (or lunch on the go), but also, be careful of dehydration.

Help Get Me Out of Here!

You may have just arrived at your destination or after a week think that you have made a major mistake and want to quit – you have not. DON'T run away and go home, or begin to murmur and complain! – for your sake, for the sake of the Good News and for those who have made sacrifices to finance your STM. Never run away from the organisation that you are part of or quit your STM because the going has got tough; you will regret it and will have missed a valuable life lesson, which you will have to learn at another time. The loss will not only be yours, but in whatever else God had planned for you, because you will be behind schedule in your life training. If you ride the storm of disappointment whilst looking to God, you will break through the darkness into the light and sail into victory.

"Endurance is a mental quality," said Captain Scott, and on that basis, he selected the members of his Antarctic expedition.

The apostle Paul passed on a message to Archippus, "Take heed to the ministry which you have received in the Lord, *that you may fulfil it*" Colossians 4:17.

Often God allows things to be difficult to help refine our character and it is only through these problems that our true motives, weaknesses and flaws can be revealed. Jonah tried to run from the call of God and only ended up going to Nineveh, because he was swallowed by the large fish, admitted his wrongdoing and confessed his sin of fleeing from the call of God.

When I first flew into India, after just days of hassle, being lied to and cheated etc. from several people, I just wanted to go home. The devil was also attacking my mind and my body was not in the best of shape. I was still suffering sleep deprivation and jetlag and the only retreat I had was my clean hotel room –

but I had to go out and eat. After one month in Egypt, I was ready to go home and in other African countries, I was happy to fly home early after various incidences and just general tiredness. Thankfully, and by the grace of God, all these STMs were completed and never once have I quit.

'Like a bird that wanders from its nest is a man who wanders from his place' Proverbs 27:8.

Terrible Accommodation

Simon Peter, a senior leader of the early church and one of the twelve disciples went on a STM to Lydda and Joppa. At Joppa he stayed with Simon a tanner (Acts 9:43 and Acts 10:32). Tanneries need urine to work the hides of the animals to make into cloths and clothes etc.; therefore the stench would have been unpleasant, hence the home (and business was by the sea for the sea breezes), but Peter embraced the experience and did not grumble or murmur. It was in Simon the tanners home that he had his vision of not calling people of other races unclean which enabled him to go to the Gentiles when Cornelius the Roman centurion summoned him. This in turn led to him preaching, the Holy Spirit falling, conversions and baptisms – because Peter was content to stay where he was regardless of outside circumstances (Acts 10:9-48). Peter did not go in search of different accommodation, but appreciated the hospitality that he had received and was obedient to Jesus' words when the twelve went out on their first mission trip, "In whatever place you enter a house, *stay there* till you depart from that place" (Mark 6:7-10).

My wife and I flew to our new home into a field of work that God had called us to at a local school. My wife and I were not happy about our accommodation and we were constantly attacked by bedbugs. After a little more than six weeks, we quit and flew home. We still refer to it as our forty days of hell! Mark and Hannah – Zimbabwe.

Faithfulness and Diligence

Faithfulness and diligence are two qualities that are sadly lacking in many Christian lives. We promise to help out, but get distracted by something of lesser importance. We rush and hurry to finish a job when our heart is elsewhere, and end up cutting corners or quitting early – this is not faithfulness or diligence and cannot be condoned. Less-than-perfect service is always better than the best of intentions and remember Jesus' words, "He who is faithful in what is least is faithful also in much; and he who is unjust in what is least is unjust also in much..." (Luke 16:10-12).

Faithfulness involves commitment; a commitment that will not casually make excuses to be exempt without hesitation or remorse for the slightest of reasons. If you are not prepared to chip in and assist in the mundane and the not-so-great things, like washing the dishes or sweeping the floor; then is a STM really for you where your duties could be many and varied?

I flew to Eastern Europe on a STM to work with an orphanage. I was greatly disturbed by everything I saw and smelt and within 24hrs of my arrival I had left and was on the plane back home. My home church who had bought my plane ticket, were very, VERY unhappy that I had wasted not only an opportunity of a lifetime, but also the church's precious resources. Ricardo – Romania.

From Missionary Artisans to STMs

The Church Missionary Society (CMS) was founded in April 1799 and in 1812, artisans (skilled workers of various trades) were sent out to relieve the missionaries.[2] These workers were known as Short Service Missionaries and in 1949, CMS had 980 full-time missionaries alongside 39 on Short Service.[3]

CMS state that Short Service is when 'a recruit only desires to offer for any period and not for life service.'[4] By the 1960s, 'opportunities for students and professional people from several months to two years, to replace missionaries on furlough or carry out special assignments' were known as Short Terms Abroad.[5] Today we call them short-term missions (STMs).

'Barnabas and Saul returned from Jerusalem *when they had fulfilled their ministry* and they also took with them John whose surname was Mark' Acts 12:25.

Chapter Twenty-Six

Duty and Character

'For the message of the cross is foolishness to those who are perishing, but to us who are being saved it is the power of God' 1 Corinthians 1:18.

'Brethren, pray for us, that the Word of the Lord may have free course and be glorified, just as it is with you' 2 Thess. 3:1.

You Have Arrived

You have arrived at your final destination to begin your STM. You have been allocated a room; you've met your room mate(s); your bag is unpacked (or plonked on the floor) and now is not the time to go wondering off! You are probably part of a STM team, having joined a mission organisation and there will need to be a team / group meeting. Listen to the leader(s) and follow their instruction. Trust me, they know best. They have had experience in these matters before (hopefully!) and I am sure that some ground rules will need to be reiterated, a tour of the mission facilities or rented home (if it's not just a hotel or hostel), alongside introductions to members of the team (who did not travel with you) and staff members who live on site.

If you have not joined a mission organisation, you need to find a place to stay, if you have not already pre-booked an apartment or a room in a cheap hotel or youth hostel. You will probably want to shower up, have a brief rest and then go outside and familiarise yourself with your local surrounding. Grab hold of a business card of your accommodation – just in case you get lost!

Depending on how long your STM is (2 weeks to 1 year), the state you are in (jet-lagged or just plain exhausted) and your condition (or that of the team) will often dictate whether you start your STM on the day of your arrival or whether it begins on the following day.

Our STM was planned for just two weeks. We spent the night at the airport because our plane left *very* early in the morning. The team leader had lots of experience and so gave us the morning off to rest. I was so excited, that along with a handful of the team, we went to the beach for a few hours. I enjoyed my rest on the beach and refreshed myself with a swim. Julian – North Africa.

Your Room – Your Home!

You have been allocated a room (or a bed in a room); try to keep it tidy! Remember your mum / mom will not be there to clean up behind you. Even if you are in a hotel or guesthouse; use the bin / trash can and do not *expect* the cleaners to pick up your rubbish because you could not be bothered to put it in the bin / trash can. Be Christ-like. Remember, you don't know who will pay you a visit or just pop in. The same applies for when you rent an apartment or home for the STM team.

Report any breakages to your leader (or host) and don't let it be a surprise for your host or mission organisation when you have departed! The quality of furniture varies from place to place and the bench that can hold four petite Asian women may not hold two burly Westerners. Don't put damp clothes on varnished furniture – the lacquer may lift.

It is very unwise to leave valuables lying around – do not tempt the cleaner or others. In hostels (amongst fellow foreigners), things go missing; and are more likely to. Never leave bulk materials, such as tracts, DVDs, Bibles, CDs etc. lying around in your hotel room, especially if you are in a country where evangelising is illegal or questionable. The hotel cleaner may inform the manager who could inform the authorities and you will get to hear about it! Some countries state that there is freedom of religion, but often the reality is very different and open to interpretation under local bylaws or the police person in charge!

I semi-unpacked my bag and placed all my Arabic Bibles and Christian materials on a spare bed. We were running late and so I had to go. In the evening I returned to the hotel; my room had been cleaned, even my Bibles and other Christian material had been neatly stacked. I informed the team leader of my mistake, who told me not to worry, "The maid probably cannot read," he said, "but be more careful next time." Nick – A Muslim country.

Duties and Chores

As part of a mission team; you are going to have to do duties and chores – perhaps those you don't like. You can grumble and complain (which is not a good thing to do), or embrace the experience, however unpleasant or difficult and get the victory. Do a good job as unto the Lord even when you are not being watched.

- 'Whatever your hand finds to do, do it with all your might...' (Ecclesiastes 9:10a).
- 'Whatever you do, do it heartily, as to the Lord and not to men' (Colossians 3:23).
- 'Whether you eat or drink or whatever you do, do all to the glory of God' (1 Corinthians 10:31).

As Bible College students, we had to do practical evangelism. I was so nervous that for the first month the lecturer excused me. In the town centre, I observed the rest of the group for many weeks and little by little, I stepped out and began to evangelise by many different methods. First, as part of a large team handing out tracts, then in pairs witnessing to people, and eventually sharing the Good News one-on-one. It was very rewarding and I am glad I overcame my fears. Samuel – Wales.

Beware of:
- The dangers of familiarity as it can breed contempt.
- Doing the right things for the wrong motives.
- Being outwardly submissive but inwardly rebellious.
- Making promises that you have no intention of keeping.
- Of deliberately rocking the boat so as to draw attention to yourself or playing the fool.
- Of usurping authority or not being submissive to those who are over you.
- Of breaking the rules – they are there for a reason.

'As the elect of God, holy and beloved, put on tender mercies, kindness, humility, meekness, longsuffering; bearing with one another, if anyone has a complaint against another; even as Christ forgave you so you must also must do. But above all these things put on love which is the bond of perfection' Colossians 3:12-14.

Let us do Good
The Bible states, 'As we have opportunity, let us do go good to all, but especially to those of the household of faith' (Galatians 6:10). Therefore, we have an obligation to help others, but

especially the brethren, and as part of a STM team there will be plenty of opportunities to help others. You can help others in a variety of ways; practical help in chores and duties, words of encouragement or in spiritual matters. But in our obligation lays a danger in which we may neglect an opportunity, thinking that someone else will do it. How many times have we left washing the dishes to another, yet we all ate round the meal table? Whilst others will try to justify their exemption from certain duties and being allergic to washing up liquid is a valid exemption, but that does not mean that they are exempt from laying the table, wiping up / drying the dishes or other important duties, like peeling the potatoes, chopping vegetables, making sandwiches or sweeping the yard!

It was only a weeklong mission; but everyday, the church had arranged for a caterer to provide our meals. I do not know why, but it was always me who did the washing up as nobody else came forward. At the end of the week, I had a go at the other team members, but should never have allowed the issue to run for so long. Daniel – Wales.

Let us not be in the habit of making lame excuses to get out of practical chores, because we are only neglecting our duty and revealing to those around us our true character. If we 'love one another' as Christ commanded us to, we will want to help the team and function at our highest level. Team leaders should organise a rota and STM-ers should comply with it!

Around one hundred and twenty years ago, an anonymous writer penned the following: 'It is a mistake to suppose that aggressive spiritual work can be successfully accomplished by setting apart a few weeks in the year for it, without the most careful preparation for it during the rest of the time.'

'For God is not unjust to forget your work and labour of love which you have shown towards His name...and we desire that each one of you show the same diligence to the full assurance of hope until the end, that you do not become sluggish [lazy or slothful in your duties] but imitate those who through faith and patience inherit the promises' Hebrews 6:10-12.

Chapter Twenty-Seven

Being Streetwise

'Only let your conduct be worthy of the Gospel of Christ, so that whether I come and see you or am absent, I may hear of your affairs, that you stand fast in one spirit, with one mind, striving together for the faith of the Gospel, and not in any way terrified by your adversaries...' Philippians 1:27-28.

'And this I pray, that your love may abound still more and more in knowledge and in all discernment, that you may approve the things that are excellent, that you may be sincere and without offence till the day of Christ, being filled with the fruits of righteousness...' Philippians 1:9-11.

Be Wise, Be Streetwise

Entering into a new country you have to learn to be streetwise. You may remember Mick Dundee from the film *Crocodile Dundee II*. He went to New York from the outback of Australia, got associated with Leroy Brown – "What's going down?" and ended up delivering stationery. Mick was convinced that the packages contained drugs, but as Leroy explained, "With a name like Brown, people expect you to be bad." Whilst it was only a film, we must be streetwise on our short-term mission (STM) and you too, will probably meet some characters!

After you clear customs and enter a new world, you should at least try to pretend that you know what you are doing; though if you are with a mission organisation, many pressures (of finding transport and accommodation) are alleviated. Stepping through the airport doors with a fresh visa and stamp on your passport (or when arriving at a bus, train or ferry terminal) touts and hustlers will quickly latch on to the foreigner, offering their assistance; sometimes they are helpful, at other times they are not! Be polite; do not feel obligated to enter into a conversation.

Your Surroundings

Be aware of your surroundings. Be cautious who you go with or follow, if they have approached you, offering to show you something. They may lead you into a dark or quiet alley to rob you or to get you lost, and will *only* take you to your accommodation for a sum of money. Be shrewd in the discernment of peoples motives. Devilish appointments lead to a chain of bondage and grief, whereas Divine appointments lead to a chain of blessing and joy. Your mission organisation will advise you of no-go areas and places to avoid.

Sometimes you may take a person to a cafe to share the Good News with them and they will try to order everything! Once, two men approached me and I invited them for a coffee (I was in eyesight of the rest of my team). As we sat down the men picked up the dinner menu looking to order. I informed them that I had already eaten and was inviting them for a tea or coffee, not a meal. One of the men ordered a beer, I quickly told him in front of the waiter that I was not buying any beers as I don't drink, but if you want it, you pay for it. He ordered a coffee!

In one Islamic country we took a man out for a meal, which is a good opportunity to share the Good News in social surroundings where people do not leave until they have finished their food! He was happy for the food, seemed to appreciate a New Testament in his mother tongue, but also wanted money. This we did not give him and explained that he has already got a lot and should be happy with that.

I met this man as we were returning to our hotel and we went for a coffee. No other member of our team would accompany us as they were too tired. So was I, but I was not going to let an opportunity pass me by. I bought this man a coffee and we chatted. He called the waiter over and got a cigarette. He wanted me to pay the waiter, I told him that I do not buy cigarettes and so he had to pay for that one himself! After a few hours, he walked me back to where we met up. I gave him a New Testament and a Christian music cassette, which he did not seem happy with and he *demanded* money! After gently explaining that I do not pay for friendship, but to no avail, I walked off in disgust. My team leader said that he might have been a rent boy (male prostitute)! Mark – North Africa.

Border Crossings and Directions

Border Crossings are the most wary places to be, but especially as your emerge from no-man's-land and into a new country, where more often than not, you will be swarmed upon like bees to a open pot of jam, or ants to sugar.

In many places of the world people *want* to carry your bags; it is unlikely that they will run off with a fully laden rucksack, but they *will* expect payment or take you to their preferred choice of bus, taxi, or hotel, where you will end up indirectly paying for it. If you ask, "Where is the nearest hotel?" in developing countries some people will want to take you to it, and expect financial recompense! Just ask to be pointed in the right direction. Others will take you to a hotel and ignore the guesthouse, hostel, B&B and other accommodation because you asked for a *hotel*. If they have gone out of their way then give them something for their time and don't let them run off with your wallet or purse!

I crossed over the border into an East African country and a teenage boy helped us find the correct bus. I gave him what seemed a fair financial recompense. He took the money with a sullen look on his face and said that I should give him double the amount. Back on the bus, after contemplation, the boy had wanted the equivalent of several hours pay for just ten minutes work! John – Ethiopia.

Money Exchanging

In some countries, you cannot buy the next countries currencies from a Bureau de Change or bank and so frequently have no option, but to buy money on the border. On the Kenya / Tanzania border we tried to exchange some money into the local currency, where a slight-of-hand trick cost us the best part of £34 ($50). We had not taken our eyes off the money that we had handed the man; but as he suddenly dropped the exchange rate from what we had agreed, we had no choice but to return each other's money – though not all of ours came back!

In Khartoum, Sudan, we came out of yet another bank, having tried to purchase Ethiopian currency when a man approached us and told us that he could exchange the money. The bank guard moved us on and the man told us to follow him. We followed him, stopping off at several places, waiting around and after fifteen minutes, something felt really wrong and we just walked away.

Touts About

Getting off the ferry at Zanzibar, we were bombarded with offers of help, taxis, hotel reps (self-employed touts), before we had even completed our stroll down the gangplank. After politely declining all offers, a man continued with us (several fell away as we continued ignoring them) and followed us into a hotel.

In India, you get people who want to "practice" their English and as you walk around the backstreets and you'll end up at the 'family business,' a carpet or silk shop. "Let's go inside," the son will say (who is often unrelated to the owner), "you can see the family business." You are taken into a room with blankets and silks and other goods stacked all around you, and given a seat in the corner, farthest away from the door. You are offered a free drink by the 'father' who begins showing you the family's craftsmanship; you look around and your unofficial I-want-to-practise-my-English "guide" has disappeared, whilst silk scarves and cotton blankets are strewn on the ground to block your exit, and you get to witness high pressure sells techniques!

In Tunisia, a common scam was for people to allege that they worked at the hotel that you are staying at to gain your confidence. We would always ask them, which hotel is that? If they guessed correctly (and in some towns they had a 33.3% chance of getting it right), then they would have to tell us who the manager was, which nobody knew!

We hired a guide for thirty minutes to take us to three specific tombs scattered amongst many over a wide area. Upon payment, the guide was very unhappy, angry and sullen and demanded more. I thought that perhaps I had underpaid him and after careful consideration gave him some extra, but still he was not happy and demanded an outrageous amount, which his friends agreed with. I realised that I had been manipulated into paying the man more than I should have done, but he never got the outrageous amount he wanted! Newton – Egypt.

Watch out Thieves About

In Rome, Italy, a group of four teenagers and children came around my brother and I and got in between us. When one of the teenagers put their hand over my watch, I knew something was amiss and in a flash, this robbery scene came to mind, having read it in a book. I heard my Velcro rip on my pockets and instantly got hold of the teenagers wrist, upturned it and raised their arm up high, thus pushing their body down so as to immobilise them. By this time, locals were on the scene, shouting, but as I could not say "pickpocket" in Italian, we let them go and shook our heads in disappointment.

In Nairobi, Kenya, known as "Nairobbery" by travellers, two Swiss girls were robbed of their bum-bags (fanny pack / belt bags). They were approached from behind in broad daylight on a busy main street. Thieves told them that they had a knife and would cut the waist straps of their bum-bags, but as long as they did not scream, they would be safe. This they did and ran off, the girls began to scream and a crowd of men went to their 'aid,' but these men were part of the same scam and hindered the girls pointing out the culprits to those who were genuinely trying to help.

On a two day bus journey in Ethiopia, one of the conductors told us that it was safe to leave our bags on the roof of the bus overnight, as it was parked in a locked bus compound. We took our bags with us only to find that the next day, the conductor of two years had ran away with all the bus money, equivalent to a year's wage. The driver had to borrow money so that we could get some diesel and move on, but what if we had been foolhardy and heeded the conductor's advice!

Just outside of the Vatican City, we were approached by a gypsy type lady holding a baby in her arms and a large newspaper. She came right up to us, but we shooed her away as the paper is merely a cover so as to pickpocket you without her hands being seen. Mark – Italy.

Touching and Interacting With the Foreigner

I have found that in both Africa and Asia, children love to touch your skin, stroke your arms (especially if you have hairs on them, as Africans and Asians generally do not) and sometimes even adults. Africans are fascinated with straight soft hair (especially blonde-haired people), and do not be surprised if someone tries to stroke your hair or arms. Adults may ask, and it is nothing to be afraid of, but if you are a woman, be aware of men and rebuke them firmly if the occasion requires it!

Several local Christians in developing countries have informed me that in their nations, just walking alongside a foreigner bolsters their own status, but to talk with one is far better, and how much more if they drink coffee or have a meal with them. These opportunities are always good to share the Gospel to those who have approached you, whilst some are best kept at arms length because you *know* they are up to no good as you feel uncomfortable in their presence. Others are just after a free meal, your contact details or will be friendly with you in an attempt to get closer to members of the opposite sex within the team. Always be ready to help a member of the STM team who may be pestered or harassed by a local – "We have to go, goodbye," and walk of together. A good test of the 'sincerity' of a local man speaking to a female member of your STM team is: Does he stay around when a male member of the team introduces himself and says, "hello / hi," and begins to join in the conversation?

Our mission leader had informed us that in Tunisia, it is quite normal to see a man holding another man's arm as they walk along the street, as it is a sign of friendship. It is one thing knowing it, but quite another when it happened to me! – But I soon got used to it. Nicholas – Tunisia.

Getting your Attention

In Africa to get your attention people will hiss as it is rude to shout, but in South East Asia the customary, "You, YOU!" or "Oi!" yelled at the top of their lungs is common. Others try to get your attention by saying, "I want to show you something," or "I want to tell you something." Sometimes you can be in the midst of a conversation and a person will interrupt (especially sellers), tug on your arm or even gently slap you on your arm to get your attention!

There are those who want you to read out a printed letter on their behalf, which they probably typed themselves at the internet café. The letter, on A4 paper, which is sometimes laminated, goes on to explain that this person should be employed as a guide or similar, or that the person needs financial help, with a recommendation from John Smith of England, or Joe Bloggs of America.

As much as these instances may be a nuisance, please remember that these people are only trying to make a living and the quality of your life compared to theirs is huge. If you were in their circumstances, you would probably do the same. Be polite and smile. In Russian culture, to smile at a stranger means you are up to no good! Some sellers have some handy items, knickknacks or snacks (especially at bus stations) and you will be thankful that they approached you, whilst some guides are real gems of local knowledge and can take you into areas where you would have never trod.

Chapter Twenty-Eight

Security, Wisdom and Safety

Jesus said, "Behold, I send you out as sheep in the midst of wolves. Therefore be as wise as serpents and harmless as doves" Matthew 10:16.

Jesus said, "…My friends, do not be afraid of those who kill the body, and after that have no more they can do. But I will show you whom you should fear. Fear Him who after He has killed, has power to cast into hell; yes, I say to you, fear Him!" Luke 12:4-5.

Security and Safety

Wherever you go to in the world, even outside of your own front door, you could encounter trouble, but wisdom and caution are the best line of defence; whether at home or on your short-term mission (STM). On very rare occasions, countries (or some areas) can break out into political instability so if you are an independent STM-er it pays to scan the local news headlines, international papers and look on your government's website as they issue travel warnings to its citizens.

To state the obvious (but curiosity can override common sense), avoid political rallies and demonstrations as they can turn nasty and you could end up in the middle of it. Tear gas, rubber bullets, and flying missiles (rocks and stones) make no distinction on whom they hit or affect. Keep away from drunken crowds.

Handbags and bum-bags (fanny packs / belt bags) are magnets for thieves. If you can loop your gadgets (e.g. digital camera or mobile phone) on your belt covered by a long shirt or jumper (sweater) then this is better. Zipped or Velcro pockets on trousers (pants) or skirts are very good for wallets, purses and passports. Some people have their passport and excess money in a pouch which is hung around the neck and tucked into one's top – out of sight, out of mind. Money belts are also VERY good.

Beware if people bump into you as they may be trying to steal from you, or distracting you at a café, as someone else takes your bag from under your table or chair etc. Hook your day-bag round your chair leg or through your arm.

Do not joke about terrorism, guns, bombs, political issues, or health scares (e.g. "I think I have Ebola"), but especially at the airport or on-board a plane.

> It was the last day of our mission; we got off the train at our stop and were walking along the platform. It was a warm evening and I had my coat looped through my shoulder bag. Before I knew it, a young man ran up from behind me and grabbed my coat and sped off. He jumped onto the moving train and was never seen again – neither was my coat! David – North Africa.

Problem People

Every once and a while I have encountered 'problem people' whilst on a mission and more often than not, it comes after something significant has happened. It is the devil's way of trying to frighten or discourage me, but these instances have only ever confirmed the good work that has happened, in that the devil's feathers are ruffled. It may be the guy who is intoxicated or high on drugs; the criminal who in envious (or who despises your presence in their neighbourhood), those who are unbalanced in mind, the plain demoniacs and those in groups who are boisterous, being egged on by the crowd.

> Someone once wrote: 'A Christian should ever keep in mind that it is not man who is his greatest enemy and opponent in the work, but it is the demons in man and you would be wise to carefully discriminate and distinguish between the two.'

Strangers and Accommodation

It is very unwise to invite a stranger into your hotel room as they may be a sex worker; regardless of the fact that they are the same sex as you. Most hotels do not permit room calls / visits because of this very problem. Also, if you do invite a local back to your hotel (and they are not a Christian worker) then it is often best that they wait in the lobby area, as people do think the worst and you do not wish to give an 'appearance of evil' (see 1 Thessalonians 5:21, NIV), and not even a 'hint of sexual immorality' to be found among Christians (Ephesians 5:3, NIV). Your mission organisation (or host) will have its (or his or her) own policy regarding visitors, find out what it is.

The leaders of Project Pearl, where one million Bibles were smuggled into Communist China on the night of 18 June 1981 had a strategy – it was 'hope and pray for the best outcome, but prepare for the worst.' They trusted the Lord to grant them a successful delivery, but also had contingency plans in case something went wrong. David fled from King Saul and fled to the Achish, King of Gath. For fear of his life, David feigned madness! (1 Samuel 21:10-15).

I had left my mission partner chatting to a young man as I was getting cold in the open-air and had returned to the hotel room. It was in the evening and within the hour my mission partner had brought this man back to our hotel. He unlocked the door and beckoned him in. I was lying on the bed resting, as we had no chairs and my friend told me that he had to pop to reception, and would be back. I shouted at him, "David come back here," and would not let him leave. Later when the man had gone, I explained the situation to him. I could have just come out of the shower, all our Christian material could have been laid out on our beds (sorting out what we had left) and at worse, the man could have thought that I wanted to sleep with him! Marcus – North Africa.

Use Wisdom
Don't invite trouble, be sensible in what you wear and where you go. It is always wise not to go out alone in a foreign country, but even pairs and groups of foreign women will attract attention. It is always best for men to witness to men and women to witness to women otherwise the one listening may have ulterior motives. Always let your team leader know where you are going and when you expect to be back.

My team were ministering in a Muslim country. On the beach, one of our girls wore revealing swimwear. Many Muslim men came to speak to her. Later she told us that she had a good day "witnessing." I was too embarrassed to say, "Get real! They were ogling!" Rodney – Indonesia.

Kidnapping and Hostage Taking
In the third week of February 2009, gunmen held two hostels in Rio De Janeiro, Brazil, hostage for several hours where groups of tourists had come to celebrate the carnival week, though

nobody was harmed. Kidnapping and hostage takings are rare occurrences, though they are more likely to happen in war zones or in isolated areas where extremists are irate at your Christian presence or just because you are a foreigner. God would not lead inexperienced independent STM-ers to these dangerous locations, whilst most mission organisations avoid them.

It was in the summer of 2007, that a group of Korean STM-ers were taken captive in Afghanistan and held for some time before members of the team were released (in dribs and drabs) as the Korean government desperately sought the release of their citizens and had to agree to certain conditions. It was with great sadness that the world was informed that one of the STM-er was martyred for his faith. Thankfully these incidences of kidnapping and hostage taking are ultra rare among STMs.

The Dangers at Night

As in your home country there are some places where it is advisable not to walk alone and not to go after dark. Unlit streets and alleyways are the norm in parts of the developing world and manhole covers may be nonexistent. Beware of potholes, raised kerbs, no sewer coverings, ditches and a thousand and one other obstacles in unlit areas.

> In one town in East Africa, a tourist fell into a ditch and broke her leg. That was the end of her holiday and an accident can be the end of any STM. John – Ethiopia.

Life is full of Dangers

Dangers lurk everywhere, but that should not paralyse us into inaction or hold us bound by fear and in trepidation. We need to understand that God is sovereign – He is in control of all things and all things are under His control, but God's sovereignty does not relieve us of responsibility. We have been given wisdom and common sense and it should be applied. God is more than able to look after us, and let us look after ourselves and lookout for each other.

> Albert D. Helser, missionary to the Sudan wrote: 'Keep in the will of God and you are immortal until your work is finished.'

Chapter Twenty-Nine

The Law of the Land

'And they called them and commanded them not to speak at all nor teach in the name of Jesus. But Peter and John answered and said to them, "Whether it is right in the sight of God to listen to you more than to God, you judge. For we cannot but speak the things which we have seen and heard" ' Acts 4:18-20.

"Did we not strictly command you not to teach in His name? And look, you have filled Jerusalem with your doctrine..." and Peter and the other apostles said, "We ought to obey God rather than men" Acts 5:28-29.

Ignorance of the Law

There is a saying that goes, 'Ignorance of the law is no defence,' and being in a different country than your own (with unfamiliar laws) does not mean that prosecution will be less swift if you break the law, nor will you have immunity because you are a foreigner. Short-term mission (STM) or no STM, laws of the land have to be obeyed unless they break the higher law of God's decrees, though every form of wisdom and discretion should be used when you share the Good News (or in the distribution of Christian material) in places where it is illegal to evangelise or change one's faith.

The laws of other lands, which may affect your STM, can range from no evangelising to the forbidding of owning or distributing unauthorised literature. The consequences can be a slap on the wrist (a telling off), a fine or a court case though most mission organisations stay on the right side of the law and would never intentionally put their STM-ers in danger, whilst those that do bend the rules know the consequences and inform the participants of such. Other laws which may differ from your own country can be: the forbidding of taking photographs of military installations, bridges and government buildings; the forbidding of importing foods (or other), such as chewing gum (Singapore), spitting in public (Thailand), dropping litter (Britain), or may affect what you can take in (or out of a country) – items or money, as well as various driving regulations.

Martha VanCise in *Successful Mission Teams – A Guide for Volunteers* wrote: 'As a rule, unusual laws or regulations will usually fall into of these categories: money exchange; traffic patterns and regulations; standards for public dress; photography; political expression; religious activities; contraband substances and antiquities.'[1]

At the end of January 2010, following the Haiti earthquake, a STM team from two American Baptist Churches in Idaho, America, were arrested at the border for trying to take thirty-three orphaned / abandoned children to their orphanage in the neighbouring country of the Dominican Republic. Local pastors had helped round up the children (to give them a chance in life), but the team did not have the adoption paperwork needed (and so it looked like child trafficking). They subsequently found out that some of the children had at least one living parent and were charged in the first week of February 2010. The following week, the STM team were cleared of "child abduction" as the judge said that there was no criminal intent and within nineteen days of the ordeal, eight of the ten STM-ers were back on U.S. soil.

Protect Yourself

Political tension has revealed to the world the inflamed anger of some indigenous peoples in certain areas of a minority of countries. At other times, if you hold a certain passport, you may be denied a visa or forbidden access to enter a country, whilst a change of regime or government can change their ruling at a whim. In some countries (because of war, economic sanctions or the countries colonial past), some foreign citizens may face added danger (or disdain – being looked down upon) thus hindering the work and possibly endangering those with them.

Just two months after the second Gulf War, we were in a North African country on a STM and on the edge of one town, we had stones thrown at us and abuse shouted by the local children and teenagers. Likewise, if you go to a district that is not familiar with foreigners, they may be extra suspicious, but more often than not, you will be greeted by the kindest and friendliest people who want to lavish on you all the hospitality they can afford.

The first Protestant missionary to China, Robert Morrison, landed in 1807 with a letter of introduction to the United States consular, noted that as an American citizen, he remained under their protection, but as an Englishman, he dared not be known!

In November 1812, A-Fo, a Chinese man approached Dr. Robert Morrison expressing his desire to be baptised, but on the condition that he did not want his brother to know of it. Dr. Morrison explained to him that if his motive was a prudential one (in order to avoid the civil authorities attention, because he would be expelled from the country) then it was allowable; but if he was ashamed to be known as a Christian, it was not.[2]

> We stayed in different safe houses at night in locked compounds and were behind tinted windows as we drove around the city with armed guards on the back of the pickup. Our indigenous associates were very concerned for our welfare and we were told that under no circumstances were we to reveal our American nationality, as we distributed food. Andy – Somalia.

Sensitive Countries

Some STMs are based in sensitive countries where freedom of religion may not be permitted, even though a country's constitution may say otherwise and so additional wisdom and caution is needed. If you are caught evangelising, you may be let off with a caution, (all your materials confiscated) or taken to the police station (and interviewed) and then told to get on the next flight, or you might may have to appear in court. If you are permitted to leave the country, those who have assisted you (or are associated with you, local Christians, the pastor, evangelist, interpreter or guide) may suffer the consequences.

> Our team was caught by the police and held under arrest for four days. Two days we were in a prison cell, whilst the next two days we were under hotel arrest. At our court appearance we were acquitted but told to leave the country immediately. We made front-page news in the local press, where the judge was criticised for letting the infidels go. Mark – Morocco.

Printed Material

Some items of literature are forbidden in certain sensitive countries, notably Christian pamphlets and Bibles, whilst in other countries, it is a crime to criticise the government or monarchy.

In 1812, Dr. Robert Morrison sent to his mission society the Gospel of Luke in Chinese, alongside a Chinese edict, which stated that to print a book on the Christian religion in the Chinese language was a capital crime! He wrote: 'I must go forward however, trusting in the Lord. We will scrupulously obey governments so far as their decrees do not oppose what is required by the Almighty. I will be careful not to invite the notice of government.' The New Testament was completed by September 1813 and the Old Testament by November 1819![3]

One STM-er in a Muslim nation, phoned up a tentmaker missionary and wanted to visit him with fresh materials for the ministry. The missionary had to cut the conversation short and later told the STM-er that he was already under suspicion by the authorities, and that his phone may be tapped. Thankfully he was able to receive the Bibles and other material and no harm was done, but it served as a valuable lesson.

On 19 January 2009, Australian writer Harry Nicolaides was sentenced to three years in prison under Thailand's draconian lese-majesty laws, which forbid criticism of the king, which is seen as an attempt by the government to stifle dissent.

In most countries, Western tourism is too important to imperil by locking up STM-ers for minor offences though policies differ between tourist and rural areas. If the police stop foreigners, it is usually to give a firm but polite telling off but this is not the case in countries who are not dependant on tourism such as Iran, Burma, Bhutan, Sudan, Somalia and North Korea.

It was dark and we realised we were being followed by a man on a motorbike as we distributed Christian materials on peoples doorsteps (no letterboxes). We tried to 'disappear' but to no avail. We got a taxi to a popular hotel and the motorbike rider caused a scene. The hotel manager took our side, he asked for a pamphlet himself and was very thankful! We waited in the lobby area as a friendly plain-clothes police officer came to chat with the motorbike rider and us. Our materials were confiscated and we had to report to the police station the next day where the 'boss' told us off and then we were free to go! Peter – Tunisia.

Whilst we are to 'submit ourselves to every ordinance of man for the Lord's sake' (1 Peter 2:13-14) we also need to obey Jesus' command, "Go into all the world and preach the Gospel to every creature" (Mark 16:15). We know it is 'better to obey God rather than men' (Acts 5:29), therefore if the laws of the land contradict God's law (a higher law) then they can be broken, but we may have to face the consequences! As we could be sent out, "As sheep in the midst of wolves," said Jesus Christ, "Therefore be as wise as serpents and harmless as doves" (Matthew 10:16).

Chapter Thirty

Look After Yourself – The Human Body

'Wisdom is the principle thing, therefore get wisdom. And in all your getting, get understanding. Exalt her, and she will promote you; she will bring you honour, when you embrace her' Proverbs 4:7-8.

'And say to Archippus, "Take heed to the ministry which you have received in the Lord, that you may fulfil it" ' Colossians 4:17.

Hazards and Due Diligence

There are dangers and hazards everywhere, but on a short-term mission (STM) we should be extra diligent because of the unfamiliar surroundings, and heed any warnings that your mission organisation or leaders inform you of. Much of what is written in this chapter are extreme case scenarios and we should not be overly concerned or even worried about what may happen or can happen as it probably never will (and God is sovereign), but we should all be wary of extreme or adventure sports as an accident can spell the end of your STM.

It is quite possible and perfectly plausible that we could get 'run over by a bus,' as the old saying goes, but that does not paralyse us into not taking public transport or not crossing the road. The information is intended to educate and inform, and not to frighten or put you off your STM.

Each country may have its own unique difficulties that can cause problems, but these problems are a minority and incidences can be very few and far between. I have travelled to more than forty different nations and the worse I have ever encountered is diarrhoea (diarrhea), mild altitude sickness, mosquito bites, pickpockets, and once in France, a snake slithered across the footpath on a Pyrenees mountain trail which made me jump in the air and set my heartbeat thumping!

I got inside my hire car and found that the steering wheel was on the wrong side of the car. I pulled out of the airport thinking that I was driving on the correct side of the road until my passenger shouted at me. I turned left at the cross junction and kept on the right-hand side of the highway, unfortunately for me, both lanes of traffic were heading in my direction and the other vehicles were all tooting their horns and flashing their lights – I did a quick u-turn! Michael – America.

Health and Safety

Whilst you are on your STM, you may have the opportunity to participate in a sport or activity, which may be a one-off opportunity. However, be aware that safety regulations and precautions may not be as stringent in some countries as in others – this is especially true in developing countries where corners may be cut to maximise profits. At other times, the excitement of being away from home, trying to stand out, or being psyched on by other team members, you may be brazen in your foolhardiness!

Travelling on public transport in developing countries should carry its own health warnings; where bald or under inflated tyres or weak brakes are common! As is overtaking on blind bends and weaving in and out of traffic. You can also fall off the back of a pickup, be bounced out of a truck or slide off the roof of a bus or a train (what were you doing on the roof?), and you would not be the first!

One STM-er was sat in front of the engine on a motorised canoe and lost his hearing for twenty-four hours, even though he was wearing a crash helmet. Cotton wool is good for keeping noise out, or use rolled tissue paper!

I was travelling on the top of a vehicle and decided that I would impress my friend by doing press-ups on the roof rail of the moving truck. I would clap my hands between each push-up, but as I later realised, if I got it wrong, my teeth would have been smashed! Charles – India.

Extreme or Adventure Sports

When it comes to extreme or adventure sports, you pay your money and take your chances. Adventure sports can include: jet-skiing, rock climbing, snowboarding or skiing, ostrich racing, buffalo riding, crocodile wrestling (just kidding!) or playing Tarzan on the vines. Extreme sports can be: bungee jumping, skiing down a near vertical mountain, white-water rafting, motocross racing or jumping out of an aeroplane etc.

There are free versions of adrenaline pumping 'sports' which people who are away from home have been known to participate in, such as: roof-riding on buses or train surfing (standing on the top of moving transport), tomb-stoning (jumping off cliffs and high ledges into water), log walking (jumping from one floating and rotating log to another). All of these 'sports' have their own hazards and dangers which should be avoided on STMs as an accident could spell the end of your mission.

I hired a powerful dirt bike and went off-road for the day. All was going well until I crashed, and I sustained some serious injuries, but after a few months I did fully recover. Ronald – France.

The Human Body

The human body can go through huge extremes and when in dire circumstances, with adrenaline flowing through its system, it can really go the distance, but only for so long until the body collapses. Food, drink and rest are essential, though within each of us we have greater endurance when pushed to extremes. Don't forget your Sabbath day of rest, your one day off per week, which may not be a Sunday.

You have probably heard the saying, "It is better to burn out than rust out," but missionary to Indonesia and Malaysia, Elizabeth Goldsmith recalled what her Vice-Principal at her women's Bible College said, "God doesn't expect you to burn *out* but to burn *on*." Elizabeth added: 'Yet there are times when He asks us to give every ounce of our strength to an opportunity which may never come again.'[1]

Most mission trips will run smoothly, though the more complex ones are when vast overland distances are travelled across different countries on public transport. In addition, if you go to remote locations where a lot of trekking through jungles or the wilderness is endured then added stress and strain can take its toll on your body. One man went on a four-month STM and on his return found out that he had lost about 50% of his hair. His doctor confirmed that he had malaria and stated that stress and shock were a contributing factor to this genetic condition.

We trekked two days in the tropical climate to a village, which should have taken six hours. Our guide got us lost – it was tough! Our hands were badly cut on the thorns, thistles, sharp leaves and grass. My clothes of just two weeks were so badly

---

torn and blooded that I had to throw them away and get a new set. James – Laos.

The Desert and Dehydration

The human body consists of between 45-65 percent water, depending on body size, age and gender. If you lose more than 5% of your body weight through loss of water; sweating, you will begin to deteriorate, physically and mentally. If this loss rises to 10% you will become delirious, possibly deaf and oblivious to pain. If moisture loss reaches 12% then death ensues. In hot climates you can lose 1 ½ litres / liters per hour and will need to drink up to ten litres / liters per day! If you lose just 2.5% of your overall bodily fluids (dehydration), then your efficiency to function decreases by a staggering 25%!

To minimise water loss, avoid talking and breathe through your nose. A cyclist in sub-Sahara Africa noted that he was able to drink quite a few litres / liters less per day than what the British Army recommended because he covered his body, to keep the moisture in, which included the Arab headscarf so that only his eyes poked through. Ground temperature can be up to 30% higher than the surrounding air (just walk barefoot on the tarmac or on sand during summer!), so if you're in a jam and immobilised, then try to raise yourself off the ground onto a log, tree stump, or ledge and be in the shade.

An army officer came to visit our group to talk about his experiences. He informed us that out of all the safety equipments and items that you could take with you as part of a survival trip; the most important item is a mirror. It has nothing to do with vanity, but a mirror can reflect the sun's rays and be seen for many miles, alerting people to your presence. A whistle is also another handy item to take with you when going into remote areas.

The Power of Nature

It is very important not to underestimate the power of nature. Whilst in some places the weather can be quite constant, in other places and especially at altitude (or during certain seasons) the weather can turn on a knife-edge and temperatures can plummet rapidly. Rain and piercing wind can chill you to the bone within a short space of time, and is often not noticeable until you stop moving. If you are going to be trekking into some remote area, glucose tablets, for an instant energy boost will be beneficial, but most importantly, always go prepared. Take fluids and foods with you, as well as adequate clothing. It is better that you have a little extra equipment than to be caught out and endanger your life.

> I slipped and fell more than fifteen feet down a bank and landed rib first on a rock. Only by the grace of God were my ribs or other bones not broken, but the bruising took months to come out and I was in a lot of pain. Jamie – Laos.

The Sun's Rays

Sunburn, sunstroke and heatstroke can all cause major problems on the mission field. The sun may be of much stronger intensity than what you are used to and relevant precautions should be taken. As a teenager I got sunstroke and was ill for two days; I now always wear a hat when exposed to the elements. One woman went out horse riding for the day and burnt her exposed arms so badly that she had to go to hospital. After treatment she was informed that had the burns been any worse, then she would have needed skin grafts.

The sea and snow reflects and magnifies the sun's rays, and gives more exposure than if you were in the countryside or around town. Guys, remember that moisturiser and lip balm are not only for girls. Whilst you may not have had chapped lips at home, it is possible to get them abroad and in some climates, un-moisturised skin can quickly deteriorate and crack.

Cloud cover does not eliminate harmful UV rays, especially in tropical climates and those countries centred near the equator. At the equator, with no previous exposure to the sun, the average person will begin to burn within fifteen minutes. Use a high factor sun cream, especially on your arms, nose, the back of the neck and possibly even your earlobes if they are prone to burn. Just being outside whilst teaching, preaching, walking or working exposes you to UV rays, so look for shade, cover up, wear a wide rimmed hat and drink plenty of fluids. Don't forget your sunglasses (shades).

Animals, Insects, Bugs, Reptiles and Rodents

Each country has its own animals, insects, bugs, reptiles and rodents, some of which can cause harm. In many developing countries, stray dogs can be a problem; but only if they bite you! A pastor in Sudan warned us, throw stones at them to keep them away, they carry rabies. In remote locations, some dogs also hunt in packs, but more often than not, a dogs bark is worse than its bite – it is only defending what it considers its patch. One missionary to the Himalayas noted that two Tibetan dogs (like mastiffs) could take down a bear!

In December 2006, Lisa McMurray, an animal worker from Northern Ireland, was scratched by a dog at an animal sanctuary in South Africa. The dog was later put down when it began foaming at the mouth. In December 2008, Lisa was diagnosed with the rabies virus and was put into isolation at Belfast's Royal Victoria Hospital, where she died in the first week of January 2009.

> I was looking around this mission compound for the first time and was wondering what all the holes in the ground were. God spoke to me very clearly and told me 'to mind my own business.' I later found out that they were snake holes. I am glad I minded my own business, as I hate snakes! Hannah – Kenya.

Leeches

Leeches can be found in tropical locations or where damp leafy-type areas are humid. They can eat through clothes and will suck all the blood they can get from you, before falling off. Lighters are good for burning them to encourage them to drop off. Beware of squeezing them as you can push their bodily contents into your wound and this may lead to an infection. One guide got a leech stuck in his urethra; he was wearing underwear and trousers (pants) and did not wade through any water! Because of this, each member of the STM team had to have a cavity check for their own personal safety!

Mosquitoes

Mosquitoes can be the bane of many a STM. I have never taken a mosquito net with me on any mission, though I have slept under many, but I have always bought anti-malarial drugs from home when going into an area of risk.

Mosquito nets are useful if the place where you are staying in has the facility to hang them! Nets that hang by one central cord are far better than those that hang by four corners; only one hook is needed rather than four. Mosquito nets are always cheaper in developing countries, though they may not have been sprayed or soaked in active insect repellents (e.g. DEET, diethyltoluamide) for additional protection.

Chapter Thirty-One

Looking After Each Other

The apostle Paul wrote: 'Let your conduct be worthy of the Gospel of Christ...' Philippians 1:27a.

'Abstain from every form of evil' 1 Thessalonians 5:22.

Be Watchful
On your short-term mission (STM) you not only have to look after yourself, but you need to keep an eye on other members of the team, to consider their welfare and serve one another in the love of Christ. As a team member you are your 'brother's keeper' (see Genesis 4:9), and are responsible to protect and to watch over each other. This is why many mission organisations do not want you wandering around the streets on your own and why you should inform your leader where you are going, instead of playing the illusionist and disappearing!

Remember to assist those in need, be chivalrous (opening doors etc.), courteous and assist members of the team who are struggling to carry their bags, even though they should have travelled light!

> We were trying to get to sleep in our hut, but all night I could hear the scuttling of rodent's feet in the rafters above. I knew they were rats and I did not like them. One ran across my legs and I could not help but scream! Timothy – Papua New Guinea.

Unwanted Attention and Clothes
It is a sad fact that women from the West are generally perceived as having loose morals in many places of the world, whilst the men are deemed as promiscuous and hard drinking. The stereotypical view is broadcast by Hollywood (via satellite) and enforced by many tourists (by their behaviour) and by what they wear, or lack of it!

In some countries, foreign women can receive undue attention simply by their very presence in public. Headscarfs[1] and flowing tops often go a long way in some cultures to reduce unwanted attention, whilst in Iran, even Iranian women who try to emulate 'Western values' of dress and style are frequently verbally abused by their own people, by both men and women!

Some items of clothing identify you with your religion, so beware of what you buy. Islamic clothing and Islamic religion are very closely connected. A pastor in Egypt informed us, "Don't wear a jilbab[2] (a long ankle length garment), only Muslims wear them, though it's OK to use them as a night gown!" Whilst in another country, one mission leader inadvertently bought a traditional Arab garment and wore it around the streets (and received strange looks from the locals), only to find out it was a nightgown!

> I was walking along the street at the front of our mixed team. A boy on the back of a bicycle slowly rode pass, put out his hand, touched my back and stroked my blonde hair. I was so shocked, I screamed, froze to the spot and began to shout. One of the local young men heard my cry, he ran after the teenage boys who were trying to get away, pulled the culprit off the back of the bike and slapped him several times! Yvonne – Tunisia.

Relationships

In some countries, mixed teams must use wisdom in how they interact with each other in public. Even married couples need to use discretion in public displays of affection, even holding hands in public in some cultures is a no-no! In Dubai (a popular upmarket holiday destination in recent years), kissing in public (and holding hands between unmarried couples) is deemed inappropriate behaviour with a possible prison sentence, penalty or deportation!

Some older unmarried female STM-ers have been known to wear a ring on their wedding finger, so as not to attract unwanted attention as they go about the work of the Lord, whilst unmarried men in certain environments arouse suspicion amongst the local males of the community.

If you are part of a mission organisation, they will be able to advise you on all things cultural (and taboo), in regards to relationships. They will probably have their own policy regarding starting a relationship with a member of the opposite sex and it will probably be "no;" or only with the leader's permission after a designated length of time. Submit to those in authority over you (your leader) and obey the rules of the mission organisation.

It is advisable to refrain from getting emotionally involved with members of the opposite sex whilst on your STM; which includes those from within the team and members of the local community. These type of relationships will only distract you on your STM and can cause MAJOR problems if the relationship breaks down. You may still have two weeks (or two months) remaining of the STM, working in close proximity to the one who ended the relationship and it can cause friction for everyone.

I was part of a team in North Africa and one of the STM-ers began flirting with me. I enjoyed the attention at first, but a few days into the STM he asked me out. I did not think that it had gone that far. I politely declined and was surprised at the distraction; his focus was on me rather than sharing the Good News with the locals. Julia – Tunisia.

Self-Control, Purity and Holiness
- 'Whoever has no rule over his own spirit is like a city broken down without walls' (Proverbs 25:28).
- 'The fruit of the spirit is love, joy, peace, longsuffering, kindness, goodness, faithfulness, gentleness [and] self-control...' (Galatians 5:22-23).
- 'Let no one despise your youth, but be an example to the believers in word, in conduct, in love, in spirit, in faith, in purity' (1 Timothy 4:12). See also 1 Timothy 5:1-2.
- 'But as He who called you is holy, you also be holy in all your conduct,' because it is written: 'be holy because I am holy' ' (1 Peter 1:15-16).

We were a large mixed team of different nationalities of varying ages, and I became friends with a member of the opposite sex. She had a lot to say and I was happy to listen. I enjoyed her company, but it was pointed out by another member of the team that she wanted more than friendship and so I began to withdraw, so as not to lead her on. She was quite hurt about it. Nathaniel – Brazil.

Narcotics, Stimuli and Other Substances
Be careful of what you are offered to chew or drink. If you are invited to smoke a substance, please decline. If you are offered a substance to chew (except chewing gum) then in all probability it will be a narcotic type stimulus. It may be perfectly legal and

culturally acceptable, or perhaps even expected, but it is advisable to politely decline. Other stimuli are snorted and any of the above, can really mess with your stomach and bowels, or head to produce a drug-like effect, hallucinations or even evil dreams. It may be beetle gum in India, chat or chad in Africa, or the more common known narcotics in Thailand, with their dozens of Western names.

A beach cafe owner asked me if I wanted to buy a happy pizza. I told the owner that I was very happy as I had Jesus in my life. Being naïve, I had to enquire what a happy pizza was and was duly informed that it was pizza mixed with cannabis! "Surely it's illegal?" I asked. The owner replied, "The authorities turn a blind eye as the tourists like to be made happy." Stuart – Cambodia.

Potions and Unknown Drinks

All cultures have strange, weird, wonderful food and beverages, but some are not so good for you as others. Yak butter tea in Tibet may be greasy, but is not alcoholic or considered dangerous nor will it alter your state of being, and it is these latter beverages that you must be very cautious of.

Local brew can be very potent and more often than not, you may be offered a drink without knowing its true contents. Juice from palm trees ferments within hours in hot climates and has a high alcoholic content. In one country, we were offered the latter. My friend, who could speak an intermediate language fluently, enquired whether it was alcoholic or not. We were assured that it was not, but after just a sip, it was very evident that we had been misinformed.

You may not be teetotal, but on a mission I would advise to abstain from alcoholic drinks, though in France and Italy, it is the norm to have a glass of wine with your meal and the choice is always left up to the individual. If you are part of a mission organisation or with the church, check with the leader.

You DO NOT want to set a bad example to younger (or weaker) members of the team or make them stumble or give offence (1 Corinthians 8:12-13). One of the team members may have previously had issues with alcohol and one glass of wine could tip him or her over the edge. For principles and practices of Christian liberty and abstention, see Romans chapter 14, Romans 15:1-13, 1 Corinthians chapters 8 and 10, (especially 10:31-33) and 2 Corinthians 6:3.

Chapter Thirty-Two

The Culture of Another

'So they set him a place by himself, and them by themselves...because the Egyptians could not eat food with the Hebrews, for that is an abomination to the Egyptians' Genesis 43:32.

'Be anxious for nothing, but in everything by prayer and supplication, with thanksgiving, let your request be made known to God; and the peace of God, which surpasses all understanding will guard your hearts and minds through Christ Jesus' Philippians 4:6-7.

Culture

On your short-term mission (STM) outside of your own continent, you will quickly discover that your concept of time and space differs, people dress and look differently, interaction with members of the opposite sex may be very different than what you are used to and values change. In the West we try to lose weight to become healthy whilst in Africa to be overweight is to be healthy!

Culture defines who you are, your social queues, familiar references and defines how things are done; because that is the way they have always been done. It is the way a group of inhabitants do things; their attitude, behaviour and values. Culture changes from people groups to people groups and from country to country. Culture can be broken into smaller segments within a country or even a county (or state) of how those in the north differ from those in the south, or east and west. Culture can vary from one city to the next and can even vary from village to village, where each group of inhabitants do things a certain way, though within each place they share common values. Culture is also broken into religious groups and then splintered into the hundreds and in some cases, thousands of ethnic groups within those religions.

The culture of another can be simply observed from an outsider's perspective, but the closer you get the more complex it is! British or American culture from the 1970s or 1950s is very different than what it was in the 1900s and even more removed from the 1990s or the present.

Culture within the same nationality can also change depending on one's upbringing. In Malaysia, a senior Chinese pastor who had been trained for the ministry in America, invited some Chinese Malaysian youths to his home. He served them the best hot chocolate, though the youths never drank anything. The pastor was highly insulted at the youths rejection of his hospitality. As it turned out, the traditional Chinese-Malaysian youths said that the Chinese pastor had taunted them by serving hot chocolate but had not invited them to drink of it![1] The youth were following their traditional culture, whilst the pastor was following Western culture!

A lady missionary in East Africa in the 1950s wrote: '...It is not only the rites [an established religious ceremony] and the formulae of which we are ignorant, but the whole way of thinking and reasoning which is strange to us, as ours is strange to them.'[2]

In October 1875, Dr. Robert Laws, of the Livingstonia Mission in Africa, was travelling with two fellow missionaries on a paddle steamer along Lake Nyssa. A local chief, Mapunda beckoned them ashore where they were introduced to the local hospitality. Mapunda began drinking his pombé (native beer) out of a huge calabash whilst his wives on their knees began to gently rub his back, breast and stomach – presumably to shake it well down to make room for plenty more. Dr. Laws wrote: 'The bowl was passed to me, but Mr Young being chief, I handed it to him to get the first draught. As he raised the bowl to his lips, I had the fun of seeing the chief's wives approach unobserved to perform their kindly office to the English chief. Scarcely had he tasted the pombé when he looked up to see what was the matter, and found to his horror the gentle hands of a fair couple and a younger attendant beginning their attentions!'[3]

The Good, the Bad and the Neutral of Culture

The best way to see or understand culture is to go to an ethnic group other than your own; ideally, one that is outside of your own country. You will clearly see the differences between yourself and them, and how you react to the way they do things or how they react to the way you do things! It is educational, funny, though sometimes an embarrassing experience, but a great learning curve, full of memories that last a lifetime.

Every culture has its good and bad points, though ethnic members of each culture may not be able to see certain negative aspects until they are confronted with the culture of another. Culture is the norm of life, the way things are done and therefore each culture thinks that its understanding of the right, good and the true is best – if only because it has always been done that way. Other options may have never been considered or the tradition is just too strong to break.

Some cultures do not use the Western idea of personal space. When conversing they stand so close that you may get their verbal 'spray' on your face; whilst others have bad breath! Try not to be repulsed!

The Traits of a Nation

A research company interviewed 5,000 Britons to determine 'the traits of the nation' – that is the Brits cultural traits, the things which make them British. Top of the list with 58% was their obsession about the weather, followed by queuing, voted by more than 50% and the third was sarcasm as their highest form of wit at 48%.[4]

Regardless of our nationality and cultural traits, we all need to be careful how we 'come across' when we interact with others, but as a STM team we must be aware that we do not present ourselves as loud and boisterous, especially on public transport and when in public places.

Time and Punctuality

In 1960, the first Overseas Mission Fellowship (OMF), missionaries were invited to assist the Karo Church in Karoland, on the Island of Sumatra, Indonesia. They soon discovered that in the Karo language there is no word for 'late' as no Karo likes to be tied to anything. Westerners were dubbed, 'Tied to the clock' because of their punctuality. Karo time was also thereabouts on the hour or every half hour (and nothing in between) because who could afford a watch![5]

Everything was so laid back in Karoland, that an hour or two waiting for the bus to fill up was nothing. Some days the bus did not even arrive! As a Christian leader said to a Western missionary, "Don't walk so quickly. They'll think you're a thief!"[6]

A local minister told the mature STM-er who had been kept waiting for over an hour, "You have all the watches, but we have all the time!" Charlie – Pakistan.

Culture Shock and Culture Fatigue

Arriving in any new destination on your STM is fun, unless you're ill, dehydrated and your baggage has been lost – everything is new, it's an adventure, it's exciting, but it can also be a big culture shock! This is an immediate reaction when you pass through the airport doors, into reality, when all your usual references have been taken away, producing sensory overload and things can become a blur. It often passes within a few days.

Culture fatigue happens over a period of time, once you have settled in, and you begin to get fed up with everything. Your surroundings, the different language and culture, alongside different foods, the temperatures, but especially the spiritual atmosphere, can all affect your mental wellbeing and spiritual perception, which can leave you feeling low or having a case of the blues. Culture shock or cultural fatigue does not affect all people – some people are not fazed by anything!

Flying into Delhi, India, was my first encounter with Asia, apart from eating in Indian and Chinese restaurants in the UK, which does not count! I was away from the familiar surroundings of Europe and had stepped into a location, which was alien to me. It was extreme culture shock, in which the mind and body struggled to cope, trying to adjust to the sounds, the sights, the smell, the noise, the traffic and the temperature. I had been taught about culture shock at Bible College, but you have to experience it for yourself to *truly* understand its meaning! Matthew – India.

Culture Fatigue

As you begin to settle into a routine and the weeks or months pass by, you can begin to have culture fatigue. You become tired, wearisome of your host, mission organisation, the people or your host country. You begin to criticize, complain, moan and whinge, "Why do they do it like this!?" You may feel frustrated over the language, troubled by the bland, day-in-day-out staple food or overpowered by the local spices, tired of the cold showers, lack of privacy, early mornings or late nights, the cold, humidity, the heat, dirt floors, the bugs, the flies, the inner city exhaust fumes, the people, the smells!

The disorientation of culture fatigue can manifest itself in many ways: stress and anxiety can make you feel less able to cope with your new surroundings and even minor incidents can seem like insurmountable hurdles. Minor irritants can become mountains in minutes and you must be careful that the volcano does not erupt! Stress can cause you to become irritable, angry, frustrated, tired and anxious and often leaves you unable to sleep soundly (see Ephesians 4:26-27). Sometimes you can start to dislike the people you are ministering to, believing that your culture is right and that theirs is deeply flawed. You may start to resent your STM or even God Himself. You have to be very careful, as the devil will try to take full advantage of this (see 2 Corinthians 10:5).

Dealing with Culture Fatigue

Where possible, talk the situation over with someone of your own nationality, a fellow worker, or your mission leader and talk to God about it. Get it off your chest; as the old saying goes, 'a problem shared is a problem halved.' However, do not tell your host how much you dislike everything or post your grievances on social networks, that is not the answer! Email some friends back home, read about news from your home country, which may reignite a spark in your heart. However, most importantly, remember why you are on the mission (see 1 Timothy 1:12), trust in God and remember to pray for love, grace and strength.

There are also some practical remedies to help combat culture fatigue. Relax and take some time out (you may be over-doing it), speak to your leaders and don't just play truant from your duties. Appreciate the beauty of your surroundings and do some exercise, as it is good to get the body moving. Catch up on lost sleep (go to bed earlier) and missed meals (you should not be too busy to eat, see 1 Kings 19:4-21) and ask God for His grace (again and again – daily in prayer). Sometimes we can be caught in the rut of a STM whereas everything seems the same, as every other day and sometimes we all need a new challenge, which can help us refocus our efforts. For reverse Culture Shock, see Chapter Forty-Eight, Back at Home.

Tim Dearborn in *Short-term Missions Workbook* recommends that you 'remember the five dimensions of GRACE' (not the acronym of God's riches at Christ's expense), but: 'Gratitude, refreshments, acceptance, compassion and expectancy.'

- Gratitude – Count your blessings and be grateful for what you have. There are literally hundreds of millions worse off than you. You will eventually leave, but your host is not so fortunate. Your little struggle is his or her daily life.
- Refreshments – Rest, relax, sleep, unwind and eat at regular times. Exhibiting grace is not easy when you're dog tired as you may growl all day. Going for a walk or taking a day off (or just a morning or afternoon) can help refresh you, as does a change of scenery – but speak to your mission leader before going AWOL – Absent without leave!
- Acceptance – Accept the people for who they are and not what you want them to be. Accept yourself, a sinner saved by grace who is still an ongoing work of sanctification – you are not perfect this side of heaven and will stumble and make mistakes. Make friends, learn to forgive, laugh at your mistakes and enjoy your time of ministry and opportunities of relaxation.
- Compassion – Show forth the love of Christ to others and yourself. Do not beat yourself up over issues or allow the devil to condemn you. We stand by the grace and mercy of God who can, and will, sustain you.
- Expectancy – We cannot change the world, but we can make a difference, even if it is only one life at a time. More often than not, our ministry may appear to be unfruitful, but we are called to be faithful, not successful. Let us sow the seed of the message and show the love of Christ towards everyone we meet. Also, never forget that the STM is also about changing ourselves; our views, values and character improvements.

Culture Confusion

You may encounter cultural confusion where you can see the good points in your host's culture and the weaknesses in your own (and vice versa) and have trouble trying to reconcile two cultures into one. It can be like standing at a set of crossroads unsure of where to go and not knowing which direction to take or how best to go about it. You may even resent the fact that you have to go home!

Chapter Thirty-Three

Christian Culture

'Love suffers long and is kind; love does not envy; love does not parade itself, is not puffed up; does not behave rudely, does not seek its own, is not provoked, thinks no evil; does not rejoice in iniquity, but rejoices in the truth; bears all things, believes all things, hopes all things, endures all things' 1 Corinthians 13:4-7.

'Therefore, let no one judge you in food or in drink, or regarding a festival or a new moon or Sabbaths, which are a shadow of things to come, but the substance is of Christ' Colossians 2:16.

Christian Culture Versus Non-Christian Culture

When missionaries first took the Gospel into various lands they had to sift through the local culture to see what was compatible with Christianity, what was not, what could be retained, and what had to go upon profession of conversion. Various cultural ways can be compatible with the Bible, but also at odds with it and on your short-term mission (STM) you may run into this:
1. It is compatible, if it is a biblical principle.
2. It is incompatible, if it is unbiblical.
3. It is neutral and can be retained.

In Hereroland, an administrative area in Namibia, Africa, the church's indigenous leaders approached matters of Herero culture with great insight. A missionary in the mid 1980s wrote: 'The leaders neither rejected traditional beliefs out of hand, nor accepted them without question. Rather these traditions were studied to find out what exactly their meaning was within the culture, and then examined in the light of biblical revelation.'[1]

Exporting Christian Culture

We need to be careful that on our STM we are not exporting *our* Christian culture or the culture of our denomination and trying to implant it, or *force* it on the Christian culture of another. This is true, if we are part of a mission organisation, going with our church or if we go with a friend or group of friends as independent STM-ers. Beware of your preconceived ideas, interpretations and opinions or prejudice (nationalistic, personal, racial, theological and denominational), which can distort biblical doctrine. See also Chapter Forty-One, Working with the Locals.

The Holy Bible reveals that the Lord's Supper, the Breaking of Bread, Communion was a meal, which originated as part of the Passover Feast (Matthew 26:26-29 and Luke 22:14-20) that became a more frequent event (Acts 2:42, 46, Acts 20:7, 11 & 1 Corinthians 11:17-34). Yet in the West we often use a small wafer, cracker or a piece of bread and a drop of wine (or red juice), which is what we now participate of, but the principle of Jesus' words, "Do this in remembrance of Me" is still functional.

Church members often think that what they do on a Sunday morning is pure Christian culture whereas it may only be British, American (or Western) church culture – it is the way we do things and our interpretation of certain Scriptures coupled with tradition. Often our opinion is formed more by our country or denomination's traditions rather than what is laid down in the Holy Bible. Are our Christian practices biblical or cultural? To answer this we each need to read the Holy Bible and see if what we do is in line with Scripture; if not then we have drifted from the biblical anchorage of truth.

Larry Kreider in *Bottom-Line Faith* wrote: 'Media largely shapes our mind and culture... Everyone gets locked into certain patterns of thinking. It's uncomfortable for us to change. And it is difficult for us mentally to challenge popular thinking generated by the press, politicians, clergy, or our peers. We may think it's impolite to do so. So we refrain from expressing an opposing view.'[2]

Biblical Christianity must be allowed to blossom and flourish within its own setting. On our STM we should export the Christ of Christianity and not *our* culture of Christianity – but we should live the culture of Christ – to love one another and to serve others.

Wherever you go and whatever you do on your STM, you must serve the people in humility and love; and remember that what works in one community (or on one STM) may not work in another. For experienced and mature STM-ers who go to plant or establish a new church, they will know that it is best not to fit the national converts into the mould of their home culture. Styles and formats may need to be altered to adapt to the country they are in when forming a church, which identifies with the people group they are working with. This will help put seekers at ease and aid evangelism.

In the nineteenth century in Great Britain, some radical churches (and ministries) in slum / poorer areas, held 'Workers Meetings' where the working class could attend "church" in their work clothes and not feel out of place. For many Christians and ministers, this was deemed a step too far, but it was an effective way of reaching the working class for Jesus Christ.

Culturally Sensitive – the Church and Traditions

Being culturally sensitive also borders between Christian communities and what is acceptable in one church or Christian culture in one setting may be frowned upon in another. In some churches, men sit on one side and women on the other; in some denominations, children and (or even young teenagers) participating in communion is a forbidden, and how church services are structured vary greatly.

Other cultural factors can be: the consumption and use of alcohol / cigarettes; the wearing of earrings, other body piercings, religious jewellery (even crosses), makeup, clothes (what is acceptable and what is not – is it too revealing?), jewellery (bangles, necklaces, rings), long hair versus short hair (for both men and women), unnatural hair colouring (pink or blue etc.), mixed bathing (swimming baths, lakes or in the sea) or types of swim wear – is it modest?

Some Christian cultures do not permit their members to wear a cross; often this is because it is associated with the Orthodox, Coptic or Roman Catholic Church. On your STM be culturally sensitive to those around you and that includes the brethren, and even if eating meat causes a brother to stumble, we should not eat it (see 1 Corinthians 8:12-13).

David C. Forward in *The Essential Guide to the Short Term Mission Trip* wrote: 'What message do you send the local Christians when halfway through your trip your team joins in the chorus of how they would kill for a Big Mac and French fries? What does that say about the foods they have scrimped and saved to proudly serve you at every meal so far?'[3]

Earrings, Piercings, Cuttings and Tattoos

Earrings and body piercings can be very problematic, but especially for men. In some countries, it is a cardinal sin for a man to have an earring (Romania), and in others, even among women it is frowned upon. You may be the youth leader, or the team's greatest evangelist, but your fashion or style statement will bring your words to deaf ears and only distance or alienate yourself (and possibly your team) towards those you are trying to reach or those you work with. In the West, earrings for men culturally grew out of the rebellion of the 1960s and 70s and became fashionable in the 1980s and 90s through numerous pop stars. Biblically, earrings for men are a symbol of slavery, bondage and idol worship, see Genesis 35:2-5, Exodus 21:5-6, Exodus 32:1-4, Deuteronomy 15:15-17 and Judges 8:23-27.

Tattoos can also be problematic. In Japan, many hotels have signs – 'No Tattoos' – because tattoos and gangsters are synonymous. You can wear long sleeves, but what if prior to conversion you got your face decorated! In the Arab world and in Hindu custom, henna tattoos are part of culture, religion and ceremonies where different patterns on various parts of the body represent or announce certain things. Henna tattoos are non-permanent and last several weeks.

Tattoos, flesh piercing and cuttings (mutilation / self-harm) in the Scriptures are linked with men involved in occult practice and devotion to the dead! See 1 Kings 18:22-28, Jeremiah 16:6, Mark 5:1-5, and Leviticus 21:5 and Deuteronomy 14:1-2. The Beast will mark his own! See Revelation 13:16-18, 14:9-11, 16:1-2 and 19:20-21. We have been sealed with the Spirit (2 Corinthians 1:21-22) therefore glorify God in your body and spirit which is God's temple (Romans 12:1 and 1 Corinthians 6:19-20).

Some women who were part of a mixed STM team, spent many days with a small group of Muslim women who wanted to express their friendship, by decorating the STM-ers hands with henna. At least one member consented and at least one politely declined. Whilst the henna tattoo was a work of art and looked very decorative, there were pros and cons which different team members acknowledged. In the evening when the team came together, there was also divided opinions as to the correct (if any) course of action.

In some countries, the host you are working with or the local Christians may want to know why members of your STM team have gone back to their ancestral tribal past with body piercings, flesh tunnels and tattoos (see Leviticus 19:28 and 1 Corinthians 6:19-20), which the missionaries told them to give up because of their roots in pagan culture and practice!

Chapter Thirty-Four

Being Culturally Sensitive

'We give no offence in anything, that our ministry may not be blamed' 2 Corinthians 6:3.

'Give no offence, either to the Jews or to the Greeks or to the church of God, just as I also please all men in all things, not seeking my own profit, but the profit of many that they may be saved' 1 Corinthians 10:32-33.

Understanding Culture – From Outsider to Insider
Understanding culture can be complex and to an outsider, some customs, rites or just the way things are done may seem absurd. Nevertheless, if we want to go from an outsider to an insider, we have to try to adapt; to do things the local way thus making it easier to be accepted into the society we are trying to serve and reach. We do not enter into the culture of another to judge them (or condemn them), but to serve them and to reveal the love of Christ through our words, lives and actions, and we certainly cannot demand or expect them to enter into our culture with all its flaws and weaknesses.

'For though I am free from all men, I have made myself a servant to all, that I might win the more; and to the Jews I became a Jew, that I might win Jews; to those who are under the law...that I might win those who are under the law; to those who are without law...(not being without law towards God, but under law towards Christ, that I might win those who are without law); to the weak I became as weak, that I might by all means save some...This I do for the Gospel's sake...' 1 Cor. 9:19-23.

When sharing the Gospel be careful not to wrap the Good News in Western Christian verbiage / phraseology, words like: 'justified,' (Romans 3:24 and Galatians 2:16), 'sanctified' (1 Corinthians 6:11 and Jude 1:1), and 'washed in the blood' (Revelation 1:5). These phrases are common to Christians, but will mean little or nothing to those from a non-Christian heritage.

These words may be difficult to translate / interpret (unless the interpreter is familiar with the particular Scripture in your language), or be translated literally – 'washed in the blood,' and stun an individual or an audience!

Culturally Sensitive

Being culturally sensitive means that we should be aware of the basic cultural do's, or more importantly, the don'ts (cultural faux pas – a slip up), and where possible find out the taboos – what to avoid, what not to discuss and abide by them! Nobody expects you to be an expert on all things cultural, but a few essential basics are well – essential! The locals will more than likely chuckle by minor misdemeanours, but may not be so forgiving on major issues of culture, especially in the context of relationships and religion.

Be cautious how you interact with members of the opposite sex; even those at church. You may be accustomed to giving strangers big warm hugs (or air kisses) as part of your introduction / greetings, but at times, it would be more appropriate to smile, say hello and just put out your hand, though in some places even this is a step too far! By being too friendly in some cultures is an indication of wanting to have a sexual relationship with them!

> We had some free time so I headed to the local oasis for a dip in the refreshing water. Five minutes later, the team leader arrived and told me that I should not have gone into the 'locals' pool whilst only wearing my swimming costume. I should have known better, it was a Muslim country and all the men were staring wide-eyed. Yvonne – Tunisia.

Mannerism and Gestures

Be careful of your mannerism and gestures, as body signals mean different things around the world. If you're in Brazil and give the thumbs up sign 'its OK, it's good,' it means you want to have sex! In Hindu and Muslim cultures, the left hand is considered unclean, so be careful what you touch and do not eat with your left hand! But how do you hold your veggie burger? In the Middle East, crossing your legs and showing the soles of your feet is disrespectful. Be very careful (wherever you are) with eye contact with the opposite sex and how your greet them (if at all). A Western glance in an Eastern setting may be taboo!

Culturally Sensitive – Wealth and Status

For younger STM-ers avoid bragging about your *own* room, your computer, TV, smartphone, pocket money or perhaps even your pet horse. Team leaders and older STM-ers – do not discuss your house at home, your car(s), annual holidays, Christmas bonus, your investments or the stock market (how much you've made or lost). What you earn in a day may take a month of hard labour for your host; don't be insensitive. Your host, a fellow indigenous worker, those you are witnessing to / or assisting may struggle to give two nutritious meals to their children a day when you are giving your children their own room, computer, TV, smartphone, or even a car upon graduation.

Your host may live in a two-bedroom home, with three children sharing one room and yours is a four bed-roomed house with two bathrooms. They may only have one or two changes of clothes and their best may be less than your worst. They may work 60-80 hours a week just to have a basic standard of living, you may work less than 40 hours and have disposable income. You may eat out once a week or once a month; 'eating out' may not be in their vocabulary. I am reminded of an internet video, a true short story which was entered into a film festival. An Asian garbage man goes to a fast-food restaurant, collects the leftovers and cycles away on his tricycle with his bins full of chicken bones and other scraps. He cycles some miles before he comes into his village where his wife sorts through the food. The children are called and with happiness, they have their meal – the leftovers of others.

In India, I spoke at a one roomed house where the three-foot wide 'double-bed' took up nearly half the home and a small 'chest of drawers' took up a further fifteen percent of the room. The villagers lived a hand-to-mouth existence and I had to be very sensitive as to how I shared my testimony, omitting many things so as not to inadvertently brag, but more importantly, so as not to put them down and thus lose the message of love that was intended.

The pastor of the church in which we were invited to minister had bought his first car. The small congregation were delighted for the pastor (and whilst it was old and rusted), we also shared his joy and made some compliments. Responding to a question, a member of our team let it slip that I owned a sports car, which greatly surprised those in earshot. Michael – South Africa.

Culturally Sensitive – Food and Pets

In the Arab world a dog is unclean, in the West it is a pet, a guard dog, or a guide dog, whereas in Korea it is a delicacy, though a minority of Koreans do keep them as pets. In many parts of the world, a horse is a work-animal, for pulling carts, carrying loads or a means of transport, in France it is also food. Showing a picture to your Arab host (or the Arab you are trying to reach out to) of you and Lassie embracing as 'man's best friend' will not help you become friends! Hindus, Muslims and Jews are all forbidden by their religions to eat pork – pigs are considered unclean, so you will do well to leave your bacon bap or ham sandwich alone or avoid them altogether!

David A. Livermore in *Serving with Eyes Wide Open: Doing Short-term Missions with Cultural Intelligence* wrote: 'In China it is customary to show respect for guests by disparaging ones own accomplishments, even the selection of a restaurant. In turn the guest is expected to repay this respect with a compliment.'[1]

> I was part of a large team in a tourist destination and we invited some Muslims to join us at a restaurant for an open-air evening meal. We had eaten most of our food when our Hawaiian pizza arrived. Several of us offered a slice to our guests, who politely refused whereas other members of the team tucked in. I offered a third and a fourth time, thinking that they were shy until I noticed a team member, shaking his head, beckoning his hand and without sound, repeating the words, "No, no" – then It came to me, Hawaiian pizza consists of ham and pineapple and Muslims do not eat ham or anything that comes from the pig! Martyn – Tunisia.

David Hill, a missionary to China from 1865 until his death in 1896, had an interesting experience related to native culture. One day, eighty men came under his leadership, professing to desire the Gospel and promising to build a chapel and support a teacher, if only he would give them his business card. This request would appear very mysterious until one understands that back then, the visiting card was used as a sort of note of introduction, but even more than that, it implied the moral support of the owner of the card. The eighty men had hoped to use the business card in a lawsuit, but Hill refused to give them one.[2]

Chapter Thirty-Five

Understanding the Locals

'So Abraham said to the oldest servant of his house, who ruled over all that he had, "Please put your hand under my thigh, and I will make you swear by the Lord, God of heaven and the God of the earth, that you will not take a wife for my son from the daughters of the Canaanites, among whom I dwell; but shall go to my country and to my kindred" ' Genesis 24:2-4.

'Now this was the custom in former times in Israel concerning redeeming and exchanging, to confirm anything: one man took off his sandal and gave it to the other, and this was an attestation in Israel' Ruth 4:7.

Customs and Culture

The people we meet on our short-term mission (STM) will be different than ourselves, in the same way that we are different to them. A Ghanaian proverb states: 'Rather let your children starve than have a guest go hungry.' In Western culture, this proverb is difficult to fathom in practice, but it brings to light the importance of hospitality. In the West we put our aged parents in nursing homes, whereas in many cultures to pass over the responsibility of those who brought us into the world and took care of us as a child would be considered wrong.

The postal worker cycled past the missionary's house on the Island of Sumatra, Indonesia, and waved to them whilst calling out, "There are too many letters for you, I couldn't manage them." Though the crowning incident came when they were told to collect a solitary parcel, which had been sent from England. At the post office, the official informed them that he was charging them for storage! They told the postmaster that in the future, not to bother storing parcels or letters but to deliver them without delay![1] We all do things differently (rightly or wrongly).

See also Chapters Thirty-Two to Thirty-Four, The Culture of Another, Christian Culture and Being Culturally Sensitive.

Medical missionary Len Moules went to North India, where he served twenty years in the WEC Himalayan missions amongst the Bhotya Indian / Tibetan trader in the Himalayas. As a trainee missionary, in the late 1930s he was initially stunned by the 'unsatisfied curiosity' of the locals. They thought nothing of entering his home (without knocking – even the bedroom), rummage through his possessions and then ask him what things were! After the first incidence, he wrote: 'I learnt that day what it meant to have no right to the privacy of home and private life; no claim to privileges or favours. I learned that if I intended to hold my prerogatives and Western rights, which were not understood or recognised in the East, then as an ambassador of Jesus Christ I was neither ready nor worthy. To win the Indian I must sit where they sit, with a life open and revealed to their gaze.'

'…The missionary must be prepared to have his daily life scrutinised and examined, often in minute detail. Shut your door and demand your privacy, and the Eastern mind will often imagine you have given yourself over to practices which naturally must be kept from public gaze.'

'…Unless missionaries lives are open and clear for all to see – pagans will never be convinced that the strangers live what they preach.'[2]

Superiority, Pride, Prejudices and Racism

Superiority and pride has no place in Christendom, let alone on STMs and if you have issues in these areas you must deal with them before you depart. Looking down upon anyone is a sin and must not be entertained. On the mission field, many things may annoy you. The enemy will more often than not, tell you that you are from the *West* and they are from the *third-world* and thus try to make you feel better by having an attitude of superiority, enabling you to rise above your discouragements by putting others down. This is exactly what a school bully does, they put others down to raise their own self-esteem. It is sin.

Racism can be a two way thing; we can be racist towards others or be at the receiving end. Both are not pleasant but the former is the worst, the perpetrator only reveals ignorance and prejudices. We are all made in the image of God. Racism and prejudice are sin, and preconceptions can be much farther from the truth than what we had once believed and cross the sin boundary when we judge another. Anyone of us could have been born in a different country, on a different continent, to different parents of different ethnicity and into a culture where education and the social or political sphere could have been very different than our present one.

I have lived, studied and worked at a training institution and was deeply saddened when two brothers in the Lord were at odds with each other. Both these men were studying towards higher theological education and both had already been used in their respective countries in the Christian ministry on different continents. Eventually things came to a head and the younger student, the perpetrator told the senior student that his pastor had warned him, "Never trust a —." The senior student was from that continent and was blacklisted by the false opinion of the prejudiced student who had been influenced by his pastor!

Georgina Gollock wrote: 'Never trifle with a *conviction*, but be utterly merciless to a *prejudice* – if it is your own! These painful prejudices are the cause of half the difficulties in Christian work and the man who is in the habit of yielding to prejudices is sure to cause sorrow to others and to himself. Prejudices grow above ground in youth; they are very apparent but easily removed; as a man gets older his prejudices are less evident, but they send roots down into the very centre of his being, and are almost impossible to dislodge. Strive earnestly...to get rid of every known prejudice, and pray for light to see those which you have not discovered in yourself yet. It is very important to distinguish between the "open mind," which readily rids itself of prejudice, and is able to weigh fairly the rights and wrongs of a case, and the "unsettled mind," which has no fixed anchorage, and is tossed to and fro with every wind or wave.'[3]

Weird, Wonderful, Wicked and Inequality

As you travel to different locations you will see some weird, wonderful and wicked (evil and terrible) sights, but the minority of a few, or the occasional negative incident should not be allowed to dim the light of your mission and rarely reflects the majority of the inhabitants.

In India or Nepal, you may come across 'holy men,' naked Sarduhs who sit around their followers and smoke cannabis as they try to attain a state of enlightenment. Going into some temples or shrines you will see the most grotesque depictions and graven images of their gods, some of whom are connected with fertility rites. Whilst other Sarduhs publicly display their deadness to sexual desires by lifting heavy loads with their genitals and dance around in wild frenzies during festival times.

In India, the cow is sacred as is the monkey and they wander freely everywhere. Some sects of Hinduism revere the rat and have them running around their temples where you have to take of your shoes to enter – so wear thick socks and beware of nibbled toes! Some worshipers will even drink milk from the same bowls as the rats and to feed them is an honour, whilst millions of Indians live far below the poverty line and many beg outside the temples and beyond.

MPs in Kenya get a minimum of £90,000 ($144,000) per year in salary and untaxed allowances in a country where half the people live on less than £0.75 ($1.20) per day![4] Adverts aired on Kenyan TV in 2008 stated that every month 500,000 schoolgirls miss a week of education because they cannot afford feminine hygiene products.

In some of the poorer areas in India, the 'untouchables' – the lowest caste (social status) in India do struggle. Within one household, three generations of the same family lived in three rooms and to each adult, a diet of just ten chapattis was allocated per day. That is VERY poor. See also, Chapter Forty-Five, Giving to the Poor and Needy.

The Locals Laughing

It is not uncommon for humans to laugh at, or at worst, look down upon others who cannot perform or do what is second nature to us. In the West, the vast majority of people can set a washing machine, surf the internet or turn on the DVD recorder, but often if we go to a developing country, we can be like fish out of water. What is normal to one community can be seen as an unusual custom for another.

Foreigners in a developing country are often deemed 'uneducated' because they do not have the basic life-skills of cultivating and tilling the ground or even of how to kill, pluck, gut and cook a chicken. Most people in the West have no knowledge of how to hunt, to trap game; to catch, kill and prepare what you have caught or are useless in the art of fishing with a spear or a sharpened bamboo stick. What about handling an axe for cutting down a tree or for chopping firewood? Whilst hand washing on a stone in the river would be beyond many of us. Let us beware of calling others 'uneducated' because if we flip the coin, more often that not we may come out tails, as being uneducated in the ways of basic life skills.

In Africa, the people have a slapstick type humour, like Laurel and Hardy, someone falls off their bike and everyone laughs, including the thrown rider! It was also very evident in many African countries that jokes and funny incidents would travel down the length of a bus and have all the passengers laughing or talking about it. Whilst disgruntled passengers would club together as a group and as one body, put pressure on the conductor or driver for their misdemeanours or delays.

I went to the bathroom / restroom to have a wash and climbed into the large barrel. It was a tight fit and the water was cool. It was only afterwards that I realised that this container was not a vertical bath, but I should have scooped the water out and poured it over myself! Alan – Malaysia.

Personal Hygiene and Water Safety

Personal hygiene varies slightly from one person to another, but in regards to nationalities, they are generally uniform. In many developing countries of the world, the priority is to get food on the table and everything else takes second place, even purchasing soap. Deodorants are available in developing countries, especially in the capitals, though their prices are often the same as in the West, which for many nationals is too expensive. Whilst you may meet people who smell, it is more often than not because they have done a hard day's work and have yet to return home and wash. In some countries, water is precious and having enough for the family and their herds is the top priority, whilst tens of millions of homes do not have running water. Washing can be a luxury (though we must be careful to maintain our personal hygiene on our STM), and I have never heard of a nomad taking a bath in the desert – though they may encounter an oasis!

I have always taken a can of deodorant with me whilst on a mission and when it runs out, it runs out and I only replace it a few weeks before I depart for home – I do not want to smell on the plane! (Remember: deodorant cans cannot be taken on a plane as hand luggage, so spray up before departure). Whilst virtually everyday I have been able to take a shower or at least wash in a bowl. Some countries are so hot and humid that after you have dried yourself, you begin to perspire. After a while you begin to smell like the locals and you blend in very well and thus become one with them on the sniff-o-meter.

In some areas, the river may be the place where you wash yourself and your clothes, though more often than not the locals do a far better job at washing clothes (and a lot quicker) and are happy for the extra income. If you have to wash in a river, ask the locals to find out where is the best place and what is the best time. At certain times of day, animals may come to feed or be watered! The locals may not appreciate your soap or washing suds polluting their drinking water. Find out what creatures lurk in the river – crocodiles, hippos, piranhas etc! Sometimes waterborne diseases or micro-organisms live in the water which can infect you. Common sense goes a long way, but a simple question can be returned by a simple answer, thus alleviating yourself of any fears or concerns that you may have.

> I was scared of ministering in the jungle – I did not know what lurked amongst the vegetation, but I soon got used to using the woods as a toilet and washing in a cold river. Geoff – Malaysia.

Can you Give Me?

Wherever you go on your STM people will ask for your telephone number, address, email, letters or possibly letters of introduction and invites – sometimes, the latter requests come after you have arrived home or have corresponded for a few months. See Chapter Forty-Three, Requests for Assistance.

Some people you meet on a STM are ONLY out to get what they can from you, whilst others need genuine help. Some think that as you are very rich (because you have flown to their country or are far from home), they only have to ask, after all, the worst you can say is no. You may be more financially secure than many people you meet, but many people will have their own land and home, which makes them wealthier than the average young STM-er who lives with their parents or who still has a mortgage on their home.

For non-Christians whom I have shared the Good News with, I have always given them my secondary email address if they have asked to keep in touch. Since the advent of widespread internet, I have never given out my home address, but on rare occasions, I have given out the ministry's PO BOX number for those who have no access to the internet. A foreign address can be a valuable asset to a scheming person, as one day you may find uninvited visitors, 'friends of a friend' on your doorstep, relating to the person you met on a STM. They have just arrived and have no place to stay, and no money! This is an extreme example, but not unknown!

Chapter Thirty-Six

Inequality, Oppression and Slave Labour

'For you are all sons of God through faith in Christ Jesus. For as many of you as were baptised into Christ have put on Christ. There is neither Jew nor Greek, there is neither slave nor free, there is neither male nor female; for you are all one in Christ Jesus' Galatians 3:26-28.

'You shall neither mistreat a stranger nor oppress him, for you were strangers in the land of Egypt. You shall not afflict any widow or fatherless child' Exodus 22:21-22.

Equality of Mankind

Christianity spread around the globe with the idea of the fundamental equality of mankind, but on your short-term mission (STM) you may witness some disturbing sights including inequality, oppression, slave labour and poor animal welfare.

Paul Backholer in *How Christianity Made the Modern World* wrote: 'The value of a human being in God's sight is so immense, that He sent His only begotten Son to suffer, die and to be raised again so that all could repent, believe and inherit His Kingdom. It was the first Kingdom the world had ever heard of where there was true equality. For this reason, those truly inspired by the Bible felt commissioned to create a world where the doctrine of the fundamental equality of all human beings shaped every area of human experience, from law and politics, to health and wealth. In the English speaking world, this helped the development of a civilisation where no one person should be allowed to be considered 'more equal' than another. 'For you brethren have been called to liberty; only do not use your liberty as an opportunity for the flesh, but through love serve one another' (Galatians 5:13)...'

'...Inspired by their faith, Christians became freedom fighters who limited the power of kings, empowered parliament and demanded civil rights for all. Believing all to be created equal in God's image, they made massive contributions to the development of liberty, democracy and human rights. They became pioneers of education, healthcare and fought for rights for children, women and workers. Great Christian reformers helped end the slave trade, slavery, child labour and Apartheid. As Christian soldiers they created modern campaigning, which brought the plight of the oppressed to the masses and forced governments to be accountable and act justly.'[1]

> Jesus said, "A new commandment I give to you, that you love one another; as I have loved you..." John 13:34.

The Status of Women

Women on the mission field, but especially young women may encounter problems on their STM, which their male counterpart will not (and vice versa). Some will be looked down upon because of their gender (or age), whilst some locals will greatly respect, value and appreciate your service to those to whom you hold no blood or ethnic tie.

All through the history of missions, women have been essential helpers, but also pioneers who have cut a path in which others followed. In many generations; especially in the nineteenth and twentieth centuries women missionaries were of incalculable value in the spread of the Good News in unevangelised lands, across China, Africa and Asia when most Christian men were too occupied in other pursuits.

Still today, in many places, it is only women who can open up doors and hearts (with their feminine touch) in which many a man could never reach. In some cultures and religions, outside of the family, only females can interact with the women. In some countries, they are out of sight, kept at home or not permitted to leave the house without a chaperone or their husband. It is to these 'isolated' women that *only* Christian women can reach.

> In Africa, one of our female STM-ers asked the locals, "Can we go hunting with you?" "No," was the stern reply, "women cannot hunt, they are inferior and weak!" Russell – Uganda.

The Oppressed and Exploited

In many countries that are not Christian, females are deemed not as important as the male and are treated as second-class citizens. Frequently in developing countries, the indigenous women have a much harder time in life than men. They are often at the beck and call of their husbands, other male members of the family or the wider family circle. They are also expected to work longer and harder than their male counterparts do, though they nearly always patiently endure it as their lot in life.

The history of missions (what missionaries witnessed) and life itself is etched with the sad stories of polygamy, the buying and selling of daughters and wives, and the oppression of the female sex. Whilst there are double standards for the male who is frequently unfaithful, who negates his responsibility to look after, provide for or be faithful to the one he is married to, and his children. Wherever Jesus went, He elevated the status of womanhood and gave them the dignity that they deserved. We as Christians should do the same as God made us in His image.

It can be disturbing for outsiders to witness the treatment of God's wonderful creation as men mistreat women. Seeing a Muslim veiled from head to toe in thick black garb, with mesh across the eyes in the blazing midday sun of an Arab country is a saddening sight; more so when you know that if they were to show their face, they could be beaten or imprisoned for it! But, these are the fortunate ones as they are permitted to walk the streets. The sight of an African girl or wife, pounding the families food, cutting the maize by hand, or doing menial tasks for little or no reward, out of duty or compulsion can be difficult to observe, whilst the son of the house receives an education, often his sister will not.

Asia is the sweatshop capital of the world where underage children and poorly paid adults work excessive hours under difficult circumstances for little fruit for their labour. It is often in these factories under these circumstances that household brands have their goods manufactured and sold in the Western market at superstores and designer outlets.

'We are called to evangelise, not civilise' – Joe E. Church, author of *Every Man a Bible Student* (1938). After evangelisation comes regeneration (conversion) and then civilisation!

Child Workers

In many countries, children have to work, but more often than not, if a family encounters financial difficulties, the son will continue his education but the daughter will have to earn her keep. Seeing a child of any age, carrying, dragging or lugging a full twenty-gallon container of water on their backs is a heart-wrenching sight.

It was in North Africa more than a decade ago when I first encountered child labour. The taxi drove past half a dozen children selling traditional bread; each spaced out dozens of metres from each other on a main highway. The team leader asked the driver to pull over and we bought several 'loaves.' We gave the girl a note and told her to keep the change. Her eyes lit up and a broad smile came across her grubby face. We drove off. The girl was about six years old, the same age as my sister and that was when child labour 'hit me,' I had a point of reference that I could identify with.

In some countries in Africa, South America and Asia, often the children have to contribute to the family income, more often than not this means that the children help in the fields or in the family business. This may be before or after school, but in some cases, they do not go to school. In many ways it is like eighteenth century Britain where children were integral to the labour force of the Industrial Revolution and later, Victorian England.

> We went into this two-story restaurant in Asia, sat down and glanced through the menu. A girl of eleven or twelve, the waitress, took our order. She spoke good English. The food was served at the same time as the school children were let out. We observed the child waitress peer over the balcony and look with longing eyes on her contemporaries who were dressed in their clean neat school uniforms. She longed to be with them, but, even at her tender age had responsibilities which were of greater importance. Stuart – Cambodia.

Animal Welfare

The Bible declares 'A righteous man regards the life of his animal, but the tender mercies of the wicked are cruel' (Proverbs 12:10), and on your STM you may find some sights unpleasant. From heavily laden animals; horses, camels or donkeys; to whippings, beatings, malnourished and overworked animals with scars and open sores – but these same injustices and cruelties can also apply to many children, women and men.

> We spent a few hours in the national zoo. Being a developing nation, the animals were not well kept. I think the tiger had been driven mad as he just paced back and forth in his small cage, with nothing to do. It was quite sad to see this once mighty beast, broken in mind and neglected in body. Toby – Nepal.

Chapter Thirty-Seven

The Isolation of the Tribe

The Lord said, "You shall therefore keep all My statutes and all My judgments, and perform them, that the land where I am bringing you to dwell may not vomit you out" Leviticus 20:22.

The Lord said, "You shall be careful to do as the Lord your God has commanded you; you shall not turn aside to the right hand or to the left. You shall walk in all the ways which the Lord your God has commanded you, that you may live and that it may be well with you, and that you may prolong your days in the land which you shall possess" Deuteronomy 5:32-33.

Collection of Incidences, Helpful Hints, Tips and Advice

Within this chapter is a collection of incidences and a compendium of helpful hints, tips and advice. For ninety-five percent of those going on a short-term mission (STM), virtually none of the things within this chapter will affect you and is confined to isolated tribes or to some degree, communities that are way off the standard mission group trail; though the declaration at the end of the chapter is very important. These tips and advice are included because you never know what is around the corner or where you may end up, as the twists and turns in the sovereignty of God may lead you into deeper areas of work in the coming years.

The type of independent missions that take you to isolated areas or remote tribes cost considerably more than your average trip with any mission organisation, though you can tie up with specialist agencies and NGOs. The tribes are isolated in their locations, and often 4x4s (even boats and motorised canoes) have to be hired (or rented), along with their driver / captain as well as a interpreter / guide. You will need to kit yourselves out with enough camping gear for the entire team and food to last you (and your helpers) the duration of the mission as well as spares and fuel. Everything adds up. Also remember that 'white man's' diseases can easily wipe out an entire tribe who have not had inoculations or vaccinations which are common to those of us in the West.

In August 1999, I went with a small STM team to a rural area in Central Asia. We did our research and took some water purification tablets, though most of the time we were able to buy bottled water. One evening we used tap water with our water purification tablets to cook our Korean noodles. The water turned blue, as did our noodles, but we enjoyed them and were fine! Qday – Kyrgyzstan.

The Chief / Tribal Elders

In some places, before you can camp in a village or interact with the locals, let alone share the Good News, you will have to speak to the chief, village elders or patriarchal figure. Your guide and / or interpreter will assist you in this cultural issue. With those in charge on your side, your ministry in that location can begin. If you are unable to obtain the consent of the chief, then generally speaking, the villagers will be afraid to go against the express wishes of their superior and you will try, but in all probability, only labour in vain. It is often better just to move on whilst still in the patriarchal's good will, rather than to offend. The leader may only be distrusting because it is the first time he has laid eyes on you. It may be possible to visit at another time, on a return trip and the door may be wide open.

Jesus cast evil spirits out of a demon-possessed man (and into a herd of pigs), which ran down the hill into the sea and drowned. The man was then clothed and was in his right mind when eyewitnesses told those who had gathered what had happened. Jesus was approached by the people of Gadarenes who 'began to plead with Him to depart from their region' and He did (Mark 5:17-20). At one time, Jesus was going to Jerusalem via Samaria and sent some of his disciples to prepare the ground, but when Jesus arrived, the Samaritans did not receive Him! James and John were furious and asked permission to call fire down from heaven! Jesus rebuked them and said, "The Son of Man did not come to destroy men's lives but to save them," and *they went to another village*' (Luke 9:51-56).

We tried to witness to the locals at one village, but the people refused to hear us until we had received permission from the elders of the village. Joseph – Ethiopia.

In some places, it is customary to bring presents to those whom are in charge or to bring assistance to their people. Staple foods, pots and pans, matches, disposable lighters, knives, machetes, axes; really anything to help open the minds of those to whom you are trying to reach and thus open doors. Your guide and / or interpreter are always your best port of call for advice in these matters and they will probably understand the culture, customs and etiquette.

Topless Women

In some cultures and more often than not in isolated communities, far from civilisation, it is perfectly normal for women not to cover their breasts. Especially in Africa and tribes located off the Amazon River in South America. In fact, in some parts of Africa, it is more acceptable to show one's breasts than one's legs! Up until quite recently in some parts of Papua New Guinea, it was just as common to see a woman breastfeeding her baby as it was her piglets!

I was in Malawi at a guesthouse and was reviewing some of my video footage from the previous country. One of the workers came over and began to watch it with me. "Is that a train he asked?" "Yes," I replied. "Oh, it doesn't have any tyres," the man said in a surprised voice. I was staggered that this man had never seen a train before! James – Malawi.

Superstition, Witch Doctors and Declarations

Do not underestimate the power of superstition and the control and fear which witchdoctors or shamans can hold over their people. Whilst these workers of unrighteousness are demonised, only a minority have real power, which comes from the evil one; many are just charlatans. Never forget that 'He who is in you is greater than he who is in the world' (1 John 4:4), and that Jesus was 'manifest that He might destroy the works of the evil one' (1 John 3:8). If you come across these workers of unrighteousness and bond-slaves to the devil, they may challenge you, or more often than not, try to conjure enchantments or cast spells against you, perceiving that you are servants of the living God. If you are born again and not living in wilful sin you have nothing to be afraid of, as you are covered by the blood of Christ and there is no greater name than Jesus Christ of Nazareth!

'Whoever is born of God does not sin; but he who has been born of God keeps himself and the wicked one does not touch him' (1 John 5:18). That is, the demons in man cannot touch you

- 203 -

if you are living pure and holy lives, but if you are in *defiant wilful sin* then you give the enemy a *legal entry* to harass and to inflict torment on you. The devil always stands to accuse but the innocent who are washed in the blood of the Lamb can declare, "The Lord rebuke you Satan" – (see Zechariah 3:1-5), because our 'Advocate,' Jesus Christ 'is the propitiation for our sins' (1 John 2:1-2).

Balaam, a false prophet who knew the demonic dark arts was hired to curse Israel by Balak, the son of Zippor. Balaam acknowledged that he could not go beyond the will of the Lord, there was no weak link in the chain because of Israel's purity. He noted that God had 'not observed iniquity in Jacob, nor has He seen wickedness in Israel,' and that 'the Lord his God is with him.' Christians have Christ in them and we are in Him – (see John 17:21, 2 Cor. 13:5, Gal. 2:20, 1 John 2:5 and 1 John 3:24). Thus Balaam was unable to pronounce a curse upon Israel but had to declare 'there is no sorcery against Jacob nor is there any divination against Israel' (Numbers 23:21-23).

Much of what happens in this world goes on in the unseen realms and the 'whole world lies under the sway of the evil one' (1 John 5:19), as the thief has come only 'to steal and to kill and to destroy' (John 10:10). The apostle Paul wrote: 'We do not wrestle against flesh and blood [humans], but against principalities, against powers, against the rulers of darkness of this age, against spiritual hosts of wickedness in the heavenly places' (Ephesians 6:12). This is why we must have on the 'whole armour of God' (another declaration and prayer, see Ephesians 6:10-17), and be 'praying always with all prayer and supplications in the Spirit, being watchful to this end with all perseverance…' (see Ephesians 6:13-18).

You should memorise some of the above Scriptures and proclaim Jesus Christ's victory – that Jesus is Lord, the Victorious Conqueror, that JESUS is the name that is above all others and that he defeated the devil. It is also important to plead the protection of the blood of the Lord Jesus Christ over your life (and that of the team) – and declare that 'no weapon formed against you shall prosper…' (see Isaiah 54:17).[1]

These truths are declarations and should come from the heart, they are not mantras. It is very important that you are not living in deliberate sin, that you keep a short account with God and your fellow team members (repent and ask forgiveness when you sin) – working in unity, with one mind, for the glory of Jesus Christ. See *Extreme Faith – on Fire Christianity* by the author.

Chapter Thirty-Eight

Food and Drink

'For the Kingdom of God is not food and drink, but righteousness and peace and joy in the Holy Spirit' Romans 14:17.

'Whether you eat or drink or whatever you do, do all for the glory of God. Give no offence, either to the Jews or to the Greeks or to the church of God' 1 Corinthians 10:31-32.

Food and Drink

The world has much to offer in the realm of culinary delight. On your short-term mission (STM) you rarely have to suffer, unless you live frugally which is often a false economy, see Chapter Nineteen, Stretching Your Budget. If you are with a mission organisation you will be well looked after – hopefully – but it may take time for your taste buds to adapt!

The global market has much to offer and on STMs it is always interesting to try different foods. You may encounter on your local menu, the familiar and unfamiliar! From rats, bats, cats, dogs, hogs and frogs, ants or plants, grubs or shrubs, snake or hake, rice or mice, snail or quail and crocodile eyes to vegetarian pies. For many, it will be a time to say 'grace' with faith, rather than by repetition, and remember to have water handy to 'wash it down' or to douse the hot spices![1]

In most major cities, there may be familiar fast food chains, or a local imitation, which you may not appreciate! Some countries carnivorous' food may well be a pet from home. For some it is a delicacy, like dogs in Korea and China, horses in France or donkey in parts of Italy, whilst for others, an animal is food to be eaten and not to be played with! In Indonesia, monkeys harvest coconuts for their masters and on a good day can pick 300!

In the West, we go to the supermarket (or by online, Click and Collect or have it delivered) and have a sanitised view of pre-packaged fresh meat, whereas in much of the developing world, you go to the market, buy your animal, kill it and prepare it.

British chef, Jamie Oliver was in Whyomy, USA, cattle raising country, where he spent a few days on a working ranch. After the bull calves were castrated; the testicles were peeled, cooked in batter and eaten. The rancher informed his guest, "Nothing gets wasted," and after tasting the 'cowboy cuisine,' even Jamie with joy and a look of glee said, "It tastes like scampi!"

> I had a meal of sago for the first time. It's a powdery starch that is found in certain sago palms (the pulp of a tree). I ate it and smiled; it looked like wallpaper paste and tasted like it! Charlie – Papua New Guinea.

Prince Philip, husband of HRH Queen Elizabeth II is well known for his verbal gaffes and the following, whilst is not intended to cause offence, does show the broad horizon of foods eaten in some countries. Whilst in China in 1986, Prince Philip said, "If it has got four legs and it is not a chair, if it has got two wings and it flies but is not an aeroplane, and if it swims and it is not a submarine, the Cantonese will eat it."

Beware of overdosing on your country's staple food that you have not eaten in months. One Korean student had not eaten rice since she arrived in Britain. When, after many months it was placed before her, she ate and ate as if there would be no tomorrow. The rice swelled up in her stomach, causing her excruciating pain and she had to be taken to hospital.

David C. Forward in *The Essential Guide to the Short Term Mission Trip* wrote: 'When living in a foreign country, realise that pasteurisation, refrigeration, and sanitary practices are suspect. Avoid rare (and raw) meat and fish...foods made with cream and mayonnaise, and the like. Do not overeat...' One saying is: 'Boil it, cook it, peel it or forget it' but this is not always practical. However, self-catering STM teams can wash vegetables, fruit and salad items in water with chlorine or iodine to help kill germs.

Forward also wrote: 'You must find out in advance how safe the water is to drink. The crystal-clear babbling brook probably contains millions of parasites and should be reserved for swimming and photo opportunities. To be on the safe side, it is a good idea in any developing region to buy bottled water (check for a sealed cap).'[2]

Eating Utensils

In many countries, you *only* eat with your right hand. Trying to separate meat with only one hand and no utensils is a real bind and tricky, that is why in Japan, meat is cut into portions to enable you to pick them up with your chopsticks; but have you ever tried to eat Korean seaweed or pick up thinly sliced vegetables from your plate with chopsticks? – It's a real challenge. And how do you eat a spring roll when you have no knife? Your eating utensils and accompanying food 'plate' could be: A knife and fork, spoon, chopsticks or by hand. Your food could be placed on a paper, plastic, wooden or ceramic plate, or saucepan lid; served on the table, on a banana leaf or in old newspaper for traditional, good old British fish and chips.

The Guest

You (and your team) may be invited into a home as the guest of honour, what they set before you may be a much larger portion than what they serve themselves, or an expensive speciality food. To refuse may be seen as an insult, whereas at other times, if you eat it all, you could be deemed greedy! You may get first pick of the bowl and when you have eaten, the host (and / or their children) will be permitted to tuck in. Remember, in many cultures it is customary to bring a gift for your host or when invited to a home for a meal.

You could be served lamb's head in Morocco, sheep's testicles in Mongolia, bats in Borneo or battered budgie's wings in the Canary Islands – just joking on the last one, but you may be served baby sparrows or a snake's heart in Vietnam! In Alaska, your STM diet could consist of: Maktak (raw whale meat), Beluga whale, caribou, seal, owl, polar bear or walrus!

On one STM in North Africa, a student whom we had got to know over several STMs invited the team for a meal at his student digs. As there were nearly a dozen of us on the team, we offered to pay for the meat and went to the market with him. The student bought many kilos of meat but at the dinner table that night, less than half the meat appeared! We did not mind, we had met his friends and had a great evening sharing the Good News and talking about many other things.

Vegetarian Meals and Food Etiquette

Being a vegetarian by choice is not the norm in most countries and in places where you can buy vegetarian dishes it may not be vegetarian enough! Encountering indigenous 'vegetarians' is often because they are too poor to eat meat, or because of religious reasons, such as the Dreads of Domenica (similar to Rastafarians). Buddhist cuisine is primarily vegetarian, in order to keep with the general Buddhist precept of *ahimsa (nonviolence – no flying swatting allowed!), though some sects eat meat. *The ahimsa ideal had its development in Hinduism.

To burp in India after a meal is considered a compliment, but not in Britain where it is rude, as is blowing your nose at the meal table in Korea. Incidentally, many Sikhs maintain their right to eat meat, but only vegetarian meals are served in the Langar (free refectories which are maintained by Sikh Gurdwaras) to avoid controversy.

In some cultures, you leave some food on the plate as a sign you're full, at other times you eat it all! In some cultures you accept a little food, move it around your plate and it's OK, in other places it would be frowned upon as playing with your food! Sometimes refusing drinks is rude, but you can accept it, put it to your lips, without drinking any and then place it on the floor or table without offending your host.

If in India, you were to dip your japatti (bread) into the main dish, those eating with you would not be able to participate of that dish and it would have to be returned to the kitchen. Whereas in the south of Tunisia, our mission team got invited into a Muslim home where the host set before us a very large bowl of couscous. We sat cross-legged in the courtyard and each person had a spoon and tucked in; whilst the cooks; the women (who do not eat with men that are unrelated to them) watched from a respectful distance.

Watch and observe the locals who are always forgiving of foreigners and will more often than not, laugh at you, rather than rebuke you if you get it wrong! It is good practice to laugh with them as a curved smile sets a lot of crooked things straight!

In conclusion, whatever is put before you partake of it (unless your conscience says otherwise), regardless of how unpalatable or smelly it may be; try to be thankful and grateful and at least look as if you are enjoying it! Jesus did say to the seventy whom He sent out (thirty-five STM teams), "Whatever city you enter, and they receive you, *eat such things as are set before you*" (Luke 10:8). And as the apostle Paul wrote to Timothy: 'For every creature of God is good, and *nothing is to be refused if it is received with thanksgiving*; for it is sanctified by the Word of God and prayer' (1 Timothy 4:4-5).

An old missionary creed states: 'Where He leads me I will follow. What they feed me I will swallow!'

Chapter Thirty-Nine

Team Dynamics – Leadership and the Team

'...Recognise those who labour among you, and are over you in the Lord and admonish you, and to esteem them very highly in love for their work's sake. Be at peace amongst yourselves' 1 Thessalonians 5:12-13.

'Let nothing be done through selfish ambition or conceit, but in lowliness of mind let each other esteem others better than himself. Let each of you look out not only for his own interests, but also for the interests of others' Philippians 2:3-4.

Leadership Skills

The leader(s) of a short-term mission (STM) team have the most demanding roles. They make the final decisions and have a whole host of other responsibilities to deal with, which includes keeping an eye on every member of the team, mediating between the host church, community or local missionary, the logistics of travel; seeing that everything goes as smoothly as can be expected, as well as "rallying the troops" into action.

During your STM, the team should ideally meet for prayer, short Bible Study and worship once a day. There should also be an opportunity for people to talk, share their concerns and for the leader(s) to keep the team up-to-date. See also Leadership and Leaders in Chapter Twelve, Picking a Mission Team.

'Be diligent to know the state of your flocks and attend to your herd' Proverbs 27:23.

Chris Eaton and Kim Hurst in *Vacations with a Purpose – A Planning Handbook for Your Short-Term Missions Team* notes that leaders should fulfil the following duties:

- Lead as a servant.
- Lead by delegation.
- Plan an itinerary for a team.
- Schedule, organise and hold team preparation meetings.

- Attempt to learn as much about your host country as possible.
- Follow up on any medical requirements and passport or visa requirements for each member.
- If you are working with other leaders, maintain open and honest communication.
- Maintain regular devotions during the trip.
- Draw out of the team members the things they are learning while on the team.
- Get the team members to the destination site and home again.
- Prepare for possible emergencies.
- Be a problem solver.
- Handle all logistics involved in travel.
- Pray, before, during and after the trip.[1]

The Dream Team

Within any group of people there will be differences, but within your STM team there should be the greatest of cooperation, but it is inevitable that problems will arise. Jesus said, "...Love one another; as I have loved you... By this all will know that you are My disciples, if you love one another" (John 13:34-35).

Within any group, stronger characters come to the fore. Your fellow team members on your STM may have just as many problems as yourself and so conflict and tension can arise. There may be many underlying issues that affect individuals, as well as their gender, age, level of maturity and preconceived ideas. Leaders have to deal with not only people and their successes, their personalities and their problems, but keep the STM team focused on its aims and goals.

I was once in a small team and the leaders had hired a vehicle for the duration of the STM. The driver and co-driver (both leaders) had a breakdown in communication in regards to who was going to drive. This engulfed the car in tension; the leaders should have known better and set a higher example.

Leonard Moules, a missionary field leader in the Himalayas noted that in the wisdom of God's sovereignty, we are often placed alongside the most uncongenial members because God has a work in us to do! In relation to difficult colleagues, Leonard noted that there are three courses of action open to us: '1. We can avoid them like the plague – With the least contact the least provocation! 2. We can grit our teeth and pray for grace to grease the friction points! Or lastly, we can see in the other the graces and gifts of God we each so sorely need to enrich our lives.'[2]

Contentions with the Team

The mother of the two sons of Zebedee came to Jesus and asked if her sons could sit one on His right and the other on His left when He came into His Kingdom. The ten disciples were 'moved with indignation against the two brothers' when they heard this. Jesus dealt with the situation by saying, "Whoever desires to become great among you, let him be your servant...the Son of Man did not come to be served, but to serve and to give His life a ransom for many" (Matthew 20:20-28).

Paul and Barnabas had such a grave disagreement over John Mark; that they went their separate ways (Acts 15:36-41). John Mark matured in the Lord and later on was summoned by Paul to accompany Timothy as he was useful to assist in the ministry (2 Timothy 4:11).

Try to be Christ like in all you say and do, remembering to be kind, courteous, respectful, gracious, forgiving and loving. Treat others how you would like to be treated. The apostle Paul wrote that the team that worked alongside him laboured night and day so they 'might not be a burden to any' at Thessalonica (1 Thessalonians 2:9). Whilst he was writing in the context of finances, let us not be a burden to our leaders, the mission organisation, the host or to other members of the team.

- 'The beginning of strife is like releasing water; therefore stop contentions before a quarrel starts' (Prov. 17:14).
- 'He who has knowledge spares his words and a man of understanding is of a calm spirit. Even a fool is considered wise when he holds his peace; when he shuts his lips, he is considered perceptive' (Proverbs 17:27-28).
- 'Let us pursue the things which make for peace and the things by which we may edify another' (Romans 14:19).

When I arrived in Kuala Lumpur to assist a Chinese mission team, I was shocked at the disunity. Two couples had a major breakdown in their relationship and were at odds with each other. God intervened dramatically and now they are very different. The staff members are amazed at their reconciliation. They were once enemies, but now they are true friends and talk and laugh endlessly. Qday – Malaysia.

Scott Kirby, author of *Equipped for Adventure – A Practical Guide to Short-Term Mission Trips* wrote: 'As [a] leader, you are going to deal with personality / relational conflicts, tardiness [the habit of being late], complainers, murmurers, romantic entanglements, slackers, substance abuse, immoral or improper behaviour, outbursts of anger and challenges to your leadership.

'When you see behavioural problems, don't procrastinate. Deal with problems promptly. Nobody enjoys confrontation. And deal with them privately if possible. Most of these things should be covered in the team covenant that each person signed.'[3]

I took a team of teenagers on a STM to a South American country. We were doing a very good work until people started making fun of others within the group. It became a very nasty situation and the group became divided. Some people thought the girl being bullied was just too sensitive. I spoke to the bully and she put things right, however, the girl on the receiving end was so badly hurt that she has grown cold in her faith. A leader – Brazil.

Duty and Responsibility
Many STM-ers between the ages of 16-25 are used to having everything done for them. At a set time every day, meals appear on the table; dirty washing is thrown into a magic basket and within a few days it reappears clean and ironed! A mess is made in the bedroom, yet, as if by magic, every week the room is dusted and cleaned. On the mission field, there is no magic fairy called "Mum" (Mom) and each individual has to take responsibility for themselves, but please help the not so adept members of the team – like boys and ironing!

Defiance of Rules
Defiance of rules can lead to open opposition, whether it is the rules of the nation or the rules of a mission organisation. Policies are frequently laid down because mission organisations who have put them in print have learnt from experience. Remember that it is possible not the break the letter of the law, but the spirit behind it. Don't be a rebel and look for loopholes!

The China Inland Mission founded by J. Hudson Taylor had a policy of dressing and adapting to the local customs – which was an innovative policy for its day, and laughed at, even looked down upon by missionaries of all the other mission organisations in that unevangelised country. Non-Chinese were known as 'foreign devils,' but the assimilation of the dress and customs over time broke down centuries of prejudice and aided mission work. But In 1867, in Siao-shan, an unevangelised area, the missionaries decided that they knew best and 'in defiance of Mr Taylor's wishes had gone back to English dress, to the serious detriment in that inland city. The mandarin, [the ruler of the city], who had left them in peace before, then determined upon their rejection. To let them know that he was not joking he seized their helper, a Chinese evangelist, Tsiu and had him cruelly beaten – six hundred stripes on the back with rods and a hundred more on the face with a strip of leather.'[4]

Team Considerations

Within any team there are many different functions and responsibilities. If members of a sports team decided to do their own thing then the team would not function well at all. If this happens within a mission team, the consequences will be bad at best and disastrous at worse. Each member of the STM must be a team player, because: 'A man who isolates himself seeks his own desire; he rages against all wise judgment' (Proverbs 18:1).

We were living in the same house together, part of the same mission organisation, but another member did not want to know me. We were from two different cultures, but I was the foreigner and really tried my best. I bought him a large packet of his favourite nuts, which he always ate, but he refused them. I invited him to join me for dinner on numerous occasions, but he always declined. For nearly a year we lived in the same house, took the same bus, did the same mission course and practical outreach, yet we never even knew each other. It hurt me greatly that this brother in Christ wanted nothing to do with me and refused to talk about it. Natty – England.

What to Do
- Be considerate of others (especially concerning bedtime and morning rising) – don't be noisy!
- Be punctual and prepared.

- Serve others.
- Look out for any lonely or weaker members of the team, befriend them and assist them.
- Be kind and gentle.
- Honour people and walk in humility.
- Learn a few local phrases.
- Be ready to share the Good News.
- Be culturally, economically and politically sensitive.

What not to Do
- Don't be selfish or lazy.
- Don't moan, murmur, criticise or grumble.
- Don't treat your host like a maid or servant.
- Don't hog the shower or use all the hot water – there may be ten people outside queuing for the shower.
- Don't keep the team waiting.
- Don't be the group joker, attention seeker or boisterous.
- Don't compare your hosts, house / car / food / clothes / possessions etc. to yours.
- Do not flaunt your wealth or brag (even inadvertently) about your possessions at home.
- Do not speak negatively about your host, leader, mission organisation, other STM-ers or country you are in.
- Do not give your advice on the church's problems of which you know nothing about, unless the leader himself has asked you.
- Do not demand better food, accommodation or privacy.

Remember
- You have come to serve.
- Love is a universal language.
- Serve wholeheartedly, joyfully and wear a smile.
- Be flexible, the best of plans often don't work out.
- Misunderstandings will arise because of differences.
- Beware of culture faux pas (a socially awkward or tactless act – a slip up).
- Laugh at yourself, but be cautious at laughing at others.
- Don't dishonour your team mates, the leader, host or Jesus Christ.
- You may share a room with six people, dozens of insects and hundreds of flies!

Chapter Forty

Testimonies and Preaching via an Interpreter

The apostle Paul wrote to the Church at Corinth, 'And I brethren when I came to you, did not come with excellence of speech or of wisdom declaring to you the testimony of God...I was with you in weakness, in fear and in much trembling' 1 Corinthians 2:1, 3.

'For our boasting is this: the testimony of our conscience that we conducted ourselves in the world in simplicity and godly sincerity, not with fleshly wisdom but by the grace of God, and more abundantly towards you' 2 Corinthians 1:12.

Language Difficulties

Language difficulties during your short-term mission (STM) combined with unfamiliar social and cultural cues can make communication problematic even on a basic level. Frustration can set in when you are unable to express yourself fully. Learn to laugh at your mistakes and laugh alongside the people you are working with and ministering to. Often, when speaking via an interpreter, there will still be misunderstandings and miscommunication – it's unfortunate, but that's life!

In certain cultures, how you address or interact with someone is deemed by his or her sex, or age and what is acceptable in your home country may not be permitted in the country you are in. Try to analyse things through the eyes of the locals and not by your standards from back home.

We must also be aware that we can listen but not hear, and look but not see. We can nod our head, but not understand; think we understand yet not comprehend. Often we have to read between the lines when we are communicating with others, and in another culture, that is even harder than at home.

> Paul stood...and motioned with his hand to the people. And when there was a great silence, he spoke to them in the Hebrew language...' 'And when they heard he spoke in the Hebrew language, they kept all the more silent' (Acts 21:40 and 22:2).

I walked into the room and there was a member of our STM team kissing a local Christian woman. Neither of them could speak each other's language and there was no intermediary language either. I disapproved strongly! Kenneth – Brazil.

Lost in Translation

Make sure your interpreter understands English and the language that he or she is interpreting / translating into! Use plain English; avoid big words, speak slowly, clearly and precisely. Keep sentences short. Avoid phrases or words that are only relevant to your culture, as well as slang and don't use words which have a double meaning or of the opposite intended; i.e. wicked – to mean evil or good? Sick – to mean great, vomit / barf or unwell? Keep clear of idioms,[1] colloquialisms, modern sayings or catchphrases, which will only make your interpreter scratch their head or raise their arms and give you a blank look.

'...Unless you utter by the tongue words easy to understand, how will it be known what is spoken? For you will be speaking into the air. There are, it may be, so many kinds of languages in the world, and none of them is without significance. Therefore, if I do not know the meaning of the language, I shall be a foreigner to him who speaks, and he who speaks will be a foreigner to me' 1 Corinthians 14:9-11.

The Sounds of Language – Pronunciation

Citizens of different countries struggle with certain sounds, simply because they are unfamiliar with them. Koreans cannot pronounce the letter 'Z,' the Chinese and Koreans cannot sound the letter 'L' which is very similar to the letter 'R' – hence why they say, "Melly Chlistmas" and not Merry Christmas. This use of 'L' for 'R' is known as lambdacisms, and the Japanese on the other hand, substitute the letter 'R,' for the letter 'L'. The English cannot hear the difference between some French words with their acute accents, whereas some people from the Orient can hear the difference between wool and wall, yet are unable to pronounce them as two individual words. Many African languages use 'clicks' where the tongue hits the roof of the mouth to produce various words. Just try it.

I was sharing my testimony at a large church through a Sudanese pastor whom I had spent several days with. I told the church, "I can see that you are spiritually hungry." The pastor looked embarrassed, smiled and translated into the local dialect, "You look hungry!" Paul – Sudan.

Preaching, Jokes and Politics via an Interpreter

Remember that preaching through an interpreter will double the length of the sermon and some interpreters will even repeat your message into as many as three or four languages / dialects! Respect the time given to you and always give words of greeting. Some churches have poor lighting or no natural light and reading from your Bible may be much harder than at home. Get a pair of glasses or a larger print Bible. Jokes rarely bridge cultural divides and can be hard to translate. Do not preach on politics, democracy or against tyrannical leaders as you could endanger your hosts or cause great offence and harm. Do not discuss these subjects in public places as 'loose talk costs lives' as the old war saying goes. Poems and songs are also difficult to translate and rarely if ever make sense to the interpreter or those listening – nonetheless they will still smile and perhaps the interpreter will tell them to clap at the end, to make everyone feel good, but especially you.

'We preach Christ crucified, to the Jews a stumbling block and to the Greeks foolishness' 1 Corinthians 1:23.

Testimonies

Most people going on a STM will not be expected to preach and teach in churches, but in all probability, the organisation you are with or working alongside will want you to share your testimony – your confession of faith – how you became a Christian. Another testimony could be what you have learnt since your conversion and how you have progressed in the Christian faith.

You may be asked to speak or share at the Sunday School or youth group so make each talk, testimony or story relevant to your age group. Sunday School talks on the Rich Young Ruler (Luke 18:18-27), the Good Samaritan (Luke 15:11-32), or the Wise and Foolish Builder (Matthew 7:24-27), always go down well. Remember with any group to raise and lower the tone of your voice and with young children, try to act it out, just walk back and forth, gesture with your hands and use exaggerated facial expressions. It makes it exciting for your young audience, perhaps funny in places, but always portray the important truths with seriousness and summarise them at the end with a brief conclusion. Sometimes you can use a Bible story, but put a modern twist to it as long as the same important truth is portrayed – this is why Jesus spoke in parables – contemporary stories that reveal an important message.

- 'Do not be ashamed of the testimony of our Lord...' (2 Timothy 1:8a).
- 'For I am not ashamed of the Gospel of Christ, for it is the power of God to salvation for everyone who believes...' (Romans 1:16).

Testimonies are generally from 5-10 minutes in length and via a interpreter, will double. I have walked into churches whilst on STMs and as a visitor, unknown to the fellowship, have been asked to come up the front and to say something. I will only speak for 2-3 minutes and give a word of greeting, state who I am, where I am from, the work of my ministry and give a word of exhortation to the congregation. After that my mission partner would do the same, but without overlapping our testimonies or work. Do not abuse the opportunity allocated to you. If they want to hear more, they will ask for it or arrange another meeting.

Testimonies for the first time may be nerve racking, but just explain the basic facts after introducing yourself and give some background information. My name is — I am from —. The essence of any salvation testimony is: I was a sinner, I repented of my sins, put my faith in Jesus Christ and I trust in Him for my salvation as I look to Him for my eternal redemption. Remember that nobody is born a Christian and the importance of any testimony is to put forward truth in a concise and relevant manner. With any testimony, beware of giving too much detail that is not relevant. Don't waffle or add unnecessary information. If you are asked to give a testimony then do just that – don't preach or lecture on your favourite theological topic!

The first time I ever spoke via a interpreter, I told the youth group that on a STM to a Muslim country, "I stuck out like a sore thumb." My interpreter had spent more than a year studying in the UK and his English was perfect without any foreign accent, but this idiom took more than thirty seconds to explain, which included mimicking hitting his thumb with a hammer, which then swelled up! Avoid idioms at all costs! Micah – Netherlands.

Testimonies Adapt

A testimony adapts depending on the audience you are speaking to, though not like the angler whose fish got bigger and bigger each time he told the story! How you share your testimony to a youth group would be very different than if you were speaking to university students, but the message you are trying to get across will always be the same. Stay clear of talking about past girlfriends / boyfriends or if you were divorced etc. as whilst your testimony is your life, it may not go down well in other cultures and could be misunderstood or misinterpreted / mistranslated. Keep it brief and simple.

With any testimony, keep the focus on God's grace and mercy rather than focusing on all the sins you committed – do not glory in the devil's former hold over you, avoid sordid details; naming the sin if you so desire is adequate, though sometimes very unwise in different cultures. Remember to smile, look at the audience and do not speak too fast. Keep to your allocated time, there may be two or three testimonies coming and people's attentions do wane.

Martha VanCise in *Successful Mission Teams – A Guide for Volunteers* wrote: 'When you relate stories of abuse, addiction, illness, divorce and other traumas, avoid the tabloid approach. Summarise problems. Save details to relate to God's encouragement and deliverance in the situation. Sordid details will only depress people; spiritual lessons will encourage others.'[2]

Practise your testimony in front of the mirror and time yourself. When you only practise in front of yourself, it never goes too well, so don't be alarmed or concerned. It will be fine on the day. You may wish to write down some important points on a small prompt card which you can refer to if you get stuck or lost when speaking in public. On occasions, I have used prompt cards when giving a presentation at a school or addressing a public audience, as there are certain key facts that you can forget in all the excitement or nervousness of public speaking.

The longest testimony I heard was 45 minutes (it was pure waffle) and the Bible College student who gave it never heard the last of it. It was a long-standing joke amongst the students. Another student who gave a ten second testimony – "I have always been a Christian," then proceeded to walk down the pulpit steps also missed the point! Edward – United Kingdom.

Don't Miss an Opportunity

William Lockhart was a well-known evangelist of the nineteenth century who had a powerful ministry in Merseyside (Liverpool), England. In 1859 he commented on a minister's teaching from which he 'derived much benefit,' of whom he was 'privileged to sit under' (to listen to) but noted: 'The only improvement I could wish to see is a little more preaching mixed up with the teaching. Every sermon [and testimony] ought to have in it a full and plain statement of the Gospel; when there is not, how awful to think that there may be present even one sinner perhaps anxious to hear the way of eternal life; and he is not told. How heavy the responsibility of the minister, and how great the blame attachable to those who neglect to continually direct their hearers to the Lamb of God who taketh away the sins of the world.'[3]

When dealing with people from abroad you need to use "export English" – Lord Alan Sugar, British entrepreneur. Slow down (to give the person time to think) and keep it simple.

Bridging Culture and Culturally Relevant Messages

Be clear in your communication, avoid specialised vocabulary, Christian clichés, be aware of your mannerisms, and hand gestures. Make sure your message is culturally relevant when you preach, give your testimony or when sharing the Good News one-on-one. Build a cultural bridge, like the apostle Paul at Mars Hill in Athens when he talked about the 'unknown god' – "Him I proclaim to you.... For in Him we live and move and have our being as also some of your own poets have said, 'for we are also His offspring' " (Acts 17:22-29).

Tim Dearborn in *Short-term Missions Workbook – From Mission Tourist to Global Citizens* noted some good points in relation to 1 Corinthians 2:1-5 – about the people to whom the apostle Paul had worked alongside. He wrote: 'Walk with humility, embrace with affirmation, live with vulnerability, practise flexibility, live as a student, work as a servant and speak as a story teller.'[4]

Chapter Forty-One

Working with the Locals

The apostle Paul wrote: 'But I know that when I come to you, I shall come in the fullness of the blessing of the Gospel of Christ' Romans 15:29.

The apostle Paul wrote to the church at Rome: 'I thank my God through Jesus Christ for you all, that your faith is spoken of throughout the whole world' Romans 1:8.

To Serve Others

You are going on a short-term mission (STM) to serve others. To serve is also a time to learn – if you're going as a team, working for or alongside a local church or missionary then ask them what help *they* need – not what help *you think* they need! Ask them, "How can we best assist you?"

The story is told of how a STM team arrived in one country and after asking the locals how best they could serve them; they responded by asking them to tear down a building. The STM team did a great work and at the end, they asked, "What was the building used for?" "We never used it," they said, "Last year a team like yours came here and said, "We would like to build you a building" – we had no need for a such a structure, and told them so, but they seemed so eager; we did not want to disappoint them and gave them our permission!"

As much as going on a STM is about helping others it is also a time for God to reveal to us our character and to help us change ourselves with the opportunities that we encounter. It will also be a time to evaluate our life, our priorities, our worldview and more often than not to see how well-off we actually are compared to the majority of the developing world.

You are not invincible, we do not have all the answers and we, like our hosts have failings and difficulties in some areas of our lives. Let us not project an image of what we are not, but be open to learn and open to receive help as well as give it when asked to. Remember people's names but especially leaders and the interpreter. In many cultures, titles are VERY important. If you are introduced to Pastor Obi, always greet your brother using the title and name "Pastor Obi." If the leader does not want to be addressed in such a way, he or she will inform you.

Preparation and Forward Planning

If you are going to work with a local church or tie in with a missionary it is important to find out what they want you to do, or what they expect from you (chat via a webcam or Skype). If you are to construct a home for the pastor, build a church building for the congregation or sink a borehole for the community, find out who is providing the bricks, tools, pumps and all the other related materials and finances. The host may not (and often will not) have the money to purchase the items needed and if you fly into the country expecting to buy a large quantity of bricks, hundreds of planks of wood or several tons of sand and cement straight from a Western style DIY depot, you may be in for a surprise! The host will more often than not need the money forwarded onto them so that the materials can be ordered and paid for. The transportation, materials or equipment can take weeks or months to arrive and so forward planning is essential.

The leader may consider flying out several months before the start of a STM (for a week or so) to help oil the cogs of preparation and communication, and to purchase or order the needed materials, working alongside the host. Is planning permission needed? To see what materials or resources are still needed, to confirm any bookings or to inspect the (transport and accommodation), to double-check all items and discuss issues with the local host church, (ministry or local missionary) so that both parties know what is expected from each other. There is great difference in logistical planning between a team of eight or eighty STM-ers! Some leaders fly out a week early, ahead of the team to finalise details and to double-check everything. Any tools or materials, which are not available, can then be purchased (weight & size permitting) by the team and flown out.

I was assigned by my superior to take a STM team and to work alongside two churches in two different towns. That was a mistake in itself as I was pulled in different directions. I repeatedly tried to phone one of the ministers to see what he wanted done in the week of outreach, whilst I told my team to prepare a drama and mime sketch. Two weeks before the STM, the minister contacted me and told me that he did not permit drama or mime in his church! Matthew – Wales.

Differences and Priorities

If you are involved in construction, take into consideration the thoughts, designs, style and workmanship of the locals. Does your host have planning permission or the required permits? There can be a danger in that locals become unemployed (their families go hungry) because foreigners are willing to do the work for free! Utilise the local expertise and work in partnership.

David Livermore is the executive director of the Global Learning Center at Grand Rapids Theological Seminary, who studies the trend of STMs. He noted that in Monrovia, Liberia, in 2005, tragedy occurred during the monsoon season, when a school building collapsed, killing two children. Visitors had built the school to their standards instead of Liberian standards. They relied on their own expertise whilst ignoring local authorities on the ground.[1]

Techniques and methods in construction or evangelism may also differ; you cannot demand and state, "This is how we do it at home" and proceed to change their set-up, style, method or architecture! How you do a thing at home may not be how it is done on the mission field (for better or for worse). In some cultures, relationships and the wider family are more important than tasks – the locals may turn up late, because they stopped to chat to a friend. The evangelist meets you an hour later than you had planned, but makes no apology, or the church service cannot 'truly' begin until the pastor arrives and so the morning church service runs into the late afternoon! You may find these situations a great inconvenience (and frustrating), but as you are in their culture, it is you who must give way. Go with the flow and embrace the experience! If the job is not completed, don't see it as a failure because building relationships with the locals is of prime importance.

David Livermore in *Serving with Eyes Wide Open* wrote: 'Before we're sure that our time spent painting a wall is the best thing we can do, let's be willing to reconsider that. With high levels of unemployment in most of the places we visit, are we taking jobs away from people who need them when we do our building projects? There are probably times when it is appropriate to do a building project, but be willing to slow down and ask the question before jumping in.'[2]

Mutual Respect and Courtesy

If you are going to work with a church or group in another area, please treat them with respect and courtesy. Be gracious if inconveniences arise (and they will), be forgiving and understanding if the host congregation, pastor or other workers are not punctual. Understanding when things are done differently than at home, loving in all situations and void of criticisms and murmurings towards all. Do not embarrass your host, the local church, or your fellow team members by your lack of concern for your brothers and sisters who may have bent over backwards to accommodate you and your team, to give you the very best of what they have.

You may see an answer to a problem, but you may not have earned the respect to be heard! How would you feel if a stranger came to your church or community and wanted to turn things inside out or upside down? On the other hand, you may perceive a problem, but to the local church (pastor or individual), there is no problem. You are not on your STM to change the world to your way of thinking, but are there to serve and to emanate and radiate the love of Christ.

If you do contact friends at home (or your church or leaders), and things are not as good as you had hoped, then a good rule of thumb is to assume that someone from your host country is reading your email, social media update / status, text message, letter or fax, or is listening to your phone call! How would they feel if they could read your mail or listen to the conversation? Do to others, as you would have them do unto you.

Just before Christmas 2008, two Scottish missionaries, David Fulton (aged 60) and his wife Fiona (aged 46) were arrested and charged with sedition, in Gambia, (a predominantly Muslim country in Africa). They had written emails critical of the countries president and sent them to friends and organisations in the West, the content of which Gambia deemed seditious. In court, at the capital Banjul, they pleaded guilty in the hope that a lighter sentence would be given, but on 30 December 2008, they were sentenced to a year's hard labour in Gambia and were each fined £6,250 ($9,250). The court stated that the emails, which the Fulton's insisted were harmless, incited 'hatred or contempt against the president or the government.' Supporters back in Torquay, Devon, England, said that the charges had been 'trumped up.'

The Freedom of Evangelism
You may live in a fairly free and democratic society where street evangelism is permitted, and in some places of Britain, open-air preachers have been around since Christianity was first

proclaimed on its shores. God first sent men to Britain under Roman rule in the early centuries and has since raised up men and women to proclaim the Good News in a variety of settings. Street preachers became widespread under the influences of such men as John Wycliff and the Lollards of the fourteenth century, George Fox and the Quakers of the seventeenth century. A century later came George Whitefield, John Wesley and other Anglican vicars alongside the Methodists, followed by William Booth and the Salvation Army, beginning in the mid-nineteenth century. The Open-Air Mission was founded in June 1853 by John MacGregor, "Rob Roy" and many British cities have their own mission organisations, such as the London City Mission or Birmingham City Mission where workers openly share the Good News in a variety of formats, on the streets, door-to-door, literature distribution etc. Whilst this freedom is permissible in most Western nations, in other parts of the world these types of open evangelism is not possible. In some places, evangelism is illegal and if a Muslim converts to Christianity (as well as some Hindus, Buddhists or citizens of Communist countries) they will be persecuted often ostracised (avoid speaking to and dealing with – ignored) from the family or community and may even become martyrs for the Christian faith! Therefore, much wisdom is needed in the type and method of evangelism in the place you will be travelling to. Good research and asking your host for their advice and opinion will go a long way to make your STM more effective and fruitful for the glory of God. Do not endanger your host, your interpreter or the local missionary who may be undercover. You will go home at the end of your STM, but they have to stay! The missionary could also be expelled from the country.

Two legs are better than one, unless they are both going in the wrong direction! United we stand, divided we fall.

The authors of *Mack & Leeann's Guide to Short-Term Missions* wrote: 'Let people know you don't want to offend and you'll find tremendous open doors in unexpected places. Be in partnership with those who are committed to sharing the Gospel.... Ask how the people you partner with in the host country are sharing their faith. Learn from them. Ask them what they would want people to know about evangelism in the place where they live. Make sure plans for evangelism are in concert with your missionary and host. And know that sometimes the best evangelism is to support local evangelists.'[3]

Doctrine and the Local Church

You are in another country to serve people. You may be working alongside a local church for a given period of time, a missionary or assisted by a local evangelist or pastor. You are not there to preach your denominational doctrine or to harp on about your pet subject – don't major on the minors. Even Jesus said, "My doctrine is not mine, but His who sent Me" (John 7:16). For guidance in public speaking, see Chapter Forty, Testimonies and Preaching via an Interpreter.

Jesus condemned the scribes and Pharisees saying, "Woe to you, scribes and Pharisees, hypocrites! For you travel land and sea to win one proselyte [single convert, NIV], and when he is one, you make him twice as much a son of hell as yourselves" Matthew 23:15.

The way you do church and the way your hosts does church can be very different. You may stand or sit for worship – the opposite of what you do at home; communion may be only for those who are adults. You may have to go to the front, to receive the bread and wine, (standing up or kneeling) or the servers may come to you. The preacher may expect feedback and the congregation may shout accolades back. Some of the congregation may be dancing in the aisles, hands in the air or clapping, or worshipping without music, others may look as grey as death.

In many societies, men and women do not sit together in church – even if married. Some do not permit a woman to speak behind the pulpit or to speak in front of men. If you are invited to sit on a raised platform or at the front facing the congregation (both an honour), be careful how you sit – legs crossed can be a no-no and legs apart *is* a no-no. Look around and observe. See also, Chapter Thirty-Three, Christian Culture.

The apostle Paul wrote: 'Let your conduct be worthy of the Gospel of Christ, so that whether I come and see you or am absent, I may hear of your affairs, that you stand fast in one spirit, with one mind striving together for the faith of the Gospel' Philippians 1:27.

Chapter Forty-Two

Remunerations and Wages for the Locals

'Render therefore to all their due: taxes to whom taxes are due, customs to whom customs are due.... Owe no one anything except to love one another, for he who loves has fulfilled the law.... "You shall love your neighbour as yourself" ' Romans 13:7-9.

'Let us not grow weary in doing good...Therefore as we have opportunity, let us do good to all, especially to those who are of the household of faith' Galatians 6:9-10.

Be a Blessing
A worker is worthy of his hire and those who preach the Gospel should live by the Gospel. If the Western adage is true – 'Time is Money,' then those who have helped you on your short-term mission (STM) should not be overlooked. They should receive remuneration (money or goods for their assistance), but especially Christians as Scripture declares, '...the labourer is worthy of his wages' (Luke 10:7).

It is one thing for a local to give you five minutes of their time, but quite another when they go out of their way to take you where you need to go. The difficulty can be in trying to evaluate how much you should give them, but bear in mind that if they have travelled thirty minutes from their home, it is still a thirty-minute return journey and you have encroached upon an hour of their time.

The pastor, missionary or interpreter who you work with or alongside should all get a fair amount of money for the service they have rendered to the mission team, as well as a love offering, an additional amount of money to bless them and their family. If you are part of a mission organisation (then these issues are not your responsibility), the mission will take care of it.

How to Bless Others
The local pastor, interpreter or other Christians may have been an untold blessing to you and the mission team, so how can you repay them? If you ask a Christian, "How much should I give

you?" they will more often than not say, "Nothing," or ask for a much lesser amount than what you can ACTUALLY give them. What you earn in a week or just a day, may take someone in a developing country a month or more to earn. Your £7 ($11.20) may be an hours wage, but that may feed the pastor's family for several days. It is always helpful to find out the average income of the country you are going to.

- Find out their needs, be discreet and try to fill them where possible.
- Pay for all their meals and transport.
- Be a blessing to them and their family.

In the mornings, the pastor used to meet us at our hotel room and charge his mobile / cell phone. In the afternoons, we would come back to our room and the pastor always used the shower. I was a little baffled at first, but the home in which he was staying at had no electricity or running water. Chuck – Sudan.

Sometimes the pastor or evangelist does not have the term's fees for their children's education or next month's rent. This is always small in developing countries in comparison to the West. Always bless individual workers but if you have worked with a local church or other ministry also try and be a blessing to the fellowship or ministry; sometimes you just need to ask – "How can we help?"

- Do they need Bibles, songs books or chairs?
- Does the church building need renovating? How much would it cost? Ask the pastor if he would like the team to employ church members to do the work?

More than 1.2 billion people – nearly one in five persons on the planet, survive on less than ($1) (£0.60) a day.

When to Bless Others
Experience has taught me that it is best to give a love offering (or an agreed wage) to a person at the end of a mission trip, but we have always paid for the pastor's and / or interpreter's transport and expenses (including meals) when we have been together, as and when the need arose. However, if you have a interpreter for several weeks or more, they may not be able to go without payment until you have finished with their services, because they have a family who are dependant on them. If you

hire a non-Christian translator (and occasionally it is the only option), then agree on a fee, so that no one feels cheated at the end. Most Christians will translate within a church setting, but this does not mean that they should be overlooked and for some, translation may be their job (self-employed) and therefore a good wage should be given to them.

You also need to ask yourself, does the pastor, evangelist or interpreter have enough money to take the bus back to his own home, or will he have to walk five miles? At times, a person may prefer to keep the money and walk because the needs of their family are very great.

One pastor had terrible toothache, which was evident at every meal. We inquired about the cost and gave him the money to get it fixed. It later transpired that he had greater needs and so used the money on more important items. Chuck – Sudan.

Many people live a hand-to-mouth existence – the Scriptures declare:

- '...The wages of him who is hired shall not remain with you all night until morning' (Leviticus 19:13).
- 'You shall not oppress a hired servant who is poor and needy...each day you shall give him his wages, and not let the sun go down on it, for he is poor and has set his heart on it...' (Deuteronomy 24:14-15).
- 'Do not withhold good from those to whom it is due, when it is in the power of your hand to do so. Do not say to your neighbour, "Go, and come back and tomorrow I will give it," when you have it with you' (Proverbs 3:27-28).

Hesitant, Reluctant or Shy

Be aware that some locals will be hesitant, reluctant or shy to order when you take them to a cafe or food outlet, as to them, the cost may be prohibitive – or just a new experience. Others are used to eating only one or two meals a day. Remind them that you are paying the bill and encourage them to order whatever they want. Some out of politeness will order a plain meal, others will order more and take the remainder home for their family. If you are aware of this, then you know at least one way to bless them. You can buy a large bag of rice, maize, potatoes or other staple food, alongside additional items which are not perishable, and give them some money so they can buy what *they* deem most important. You may find that on occasions, the local Christians may get over-excited and order too much food. In Kisumu, Kenya, our team had some food left over, as the portions were much bigger than we had expected. I was loathed to leave the plate of hot potatoes on the table and so went outside and gave them to the first beggar I came across. She was very pleased.

In Malawi, the team were staying at an old mission station. As we were going to visit the market, nearing the end of our stay, we asked the housekeeper what *she* needed for herself. She was a young Christian widow with two children and had been very kind to us. She gave us her small list of items, which included food, toiletries, medicine and mobile / cell phone credit. We urged her not to be shy and told her that God cares for widows and the fatherless, and as ministers of the Gospel, we wanted to bless her and her children. Everything except perishable items, we got more than what she asked for. As she often went barefoot, we bought her some sandals, the same as her neighbours. The night before we left, we settled the bill and gave her nearly as much in cash for herself and her children.

A Christian approached us and told us that she could get us some preaching appointments. At the end of the several days of ministry, we said goodbye to our helper who looked a little disappointed. The team leader did not financially recompense her and she had not been given a present from us. I asked the team leader why we had not been a blessing and *politely* made known my dissatisfaction. Apparently, it was an oversight, but the woman had given up three whole days and got nothing in return. It would not surprise me if she will not be so quick to assist other STM-ers in the future. Rodney – Indonesia.

Fixers
Fixers as the name suggest fix things. If you have a problem, they will deal with it or find a solution, whatever the problem. However, if you are working with local Christians they will probably be able to assist. Most fixers receive payment for their help whilst many issues can be solved for free by asking someone on the street! However, top-end fixers intervene with the authorities on your behalf, like when a group needs a visa in a hurry or when the consulate is closed.

Chapter Forty-Three

Requests for Assistance

'But whoever has this world's goods and sees his brother in need, and shuts up his heart from him; how does the love of God abide in him? My little children let us not love in word or in tongue, but in deed and in truth' 1 John 3:17-18.

'The leech has two daughters, crying, "Give, give!" ' Proverbs 30:15.

Asking for Assistance

Meeting and working with the locals brings new and unexpected challenges to bear and because you are fellow Christians – one in Christ – there are those in developing countries who will ask you for assistance – financially, practically or in other ways. There are different ways of looking at this (though it varies between cultures) and the outlook between the West and other countries differs. The West has a Protestant work ethic: 'If you work hard, you will succeed and you will reap the reward of your labour by the sweat of your brow.' Whereas others view it differently: 'We're brethren; you have, I need (or want), therefore I will ask!' Time and money is part of Western thinking, whereas relationships, friendships and community takes a higher priority in many developing countries, and when you return home, you may still receive requests.

Whilst this chapter is largely focussed on independent STM-ers and churches that take teams on STMs, requests sometimes filter to individual STM-ers who have completed their STM with a mission organisation and have returned home. In an ideal world, this should not happen and all requests should be forwarded on to the mission organisation. It may be a situation (or an escalating problem) that needs to be addressed because policies of mutual respect, honesty, trust and cooperation need to be adhered to. It is not right for host churches (whom mission organisations work in partnership with) or individuals from within those churches (even the evangelist or pastor) to try and solicit finances from STM members. See also, chapter Forty-Five, Giving to the Poor and Needy.

There is a BIG difference between your host asking for assistance (or other people who have helped the STM team), and a relative stranger. Many STM teams work with the same church or community and therefore long-term commitments and strong relationships are formed. Visits from a senior leader (of the host church) are often reciprocated, whilst the Western church (which is generally financially stronger than those in developing countries) covers the expenses and will arrange meetings for the leader.

How to Handle Requests

So you get asked for money (or items) – what do you do? You can acknowledge the request, ignore it, play ignorant or be like an ostrich with its head in the sand. There are Christians who work very hard and put in long hours for a small wage, and often they have nothing to lose by asking, but everything to gain. Perhaps if we were in their situation we would also do the same. On the other hand, there are some 'Christians' who abuse STM-ers friendship and resort to underhanded tactics to get what they want. Some will play one member of the STM team against another or individually try to solicit money from as many members as they can, or like a wolf, seek out the weaker members of the flock. Some are even so brazen as to pick up items which belong to STM-ers and walk away with them, or are subtle and admire an object whilst dropping so many hints that it becomes embarrassing.

One foreign student asked (and pleaded) for money for his family and so I helped him. The more I gave, the more frequently he asked. Nearly one year passed before we realised that this "needy student" was not in need! He had spun the same story to a lot people and had received the largest amounts from those who were most vulnerable. We were all conned! Pastor — Wales.

Not everybody who asks is in need – it can be just greed. Sadly, some STM team's donations, gifts or love offerings, which have been given for a specific project (or person), have been embezzled by church leaders (or others), or have been misappropriated, and the West is no exception to these sins. Some people will want your money without accountability (and resent it) whereas some are delighted to inform you of the right use of the money. Being accountable is normal in the West, part of routine life, whereas in many developing countries it is seen as a sign of mistrust – "How dare they ask!"

> The founder of a mission in a developing country repeatedly dropped hints, stating that the ministry vehicle needed 'x' amount of repairs. In his area, he was the only person who owned a vehicle outside of the public transport sector. I told him how he must be very happy to be able to afford a vehicle that was five years newer than my own! Scott – England.

Letter of Invite – Further Education
There may be occasions when a church or a wealthy individual feels called of God to sponsor an individual and each one must be obedient to their heavenly call. On the other hand, there are those who see the potential in an individual and act out of an emotional response, or from a business mind, but neither is being led of the Spirit, and what is the will of the Lord in each individual case? If an anointed preacher (or other Christian worker) leaves his or her own country to study in another, (and may never return), it would be a great loss to the home country where perhaps the need is greater. By writing a letter of invite (which is used as part of a visa application process) you may be designating yourself (even unknowingly), as the financial guarantor of that person whilst he or she is within your country! The person concerned is your liability and responsibility. I had one such letter from a young man with whom I had only met with for twenty minutes, though we had corresponded for years.

> I was travelling in the bus alongside this teenage lad. He had told me that he had gone on holiday to visit his uncle in another part of the country. After several hours, the bus ride ended and we were about to part company when he asked me for money for his next month school fees. I told him "no," thinking to myself, if he can afford to travel half the country on public transport to enjoy a holiday, he can afford his fees. John – Ethiopia.

Bible College and Scholarships
There are some Christians who *only* want to attend Bible College in English speaking countries in the West, yet English is not their first language and they have Bible Colleges in their own countries in their native tongue. Often it is not a case of wanting

to study theology as a first priority, but to get 'a foot in the door' of a Western country. Upon graduation, some never return home to their country. As a dean of men's students at a Bible College in Britain informed me, "It has made it a lot harder for genuine applicants from — to be granted visas (due to the abuse of the system), because they refuse to leave the country." On the other hand, a former Muslim who was won to the Lord via repeated STM trips was given a full scholarship to a Bible College in the UK and went into full-time Christian ministry.

In Calcutta, the cost of our hotel for four nights in 2003 was the equivalent of a months rent for one pastor. It was the cheapest hotel we could find with a Western style toilet and cost us just £4 ($6.40) per-night! Mark – India.

- 'The love of money is a root of all kinds of evil' (1 Tim. 6:10).
- Money can buy many things, but not meaning.
- Money increases your appetite but not your satisfaction.
- Money is a universal provider for everything but happiness and a passport to anywhere but heaven.
- 'It is more blessed to give than to receive' (Acts 20:35).

Prayerfully Give or Politely Decline
I have found that those who do not ask are frequently those in most need, and at times, I have appreciated needs being brought to my attention so that I have been able to assist in a more intelligent way.

Bible teacher, Derek Prince as Principal of a teacher training college in Kenya, (who taught in the native language of Swahili), said that part of in the African culture was, "There is no harm in asking." He went on to explain that if you gave someone a pair of shoes, you should not be surprised if they ask for socks, because "there is no harm in asking!"

John Wesley was the founder of Methodism, who received financial support from Lady Huntington (as were dozens of preachers) so that they could get on with the business of preaching the Good News. Lady Huntington also financed the building of around one hundred chapels ('church' buildings)! John Wesley said, "Make all you can, save all you can, and give all you can, do all the good you can, by all the means you can, in all the ways you can, in all the places you can, to all the people you can, as long as you ever can."

Chapter Forty-Four

The Love of Christ in Action

'...For I was hungry and you gave Me food; I was thirsty and you gave Me drink; I was a stranger and you took Me in; I was naked and you clothed Me; I was sick and you visited Me; I was in prison and you came to Me.... Assuredly, I say to you, *inasmuch* as you did it to one of the least of these My brethren, you did it to Me' Matthew 25:35-36, 40.

'The blind receive their sight and the lame walk; the lepers are cleansed and the deaf hear; the dead are raised up and the poor have the Gospel preached to them' Matthew 11:5.

Good Deeds Wrapped in Love

Humanitarian work and development aid is to relieve or alleviate the suffering of others and when Christians are involved, it can be the love of Christ in action, and often it is these acts of love that opens hardened hearts to the truths of the Gospel. This chapter focuses on the love of Christ in action whilst Chapter Seven, Types of Mission Work – Preaching and Humanitarian, covers the various aspects of humanitarian ministries. With some 'closed' or difficult-to-get-into countries the only way of getting a visa is joining with a humanitarian-based (Christian run) organisation / charity or a non-governmental organisation (NGO). However, frequently, even in countries with little to no visa restrictions, it may be the *only* way to share the love of Christ (by practical deeds). Our faith in Christ must be demonstrated by Christian works in a practical demonstration of love for others – 'For as the body without the spirit is dead, so faith without works is dead also' (James 2:26).

Doing good deeds without sharing the Good News is often called the social gospel; and this topic has been hotly debated over the last two centuries. Some say you should always share the Good News; whilst others are content with only healing the physical aspect of a person by humanitarian or development aid.

A missionary once noted that it was easy to preach sincerely and diligently on the mission field, as well as to pray faithfully and to labour whole-heartedly yet rarely to feel really moved with compassion towards the people he was ministering to. He went on to speak of the 'ill-clad, ill-fed, ill-protected population' most of whom had no fuel (for cooking or for warmth) and often without bedding, and that 'if some feeling of compassion would not move a labourer at such a sight then let them go home and abandon their mission work' till they learn to have compassion. This compassion will soften their hearts, melt away indifference and change their characters to be more Christ-like.[1]

One evening I got chatting to two men who were staying in the same hotel as our STM team. They were Congolese refugees and had lived in a refugee camp for ten years! I tried to comprehend what it must have been like – having to flee your home and country to seek refuge in another, leaving everything behind and looking to others for help. Richard – Tanzania.

An associate wrote the following testimony: 'In the 1990s I closed down my business and joined a humanitarian organisation in Romania. When I went to Eastern Bloc Europe, my worldview changed and change does not always feel good. The first time I saw a "home" on a garbage dump made from junk – the family inside huddled together – my worldview began to change. Sometimes I recoil from the memories of children. Many street kids escaped the abuses they encountered by crawling into sewers near the factories. The children selected these rat and cockroach infested hellholes because the pipes from the factories helped to keep them warm in the winter. Children are closer to [the] Father's heart than I think we will ever know. He sees the street kids and His awareness of their needs moves Him deeply. He knows that they are children without parents and He wants to parent them. I went to Romania to give children a fighting chance and to help establish an orphanage. My life has been deeply impacted by the broken and needy people that I have encountered.' Jim – America.

General Booth, the founder of the Salvation Army said, "You cannot preach to a man who hasn't eaten in two days;" whilst a missionary in Zaire said, "An empty stomach has no ears."

Holistic Ministry
William Booth's passion to help people practically never overshadowed the Gospel message. He said, "To get a man

soundly saved, it is not enough to put on him a pair of new breeches (trousers / pants), to give him regular work, or even to give him a university education. These things are all outside a man, and if the inside remains unchanged you have wasted your labour. You must in some way or other graft upon the man's nature a new nature, which has in it the element of the Divine."[2]

One Christian mission organisation has a Disaster Relief Fund, which provides aid such as medicines, tents, blankets, food and water, as well as rebuilding homes etc. after natural disasters. They state: 'The Christians we partner with take every opportunity to share the Gospel and thousands of people have come to know Jesus Christ. This long-term fund helps us to respond immediately whenever a disaster strikes.'[3]

Jesus healed the whole man having a holistic approach to ministry (not humanist), because He knew the interrelation between the mind, body and spirit, and wanted all people to enter into a living relationship with Him.[4]

John Perkins said, "Unless the Church fulfils its responsibility to proclaim by Word and deed the Good News to the poor, the poor have no real hope. We the Church, bear the only true Gospel of hope. Only through us can the power of Christ's love save and deliver them."

Jesus said, "The Spirit of the Lord is upon Me, because He has anointed Me to preach the Gospel to the poor. He has sent Me to heal the broken-hearted, to preach deliverance to the captives and recovery of sight to the blind, to set at liberty those who are oppressed, to preach the acceptable year of the Lord" Luke 4:18-19.

Humanistic – Silver and Gold

Whilst we have looked at holistic ministry, this is not to be confused with humanistic organisations that often reject religion whilst trying to uplift humankind. Sadly, some Christian ministries are more humanistic in their approach and are therefore more secular than sacred, whilst charitable, not Christ-like – they have a name but they are dead (see Revelation 3:1-3). They uplift humanity but ignore the Good News – the one thing that is needed!

Indian born K. P. Yohannan, founder of Gospel for Asia noted the massive imbalance between maintaining Christian institutions and proclaiming the Gospel. In his travels he 'constantly uncovers preoccupation with so-called "ministry" activities' which are 'operated by Christian workers, financed by church monies, but with little else to distinguish them as Christian.'

K. P. Yohannan wrote: 'There is nothing wrong with charitable acts – but they are *not* to be confused with preaching the Gospel. Feeding programmes can save a man dying from hunger. Medical aid can prolong life and fight disease. Housing projects can make this temporary life more comfortable – but only the Gospel of Jesus Christ can save a soul from a life of sin and an eternity in hell!

'When God changes the heart and spirit, the physical changes also. If you want to meet the needs of the poor in this world, there is no better place to start than by preaching the Gospel. It has done more to lift up the downtrodden, the hungry and the needy than all the social programs ever imagined by secular humanists.'[5]

Jesus told the story about the rich man and Lazarus (Luke 16:19-25). Lazarus ate the crumbs from the rich man's table, and eventually died, but was right with God – his priorities had been focussed correctly and he was now comforted in Abraham's bosom. Whereas the rich man died and ended up in hell, tormented greatly and was the most poor indeed! As Jesus said on another occasion, "What advantage is it to a man if he gains the whole world and he himself is destroyed or lost?" (Luke 9:25).

The religious rich young ruler had everything, but still lacked one thing. He went away saddened because his wealth was his idol, and so he was not able to receive the treasures of heaven (Luke 18:18-27). Jesus' teaching in Luke 12 (as in Matthew 6), focuses on seeking God (and not being concerned with wealth). One man said to Jesus, "Tell my brother to divide the inheritance with me!" Jesus responded, "Man who made Me a judge or an arbitrator between you? ...One's life does not consist in the abundance of the things he possesses" (Luke 12:13-21).

Peter and John went to the temple where they met a lame beggar who asked for alms. Peter looked at him and said, "Silver and gold I do not have but what I do have I give you. In the name of Jesus Christ of Nazareth, rise up and walk." Peter took the man by the hand, lifted him up and the man was healed! He began to leap and run around, praising God and when a crowd had gathered, Peter preached the Gospel to them, telling them to 'repent and be converted,' putting their faith in Jesus Christ (Acts 3:1-26).

Is the salvation of souls included in your goals? – Cyrano De Words-u-lac.

The Church and the Government

In September 1947, (the year that India was partitioned into India and Pakistan), three church denominations united to become the Church of South India, J. E. Lessie Newbigin became the Bishop in Madhurai and Ramnad of the Church of South India. In his extensive travels to the 550 churches under his care, he noted the primary work of the church was overshadowed by the sheer volume of work. 'Ministration [assistance in time of difficulty] is swallowed up in administration. Yet the problem cannot be evaded by cutting the educational and medical work loose and letting it steer its own course. Whatever may be true in a country of preponderantly Christian tradition, in a non-Christian country that is simply to invite destructions by absorption. The younger church has to take responsibility given to it by the older.... Yet there is a terrible danger that the Church should become a large social service organisation with its centre in a modern streamlined office rather than God's family with its centre in 'the apostles teaching and fellowship, the breaking of bread and in prayers' ' (Acts 3:42).

The Bishop also wrote: 'This vast educational programme of ours [which ran into four figures] needs constant vigilance if it is to serve its real purpose... It is no use denying that they are an area of tension between church and government. It cannot be otherwise. It is important that this tension should not break out in unnecessary conflict.... We intended to give an education centred in the Christian revelation. In fact, we have more and more tended simply to teach a Government-imposed syllabus, with Bible added. Our schools have been evangelising agencies, but their witness has certainly not been as clear as it should be. Now Government is severely restricting our right to teach the Bible.'[6]

Helping the Less Fortunate

Charles Kingsley (1819-1875) fought for the rights of man in England, and became chaplain to Queen Victoria in 1859. He said, "The age of chivalry is never passed, so long as there is a wrong left un-redressed, or a man or a woman left to say, 'I will redress that wrong, or spend my life in the attempt.' "[7]

Will Crooks (1852-1921) a working class man was elected a Member of the House of Commons in 1903, having fought for people's rights since 1890. In a sermon he once said, "Give part of yourself rather than part of your wealth."[8]

Hand, Heart and Mouth

The love of Jesus Christ is demonstrated by our works (and by our words) because the love of Christ constrains us, as we love our neighbour as ourselves (see Matthew 19:19, Ephesians 2:10 and James 2:14-18). James wrote: 'Pure and undefiled religion before God and the Father is this: to visit orphans and widows in their trouble and to keep oneself unspotted from the world' (James 1:27). In desperate circumstances, the deed can often speak the loudest and can be the most effective, but good deeds, with a closed Gospel is not efficient ministry.

There has to be balance between the physical and spiritual need, as the former can consume vast amounts of resources with little to no eternal fruit, whilst the latter is the most important as the destiny of souls is at stake. Jesus said, "What would it profit a man if he gains the whole world, and loses his own soul?" (Mark 8:36), and in response to a question from John the Baptist's disciples, after citing some of His works (healings etc.) He said, "...and the poor have the Gospel preached to them" (Matthew 11:5).

As the apostle Paul reiterated, 'Whoever calls upon the name of the Lord shall be saved...how shall they believe in Him of whom they have not heard, and how shall they hear without a preacher?' (Romans 10:13-14). Regardless of circumstances, people still need to hear the Good News because there is no salvation outside of Jesus Christ, as 'there is no other name under heaven given among men by which we must be saved!' (Acts 4:12). Because salvation is a 'must,' we must deliver the message of Jesus Christ and not just the practical mercy of Christ's love. We must proclaim in an intelligent and relevant manner, Jesus' life, death and resurrection because 'whoever calls upon the name of the Lord will be saved,' and they must repent, accept the free gift of eternal life and live for Him. They will become 'born again,' (John 3:3, 7), passing from 'death to life' (John 5:24 and 1 John 3:14), and will receive forgiveness of sins; being washed (spiritually speaking) by the shed blood of Jesus Christ because of their faith in His atoning work.

Chapter Forty-Five

Giving to the Poor and Needy

'There is one who scatters, yet increases more; and there is one who withholds more than is right, but it leads to poverty. The generous soul will be made rich and he who waters will also be watered himself' Proverbs 11:24-25.

Jesus said, "Even the Son of Man did not come to be served, but to serve and to give His life a ransom for many" Mark 10:45.

The Open Face of Poverty

In developing countries, poverty is more apparent; more in your face and beggars are more numerous than in the West. I remember arriving in Calcutta train station in the early hours of the morning (our train having been delayed by 9hrs!); a city in which there are 100,000 street children; and an unknown number of homeless families. As we drove into the suburbs of the city with two native pastors; the streets albeit deserted of people, were not deserted of 'homes' made of cardboard and tarpaulin and in the daytime, you could expect to see a mother and several children emerging from their dwellings.

More than 1.2 billion people survive on less than 0.60p ($1) a day. At least 1.2 billion people do not have safe drinking water. Nearly fifty percent of Africa's population have no access to a hospital or even a doctor and the average life expectancy is just 41 years. Each year, more than six million children worldwide die from preventable causes like malaria, pneumonia and diarrhoea (dirrhea), whilst 75 percent of blindness results from causes that are preventable or could now be reversed.[1]

Paul Hallam, director of Lighthouse International Ministries (LIM) in the June 2009 edition of *LIM* wrote: 'We often have enough food, finances and have no shortage of basic things we take for granted. Clean water, clothing, accommodation and employment, or indeed back up and support if we do not have a job. The truth is in our world we are in the minority. It never ceases to amaze me how many people are literally just 'existing' on our planet. You could hardly call it living. Even today, in Europe, in places like Romania, Bulgaria, Albania and the Ukraine there are people who live a day-to-day existence. They have no assurance of a good meal, warmth or even clean water.

'As you travel east, the poverty becomes even more acute and widespread in places like India. A nation of contrasts – billionaires bankrolling international sportsmen in cricket. Film stars who have more rupees than they can handle in Bollywood, businessmen who seem to be taking on the world! This is still a nation with over 300,000 children homeless, with millions illiterate and millions on the brink of starvation in agricultural areas. This is the reality in which we seek to bring hope, love and transformation. Whilst we do it against insurmountable odds, I am convinced a life receiving compassion is a life that will also give compassion.'

'One in three United Kingdom students live in poverty' – Save the Children and Oxfam[2] – Two British charities, 2009.[2] Poverty within the European Union is calculated to earnings below sixty percent of the average, after housing costs, whilst poverty in developing countries is living a hand-to-mouth existence.

God's Heart for the Poor

God has a heart for the poor (for widows, orphans and the fatherless), but how STM teams respond to appeals (from those on the street) can be complex. However, there are some Scriptures that can help guide you. Jesus said, "Give to him who asks you..." (Matthew 5:42), but He also stated, "You will always have the poor with you" (Matthew 26:11). You will not solve the problems of world poverty, but you can make a difference in individual's lives, though how and when may be directed by your mission organisation or the leader's STM policy.

Peter, James and John, pillars of the early Church, gave Paul and Barnabas the right hand of fellowship – 'They desired only that we should remember the poor, the very thing which I was also eager to do' (Galatians 2:9-10).

The Poor and Needy
- 'He who has pity on the poor lends to the Lord and He will pay back what he has given' (Proverbs 19:17).
- 'The righteous considers the cause of the poor...' (Proverbs 29:7a).

- Jesus said, "Give to him that asks you and from him who wants to borrow from you do not turn away" (Matt. 5:42).
- Jesus said, "Give to everyone who asks of you and from him who takes your goods do not ask them back. And just as you want men to do to you, you also do to them likewise" (Luke 6:30-31).

Various Policies and Recommendations

The policies of STM organisations and local churches concerning 'hand-outs' or gifts vary between each ministry in different countries (even districts and provinces), as no two locations are the same and may vary depending on the circumstances (times of war, famine or devastation). Whatever rules they have, they have for a good reason and even governments (and some tourist information agencies) have their own policies:

> Did you know? Giving money, food and clothing to children on the streets encourages them to remain on the streets. Your assistance can make a difference if given through established childcare facilities. – On a Billboard, by the Department of Social Welfare – Lusaka, Zambia.

> The issue of Cape Town's street people is becoming increasingly problematic. As citizens, we feel helpless and empathetic, and thus donate what we can. In reality, this does not contribute to solving the bigger picture. Don't give to street people directly, here's why: Giving your donations of money, tips, food and clothing directly to street people who stand at traffic intersections or on the streets does not help the problem, it AGGRAVATES it. Instead of making a real difference, it condemns street people to a permanent life on the streets. It can also result in associated problems of drug and substance abuse and crime. – Leaflet by the City of Cape Town, South Africa.

Finding Your Own Policy

Every guidebook to foreign destinations discourages the giving of independent gifts and money, as it encourages a culture of begging; it can cause problems for others and money can be used on substance abuse – glue, drugs and alcohol. They all suggest giving to charities who can distribute to those in need in the most effective manner. However, as a disciple of the Lord

Jesus Christ on an independent STM (not a tourist on holiday, nor breaking a mission organisation's policy), there may be some individuals who through no fault of their own are in dire circumstances, and to pass them by (to ignore their need), would be wrong. See the story of the Good Samaritan (Luke 10:29-37), where the one who did right was not the religious priest or Levite, but the one who had mercy on the man who fell among thieves and was stripped of his possessions. I am reminded of two STM-ers; one of whom broke down behind the pulpit whilst he shared how he walked past a dead child in the street, and a woman (on a different STM in another country), how she witnessed the same. For the woman, this was her call to set up a children's home, which has been in operation for over a decade.

'Indiscriminate charity does more harm than good' – anonymous author of the *Life of General Gordon* (c.1895).

If you are an independent STM-er you can make your own policy in regards to giving to the poor and needy, which will inevitably adapt over time and from one STM to another. Before I went to Africa, God gave me the following Scripture: 'Whoever shuts his ears to the cry of the poor will also cry out himself and not be heard' (Proverbs 21:13). In its most basic sense, the Scripture is easy to understand but the application of it varied from country to country. Regardless of where you are in the world, the how, what and when to give, always vexes the most compassionate and kindest of people.

A missionary wrote: 'It is more difficult, more thankless, but really a kinder act to put a person into the way of helping himself rather than doing all for him; which [the] latter is often much easier. This applies both to the conduct of missionary operations and almsgiving.'[3]

The Rich Foreigner
On your STM many people you meet will perceive you as the rich foreigner – and depending on how far you have flown, your plane tickets could have cost more than the locals earn in several years! If you were to sell your electrical gizmos (digital camera, iPod etc.), you would find that many families in developing countries could feed themselves for a month or two!

In some cultures it can be common for Christians in developing countries (as brothers and sisters in the Lord), to ask for money (or other items), which can come as a surprise to many first time STM-ers. Do not be offended if a Christian asks you for money; if you were in their circumstances you would probably do the same. But before you begin to act as the mobile ATM and dispense the contents of your wallet or purse, you should ask your team leader for his or her advice, as experience has probably taught them a thing or two, but ALWAYS adhere to your mission organisation's policy.

Not everybody who asks has a *need*, but a person may *want* some of your perceived wealth, whilst on the other hand, your little gift may go a long way to help a genuine Christian in need.

One local pastor repeatedly dropped hints about his *need*, I politely said, "I wish I was rich like you, you're married, have children and have your own home; I cannot afford to get married and start a family!" Edward – Africa.

Walk in the Spirit

We are called to be 'led of the Spirit' (see Romans 8:14 and Galatians 5:18a), and not of our emotions. We are to 'walk in the Spirit' (Galatians 5:25), and should make intelligent decisions based on our financial circumstances. It is a sin when we have the power to help someone, but harden our hearts towards them and clench our fists: 'Do not withhold good from those to whom it is due, *when* it is in the power of your hand to do so' (Proverbs 3:27). 'Whoever has this world's goods and sees his brother in need, and shuts up his heart from him, how does the love of God abide in him?' (1 John 3:17). When a 'brother or sister is naked and destitute of daily food and one of you says to them, "Depart in peace, be warmed and filled," but you do not give them the things which are needed for the body, what does it profit?'(James 2:15-16).

God is 'a Father of the fatherless, a defender of widows...God sets the solitary in families' Psalm 68:5-6a.

For many STM-ers who have taken a year out, (or those not long out of school or college), they will probably not have the disposable income compared to someone who has worked for many years. Therefore, they may not be in a position to help local Christians who ask for financial assistance – and that's OK. The best way to invest your money is to lend it to the Lord because, 'He who has pity on the poor lends to the Lord, and He will pay back what he has given' (Proverbs 19:17).

Amy Carmichael, missionary to India, said, "You can give without loving, but you cannot love without giving."

> Within two days of our ministry, we had been into three indigenous people's homes all of whom lived in the same district and within a short bicycle ride of each other. One home was just a room; another was a small building with a courtyard, whilst the third residence was in a gated community and consisted of Western amenities. Mark – India.

True Worship

Religious observances, including worship and praise is made null and void (and is not desired of God), when justice and righteousness is forsaken (Amos 5:21-24). 'Defend the poor and the fatherless; do justice to the afflicted and needy. Deliver the poor and the needy; free them from the hand of the wicked' (Psalm 82:3-4). Society does not always stand up for those who cannot defend themselves and Christians should always be at the forefront of this. We are called to worship God 'in Spirit and in truth' (John 4:23), and true worship consists not only of our social concern, concern for our neighbours, and our treatment of others (treat people how you would like to be treated), but of our lifestyle and our heart attitude. To have 'clean hands and a pure heart' (Psalm 24:4), to be holy, to walk in the fear of God and to uphold and adhere to the statutes and commands of God. If we fail in these areas then God cannot accept our worship and our STM will not be as successful as it should be.

God said, "Is this not the fast I have chosen: to loose the bonds of wickedness, to undo heavy burdens, to let the oppressed go free and that you break every yoke? Is it not to share your bread with the hungry and that you bring to your house the poor who are cast out; when you see the naked, that you cover him and not hide yourself from your own flesh?" (Isaiah 58:6-7). See also what Jesus said in Matthew 25:35-46.

John Wesley from the eighteenth century, noted that as Methodists increased in wealth, they tended to decrease in godliness. It is in this connection that he often repeated his maxim: "Get all you can, save all you can, give all you can."

Chapter Forty-Six

What you Hope to Achieve

'I planted, Apollos watered, but God gave the increase. So neither he who plants is anything, nor he who waters, but God who gives the increase. Now he who plants and he who waters are one, and each one will receive his own reward according to his own labour' 1 Corinthians 3:6-8.

'Ask of Me, and I will give You the nations for Your inheritance, and the ends of the earth for Your possession' Psalm 2:8.

Hopes and Expectations

You may go on your short-term mission (STM) with great hopes and expectations (and you should), but sometimes the reality is very different from the preconceived idea or dream. It is like the famed travel writer of the 1930s, H. V. Morton who contrasted between his memories of a snowy Christmas card scene of the Nativity and what he saw in Bethlehem. He wrote: 'Every Christian nation has translated the story of Christ into its own idiom and cradled Him in its barns. The great medieval painters have, each man in his own way, painted in the national background of his own country and his own time. And we who come from Europe to Palestine [the Holy Land] come from an enchanted country to the bare rocks and crags of reality.'[1]

Preaching to crowds of thousands of eager listeners is not the reality of most STMs and for many mission organisations, it is not possible, as they specialise in one-on-one encounters, small meetings or participate in humanitarian or development aid as an expression of the love of Christ.

Georgina A. Gollock in *Candidates in Waiting – A Manual of Home Preparation for Foreign Missionary Work* (1892) wrote: '...Study of contemporary missionary history and of missionary biography as well, will also help to rid you while at home of the unhealthy glamour which may distort your view of your future work.... Spiritual results are beyond all human comprehension in their origin and can be commanded by no methods.... You will find that men who died after long years of apparently fruitless labour have yet done service for which all succeeding workers have given glory to God...'[2]

I have never known anyone to go on a STM who was not impacted by their time away, whilst many received more than they gave.

In 2000, a senior Christian leader gave advice for those wishing to work in China. 'Come and see how you can serve the vision God has given the church in China. Together we can seek God about ways to cooperate. You have gifts and resources we don't have, and we have gifts and resources you don't have. Together we can serve the Lord in an effective manner.' Be a servant and serve one another in Christ, see Mark 10:42-45.

In October 1990, I joined a small STM mixed team of six people and travelled to the south of Spain, where a mission organisation had just bought a large, rather abandoned house and were turning it into their mission base. We went mainly to do some work on the house; though after a day, the duty of cooking was assigned to me, which I enjoyed. It was my first overseas mission trip and I only stayed a week, but I was so impacted that I went back the following year for three months and some years later joined the team in Spain for six years. Bridget – Spain.

The Complexity of Evangelism

If you are an independent STM-er going from one country to another, this adds to the complexity of evangelism, but often a local is more eager to hear from or listen to a stranger than a local Christian. Steve Collins on shorttermmissions.com wrote: 'Be realistic about the depth of evangelism you will be able to do in the particular cross-cultural setting you are involved in. Many people expect that their cross-cultural efforts during a two-week period will result in conversions for Christ. [How many people have you led to the Lord at home within a two-week exposure?]. Realistically, a group of high school students working cross-culturally without foreign language skills probably will not see many people accept Christ personally. This should not diminish the impact their participation will have in a process that brings those individuals to receive Christ as Lord.'[3]

Some mission fields of the world have good soil and the seed sown, quickly grows and bears fruit as people respond to the Gospel message. Whilst other places are very difficult to work in, the ground is hard and stony and the people are unresponsive.

Missionaries of twenty-five years in Papau New Guinea, were telling some STM-ers that the indigenous Christians (in their area) are still frightened and held bound by the mystical powers of the sago tree in the Sepic River and refuse to go near it. "It makes you wonder," said the missionaries "what have we achieved in all our years of service?"

Many Links Make One Chain

Dr. Robert Morrison of China, Robert Moffat of Kuruman, South Africa, and Adoniram Judson of Burma, all pioneering missionaries in the early nineteenth century saw their first converts in their unevangelised fields after seven years of hard labour. Often it is a case that the grain of wheat has to fall into the ground and die – and if it has died, it can sprout and produce much fruit (John 12:24), but the majority of STMs are based in areas where the Good News has been proclaimed before; so the fields have been ploughed to some degree or other.

There are many links that make up a chain, and often our witnessing is part of a spiritual chain that leads to a person's conversion. The longer you stay in one destination, the more noticeable the impact that you will have made on individuals, a village or a community. Sometimes, our impact is unbeknown to us (good or bad) and the good influences can be part of a chain of grace that eventually leads someone to Christ. To prove this point, I asked a group of Bible college students (in evangelism class) how many times they had interacted with the Gospel (via personal witness, a tract, reading the Bible, attending church etc.) before they became a Christian. Not one person had a solitary interaction (whilst the majority received multiple encounters) before they surrendered their lives to Jesus Christ.

Some STMs can be a case of sowing and planting the seeds of the Good News into people's hearts, whilst another team may see the fruit of the collective labour, as Jesus said, "One sows another reaps," but "both he who sows and he who reaps may rejoice together" (John 4:36-38). The apostle Paul wrote: 'I planted, Apollos watered, but God gave the increase…and each one will receive his own reward according to his labour' (1 Corinthians 3:6, 8).

Inspiring Mission Related Scriptures
- 'Declare His glory among the nations, His wonders among all peoples' (Psalm 96:3).

- 'Arise, O God, judge the earth; for You shall inherit all nations' (Psalm 82:8).
- 'I will go in the strength of the Lord God; I will make mention of Your righteousness, of Yours only' (Psalm 71:16).
- 'That men may know that You, whose name alone is the Lord, are the Most High over all the earth' (Psalm 83:18).
- '...The people who know their God shall be strong and carry out great exploits' (Daniel 11:32b).
- '...Be steadfast, immovable...your labour in the Lord is not in vain' (1 Corinthians 15:58).
- "I have come to do Your will O God" (Hebrews 10:9).

Jesus said, "Go into all the world, and preach the Gospel to every creature" (Mark 16:15). The apostle Paul wrote: 'For whosoever shall call upon the name of the Lord shall be saved. How then shall they call on Him in whom they have not believed? And how shall they believe in Him of whom they have not heard? And how shall they hear without a preacher? And how shall they preach, unless they are sent? As it is written, 'How beautiful are the feet of them that preach the Gospel of peace, and bring glad tidings of good things!' So then faith comes by hearing, and hearing by the Word of God' (Romans 10:13-15, 17).

The apostle Paul became all things to all men to save some (1 Corinthians 9:19-22). As we are called to be fishers of men then like fishermen, we need to use different types of bait (methods or approaches) to catch different types of fish.

We must remember that when we try to catch fish, by sharing the Good News, that people will be dirty and will need a lot of cleaning up, training and discipleship. Sadly, many churches expect the fish to be clean before they can be caught, but this is not what Jesus taught, saying, "Those who are well have no need of a physician, but those who are sick. I did not come to call the righteous, but sinners to repentance" (Mark 2:17).

Jesus said, "...Behold, I say to you, lift up your eyes and look at the fields, for they are already white for harvest! And he who reaps receives wages and gathers fruit for eternal life that both he who sows and he who reaps may rejoice together. For in this the saying is true: 'One sows and another reaps.' I sent you to reap that for which you have not laboured and you have entered into their labours" John 4:35-38.

Realistic yet Expectant

Whilst we should be realistic on our STM, we do serve the God of the impossible, and who knows what might happen in expectant faith. The prophet Jonah was most reluctant to preach to the Assyrians in Nineveh, and tried to run from the call of God. But when he preached to the unevangelised city of Nineveh declaring the Word of the Lord, "Yet forty days and Nineveh shall be overthrown!" (Jonah chapter 3). The people believed the Word as from God, repented and turned from their evil ways!

Laurel A. Cocks under the subject of Culture Clash in *Stepping Out* wrote: 'It's unlikely that you'll meet all your expectations. One short-termer in the Philippines thought he'd be able to speak the language much sooner than he could. Another common expectation is that "successful" ministry is possible the minute you step off the plane. Remember that success is not your primary goal. Instead look for ways to link up with what God is doing there. He'll use you all right, but perhaps not as you expected. Positive, realistic expectations are a most effective antidote for cultural stress. Don't leave home without them.'[4]

Success Versus Faithfulness

We all want to be successful, but what is success? The expectation of a STM differs from one to another. God has not called us to be successful, but faithful and that is our ideal, whilst our aim is to be in the centre of God's will, and we leave the results up to Him. One sows, another reaps, but we all work towards building His Kingdom. God is glorified when we bear fruit, see John 15:7-8, but fruit has many aspects, and the only place you'll find success before work is in the dictionary!

A missionary once stated, "People ask me, when am I coming home? I answer, when the Lord commands! My duty appears to be to sow the seed of God's Word. I may not reap the harvest, but the sowing is what I am called to. God has rested the reward on my labour for Him and not on success."

Mary Slessor, the 'White Queen of the Calabar' (Nigeria), said, "Christ sent me to preach the Gospel and He will look after the results." In 1876, she sailed for West Africa and by the time of her death in 1915, she left behind many adopted children (many of whom had married), hundreds, if not thousands of converts, a string of mission stations, multiple churches, schools, a training centre for women, homes of rest and a name which has endured forever, as a pioneer for the Calabar Mission.

Miar Davies was sent out as part of a mission team to France in 1947. After a short time in Paris, she was invited to speak at the Every Creature Conference that was held annually at the Bible College of Wales (BCW) in Swansea, UK, where she had begun her training in 1935 under Rees Howells. Miar was concerned because many of the speakers were well known and had done mighty exploits for God, whereas she was new to the mission field. Rees Howells introduced her as a missionary to France, who was sent out from BCW and one who had been "faithful to her calling," which put her at ease and set the scene for her testimony.

Back in France, Miar received a vision from God, which showed her how to reach the neighbourhood, which the team implemented. A church was founded and Miar spent forty-two years on the mission field before returning to BCW where she spent the rest of her life.

Henry Martyn, missionary to India and Persia, said, "Let me labour for fifty years amidst scorn and never see one soul converted...the Lord who controls all events is my friend, my Master, my God, my all."

Unexpected Results

J. Manton Smith, one-half of the Fullerton and Smith evangelistic team noted: 'We are responsible for fidelity [the quality of being faithful] and not for success.' He had been telling the story of a man's conversion who attended one of his campaigns in Southampton, England, six or seven years previously, but was not converted until a week after the campaign, and the man had spoken to both evangelists. Smith went on to state: 'Who would wish to count the converts at a mission...when unexpected fruit like this appears?'

'...If we are faithful witnesses for God and proclaim the simple Gospel of Christ crucified for sinners, telling it out clearly in the language of the people, then like the Master Himself, the common people will hear us gladly and Jesus Himself will bless our simple message to the salvation of people.'[5]

'Let us not grow weary in doing good, for in due season we shall reap if we do not lose heart' Galatians 6:9.

Chapter Forty-Seven

Getting Ready to Return Home

'He has taken a bag...with him and will come home on the appointed day' Proverbs 7:20.

'For here we have no continuing city, but we seek the one to come' Hebrews 13:14.

Debriefing Meeting

If you are part of a mission organisation, at the end of the short-term mission (STM), either in your host country or when you arrive back at home, there should be a debriefing meeting, which should consist of every member of the team. It is an opportunity to try to adjust to some level of normality as you try to fit back into your home settings, and a time where you talk and discuss the STM. Each member of the team should have an opportunity to share their thoughts, highlights, (their lows), experiences and what they have learnt. The team, (not the leader) should do the majority of the talking. Ideally, there should be an anonymous questionnaire to fill out where each member can comment on all things concerning the mission and generally evaluate the trip from their perspective, which will aid the leader or mission organisation with planning and implementing future STMs.

Jesus sent out the seventy on their STMs and when they came back, they reported to Him all that had happened; Jesus told them a spiritual truth and they all rejoiced together (Luke 10:1, 17-20).

I went on a STM with a friend to North Africa where we saw some wonderful miracles of God's provision and protection. Nevertheless, we did not do very well, because we needed to save money. Back at home, we evaluated our trip and my friend said, "Next time I think we could eat better." After such a wonderful trip and so many miracles, I was disappointed that all he could think of was the food. It reminded me of the Exodus story, when the Israelites began craving for the food they had in Egypt! Frank – Morocco.

Before I Depart for Home

Before you leave your STM, there are things you should do and other things which you may like to do. Tidy your room, dorm or rented apartment. You should always thank the team leader, interpreter, guide, the cooks, the host church and whoever else has helped you. Say your goodbyes to the rest of the team (if you are not flying back together), get their email addresses (if you intend to keep in touch), but do not make promises (especially to the locals) if you cannot keep them.

As a local Christian leader, I helped a STM team from Canada, but after they returned home, they ignored all of my emails and I never heard from them again. It was very strange. Pastor Joseph – Sudan.

The leader of a STM team should confirm the flight details three days (or thereabouts before departure); the day before departure, settle all the bills (accommodation, gifts and other expenses) and confirm that the team has transport to the airport. Pack your bag. If you have stayed with a host or at a mission compound, tidy up! Check-in online 24hrs before departure (and you get to pick your seat home). On the day of departure, (check the rooms) and leave in plenty of time, as it is better to wait around for three hours at the airport than to miss the flight because the vehicle broke down or because the train was delayed. Keep your plane ticket and passport on you!

As full-time missionaries of over twenty-years, my husband and I supported the large STM team that stayed on our mission base. Unfortunately, they left everything dirty, unwashed and in a mess. It took me two days to clear up behind them, including scouring all the burnt pans! Judy – Papua New Guinea.

Intelligent Distribution of Items

You may have some items of clothing or other possessions (books, penknife, teddy bear, sleeping bag, construction tools etc.) that you brought to the mission field which would be far better used (or appreciated) by the locals – but can you really give up your teddy bear? Don't be like the student who took all of his tinned food and various food packets (two boxes worth) back to his own country instead of being a blessing to others! If you are with a mission organisation, speak to your leader

BEFORE you give items or money away – seek their advice as what to do. Problems arise when someone receives a gift and somebody else does not. It can cause friction and tension. There is a danger that individuals will be friendly to future STM-er because of what they can get out of it and it can lead to a culture of begging.

You could give your excess items to someone you work alongside (a local) or a person you ministered to, a new friend or someone who looks in need. You may wish to leave some money behind, instead of converting your spare cash back into your own currency (but leave some money for the airport!) or use this money to buy present(s) – something which an individual or a church needs. You may be in a position to hand over some of your own currency (pounds, dollars or euros). $16 (£10) may *just* be a monthly phone top up for someone in the West, but it can pay for half a months rent in a Mumbai slum shack; and is sixteen days living expenses for the 20% of the world who live on $1 (£0.60) a day!

Sometimes money is given to the church you have worked with (or the local missionary who has arranged things for you) and in this way, it can be better utilised. If STM teams frequently work with the church, it can cause problems when one team gives x amount and another team gives less. On occasions, money, which has been given to a church, a project (or to be passed on to others) has been misappropriated by those to whom it has been entrusted. I know of at least four occasions when this has happened. Money has been commandeered by the pastor or leader of the local mission because in their culture, their need (or greed) was greater than what the money was designated for. Perhaps the temptation was too great. God will be their judge and we have to do the right things in His eyes and bless people.

The pastor said he needed a brick church built for his small congregation, but did not have the money. We gave him enough money to cover the cost of the materials, which was less than $1,000 (£625). After three months we returned to visit the pastor and to see the progress of the building. The pastor has disappeared and so had the money! William – India.

Requests for Help

In the developing world, requests for help from the local church or individuals are common, but not all are pure and honourable, feasible, practical or even Scriptural. As one Bishop wrote about his own diocese: 'The old hereditary beggar mentality does not die easily and 'The Mission' is still often treated as a sponge to be squeezed.'[1]

There are times when our brother or sister in the Lord is in desperate need and to refuse help would be hypocritical. 'Whoever has this world's goods and sees his brother in need and shuts up his heart from him, how does the love of God abide in him?' (1 John 3:17), but if you are part of a mission organisation; then the person making the request should not be approaching you, but your leader. For the person asking (and the leader responding), there is a difference between an 'immediate need' of food and clothing (see James 2:14-17), and of wanting something because it is perceived that they have the means to help. See also, Chapters Forty-Two to Forty-Five, Remunerations and Wages for the Locals, Requests for Assistance, The Love of Christ in Action and Giving to the Poor and Needy.

> One man asked me to pay his university fees; I felt quite grieved by his request as I never had the opportunity to go to university. I had to leave school and get a job. Jack – Tunisia.

Your Contact Details

Be sensible to whom you give your contact details to. You will probably be asked for your home address; email and telephone number by many people, though there is a great difference between a relative stranger that you talked to for twenty minutes on the street and the person you have worked alongside for days, weeks or months. In your home country, would you give your personal details to a stranger? The internet is still not available in places or it may cost too much, and international phone calls can be expensive.

A visiting speaker (and his daughter) came to a church that I was a member of. The daughter was a youth leader (like myself at the time), and so we discussed youth things. After about ten minutes, she asked for my address, which I freely gave though noticed as she pulled out her A5 pad, it was full of contacts. Two months later, I received a letter telling me that her youth group has decided that our youth group should make a collection every week and send them the money every month! I took the letter to my pastor and asked him if he knew that his guests were trying to solicit finances from us. He read it, smiled, and having lived for many years in the country of which his guests had come from, said, "Mathew, in — that is the way they do it."

Promises and Emotional Bonds

In the Western world there is an underlying culture of misleading politeness, which entails not telling the truth. A common form is making promises (albeit unintentionally) and not fulfilling them, "I'll keep in touch," "I'll never forget you" (and you never write, email or phone), "I'll send you the book / photo / clothes / DVD" etc. and don't. It is a culture that has developed out of politeness (and / or good intentions), but in different countries is taken as a promise; not just a loose saying.

I did a STM in the United Kingdom and stayed on as a full-time Christian worker. Several people said to me over the years, "You must come round for dinner some time." But I never did. I was perplexed by this and so asked a national, "Was I meant to phone them to tell them when I would like dinner?" Yong-shin – Wales.

In the heat of the moment, the emotion of the mission or whilst saying our goodbyes we are prone to say the most normal, yet bizarre statements – "You must come and visit me sometime," – "If you're in — look me up." Even Peter told the Lord that he would never deny Him; yet in less than eight hours, he had denied Jesus three times and swore he never even knew the man! The statements that we make out of politeness can be taken as a promise in other cultures. Even after the STM has ended it has been known for the host or a member of the church to phone the STM-er from the airport or even turn up on the STM-ers doorstep unannounced, (surprise!), with no place to stay, little money and a three month visa! (This is not so common now due to tighter visa applications and fear of international terrorism. In many countries, they will not let you pass through immigration unless you can prove, that you have the financial means to support yourself, or unless they have a friend or relative within the country who will vouch for them).

Don't make a promise that you cannot keep and if you agree to something then do your utmost to fulfill your obligation. The statement, "I'll think about it," in response to a request, can also be interpreted in other cultures as a yes, or that you will get back to them, whereas in the West it is often used as polite way to get someone to stop pestering you!

Don't be foolish like some STM-ers who have offered scholarships, visas, plane tickets, money for schooling / buildings, trips to Disney Land (not joking!), mobile / cell phones, books, DVDs, CDs, designer trainers (sneakers), letters of recommendation / invites and even a promise to return next year. Broken promises can shatter dreams and hopes. Breaking your word tarnishes your reputation (that of the mission organisation), shows little regard to the one you have promised and dishonours the name of the Lord. Write any promise down and if you are unable to fulfill your obligations / promises, then let the person know, and give a good valid reason wrapped in love and sympathy for your backtracking. Sometimes we do forget things – one STM team bought two shopping trolley loads of supplies and drove back to the mission base, not realising that they left the food in the trolleys in the supermarket car park (parking lot)!

As part of our six week STM we drove across the border and stayed in a Christian run orphanage. I had been there a few times before and I knew most of the children's names. It was great to see them. Leaving was very hard for all concerned, the children hugged us and we all cried. Chris – Mexico.

Working with the locals can produce emotional bonds, ties of friendship, which can last for years or even decades and can be emotionally traumatic when you have to part. Don't be ashamed of crying, and if your host comes and visits your country (by appointment!), try to be as helpful towards them as they were to you, or better!

Someone once said, "It is not great men who change the world, but weak men (and women) in the hands of a great God."

Chapter Forty-Eight

Back at Home

When Paul and Barnabas completed their first missionary trip, they returned to their church at 'Antioch where they had been commended to the grace of God for the work they had completed. And when they had come and gathered the church together, they reported all that God had done with them and that He had opened the door of faith to the Gentiles' Acts 14:26-27.

'I went out full, and the Lord has brought me home again...' Ruth 1:21a.

Back on Native Soil

Your short-term mission (STM) is over – when you arrive back at home, you could be greeted with all sorts of emotions, from jubilation to depression, loneliness, disorientation or reverse culture shock; and there will be many things that need to be done. There will be your bag to unpack, clothes to wash (a washing machine at last!), friends or family wanting to know how the STM went, or for the undiscerning churchgoer, "How was your holiday / vacation?" There will be a small mountain of correspondence to deal with, bank statements to check, junk mail to wade through and a whole host of other things.

Reverse Culture Shock

Arriving back at 'home' can be daunting – especially the affluence, excess and waste of resources – this is most noticeable when you return from a developing country. You can feel ashamed at yourself for having a wardrobe full of clothes, numerous pairs of shoes, the latest gadgets and three meals a day whereas the people you were working alongside or ministering to, were poor, some of whom may live a day-to-day existence. Do not make any rash decisions like throwing your wardrobe away (well its contents!), but prayerfully ask yourself, "What can I learn from this?" Instead of buying all the latest clothes, music and accumulating so many items, the money could be better utilised to help those whom you left behind, to assist others to go on STMs or support indigenous evangelists.

One missionary had spent years in a famine zone, where too many suffered and multitudes starved to death. On returning to the UK, he went into a supermarket and was transfixed on the spot in the middle of an aisle, gazing at the abundance of rows and rows of perfectly formed and unblemished fruit. Nobody could move him and he seemed unable to speak. A minister, who evidently knew the missionary went over to him and stood alongside him and the store manager. The missionary under his breath mumbled out the words, "Oranges, oranges." The minister realising the situation asked the missionary if he would like one. "Yes," replied the missionary softly. The minister picked up a juicy orange, began to unpeel it, and gave segments to the missionary who began chewing slowly and came out of his trance-like state.

'...Whatever things are true, whatever things are noble, whatever things are just, whatever things are pure, whatever things are lovely, whatever things are of a good report, if there is any virtue and if there is anything praiseworthy – meditate on these things' Philippians 4:8.

Things to Do on Your Return
1. Give thanks to the Lord!
2. Unpack your bag.
3. Put the washing machine on (if mum is not around!), "Mum / Mom, can you help me!"
4. Have a hot shower or bath (it could be your first bath in months!).
5. Have a powernap or sleep, especially if you have had a night flight.
6. Put washing out to dry, "Mum / Mom!"
7. Open your correspondence, throw away the junk mail – leave checking your bank statements for another time.

When the twelve disciples returned from their mission trip they had to have some time to rest before the 'normality' of their lives continued (Mark 6:30-31).

Within a Few Days you Will Need To
1. Let your friends, family, supporters and church know that you are home (in case they don't know). Phone, email, SMS or social media; elderly people appreciate letters.

2. Write a summary or report of the mission – if not for yourself, for those who have prayed or financially supported you. Go through your journal for highlights and / or look through your sent emails whilst you were on your STM and use that as a framework. Your church may want you to give your testimony of your STM, or you may want to tell them (and you should) – go see your pastor or youth leader.
3. Fulfill your obligations / discharge your duties, by sending photos, CDs or books etc. to those you have promised. These items do not always arrive and don't expect an acknowledgment of thanks.
4. Write letters, send emails, or use social media keep in contact with those whom you said you would. Send thank you emails or letters to those who helped you and don't forget your host (if you worked with a local church). Be cautious if your worked in a sensitive country!
5. Get a job or continue with your studies, but try to have a few days rest on your return before resuming a routine. You may still be jetlagged or may even be unwell for a few days.
6. If you think you may have caught something (not a fish), see a doctor and tell them that you have come back from —. Malaria (and other diseases or infections) can appear after months of your return and even after two years!

> I spent five incredible months in Africa working with a mission organisation in several countries, but upon returning home, I realised that I was not 100% in health. After one month, I was fine and began filling in job application forms. Jason – England.

Other Helpful Things

Add up the total cost of your STM. This is easier if you joined a mission organisation as you only have a few items to add. However, working out the cost of your mission and dividing it by the number of days you were there is an interesting sum and helps you budget for future missions. By now, you would have probably have written a report of your trip (for the church newsletter and your supporters), but for your own record, evaluate the STM and make a note of several factors:

- What you learnt and what God taught you.
- How could I have been more effective?

- What things would I have done differently?
- Things to remember for the next time (what items would have been great to take and what to leave at home) etc.
- Total cost of the STM.

> I came home from my North Africa STM and on the Sunday asked the pastor if I could give a testimony about the two-week mission. I was only given five minutes (I had hoped for longer) and so was as concise as possible. George – England.

Freedom and Caution

The West has huge amounts of freedom which has arisen from our Christian heritage and our forefathers who fought for those rights. See *How Christianity Made the Modern World* by Paul Backholer.[1] In other parts of the world, these "rights" do not exist. You have to be wise whilst on your STM, but just as wise on your return. Be careful what you publish, email, write in a newsletter / social media or allow to be put into print, especially if you have worked in a Muslim, Buddhist or Communist town, district or country. It can cause problems for the locals, new converts, the local church or highlights the authorities that stricter controls are needed in the future. Being too open can hinder future mission work in some towns, districts or countries.

Korean Christians told me that during the Seoul Olympics (1988), spies from different governments went into churches and read the news from the mission boards of the missionaries who were working in sensitive countries (with their names, photos and locations displayed). Many missionaries were then expelled from these countries because of these indiscretions and oversights.

The Next Step

Your STM would have been a life changing experience at best, but on the lower end of the scale you would still have learnt many things (about yourself and others). Where you go from now, is between you and the Lord. You may have got a taste for STMs and hunger for more or feel that they are not for you, but you still want to see the fulfilment of the Great Commission. Why not be the missionary in your workplace, college or university? Consider using some of your disposable income to help others to go on STM, or support Christian workers at home or abroad!

For others, their STM may be a stepping-stone or a turning point that will eventually lead them to become a full-time missionary or other Christian worker. For some, they will be infused to become a mission mobiliser, one who mobilises / encourages others to go on missions and helps raise support and awareness for missions, both prayerfully and financially.

Remember To

- Continue to pray for the mission organisation or local church that you worked with, as well as those you met, helped and ministered to.
- Keep in touch with other members of your team.
- Encourage others to go on STMs.
- Perhaps you are already planning on going on another STM next year!
- If you are able to, I would encourage you to give more of your disposable income towards the fulfilment of the Great Commission: support mission organisations, missionaries, Bible translation; perhaps your church could support others to go on a STM? If this book has blessed you, then why not bless others with a copy. ☺

Nearly two decades ago I went on my first overseas mission trip. I only stayed a week in southern Spain, but the following year I returned for three months and some years later joined the same mission in Spain where I spent six years. What impacted me was the sense of *really* living for a purpose. I saw a number of very different people, some highly educated and intelligent, some very practical, some of varying ages, couples and singles, all joined together in heart and in spirit, to see that place reached for Jesus Christ. They had given up careers, homes, incomes, left family members behind, and they seemed to be so happy and at peace. What they were doing was, in the world's eyes, foolish, but in the Kingdom, it was of real value and importance. I think in my heart I knew then that I did not want to pursue things that only had value in this world, I wanted to live for what was *really* important; I wanted to be a part of what God was doing in the world and I'm thankful to the members of that team for showing it to me. Bridget – Wales.

Appendices A-G

Appendix A

American STM Statistics 1965-2008

In 1965, student researcher, Thomas Chandler noted only 540 individuals from North America involved in short-term missions (STMs).[1]

Douglas Millian, co-founder of Discover the World Inc. noted that according to some estimates, in 1975, 6,000 people from the USA went on a STM which increased to over 60,000 by 1987. Jim Rogers of YWAM Publishing, stated that in 1976, approximately 6,000 North Americans went on a STM but ten years later this number increased ten-fold to approximately 60,000.[2]

Douglas Millian in his doctoral dissertation (about STMs) states that between 1979 and 1989 the annual number of participants in STMs rose from just over 25,000 to approximately 120,000. Concurrently, the number of agencies involved in STMs rose from fifty to more than four hundred.[3]

By 1992, there were more than 250,000 STM-ers. By 1998, John Kyle of the Evangelical Fellowship of Mission Agencies put the figure at 450,000.[4] Whilst the Mission Advanced Research and Communication Center of World Vision, estimated that the number of U.S. lay people involved in short-term projects increased from 22,000 in 1979 to 120,000 in 1989. Later estimates held that 150,000 were sent out in 1998. The *Mission Handbook*, meanwhile, says the 'number of short-termers sent by mission agencies and serving from two weeks to a year increased from 38,968 in 1992 to 63,995 in 1996 to 100,386 in 1999.'[5]

In 2003, Peterson, Aeschliman and Sneed estimated at least one million STM-ers were being sent out from a globally-sent perspective each year. In 2004, Robert Priest, director of the doctoral program in Intercultural Studies at Trinity Evangelical Divinity School, reported he was beginning to locate data suggesting the number could be as high as four million STM-ers.

In the USA, there are at least 40,000 sending entities (35,000 churches, 3,700 agencies and more than 1,000 schools) that do the sending.[6]

A Princeton University study found that in 2005, 1.6 million church members took mission trips of an average of eight days.[7]

In October 2008, The Barna Group reported that 8 million of the 228 million adult residents of the U.S. have been on a STM trip in the last five years, though 33 percent of the STMs were locations within the U.S.[8]

Appendix B

Giving to Christian Missions

Scott Kirby, author of *Equipped for Adventure – A Practical Guide to Short-Term Mission Trips* (2006) noted that with his own doctoral research project: 'Over three-fourths [three quarters] of the respondents reported increased missions giving as a result of their short-term mission experience....' With that, 'Over half of the people mentioned the word *need* in their answers.... They are now giving more to global missions because the short-term experience allowed them to personally see the needs.'

Scott Kirby also noted STEM Int'l Ministries study, which revealed that STM participants 'on the average doubled their missions giving as a result of their short-term experience.' Whilst 'James Cecil's doctoral study found that seventy percent of short-term volunteers surveyed increased their mission giving as a result of their volunteer experience.' Whilst 'Tommy G. Purvis's research project found that seventy-six percent of the volunteers reported increased missions giving as a result of their volunteer mission trip.'

Scott Kirby also reported on a study by Dan Ray of all Southern Baptist Churches from South Carolina, USA, who participated in mission partnership projects from 1989-1992. The churches participating increased their average financial giving by 16.16 percent towards the denomination Cooperative Program, whilst the average South Carolina Southern Baptist Churches increased its giving to the Cooperative Program by 2.77 percent. Kirby noting: 'When people personally see the needs, they are motivated to give.' Kirby also notes a link between those who go on STMs and those who become full-time missionaries. The conclusion being: 'The short-termer stream has been the single greatest pipeline for flooding the world with new long-term missionary recruits.'[9]

Appendix C

A True Christian

Georgina A. Gollock correctly stated in *Candidates in Waiting – A Manual of Home Preparation for Foreign Missionary Work* (1892) that 'the fundamental principle of all true missions [is] – "Spiritual men for spiritual work." You must yourself be in living union with Christ, by the Holy Spirit, before you can lead others to know and love Him.'[10]

Marie Monsen was a Norwegian missionary who arrived in China in 1901. She saw revival across China from 1927-1932, in every mission station she visited (of differing denominations), in numerous provinces. In November 1931, she arrived at Chenping,

- 265 -

one of the mission stations of the Norwegian Lutheran Mission in Honan and saw revival. In the second week she spoke at the Chenping annual three day conference. At the end of the day, as her custom was, she would take her stand at the door and as the people left, she pointedly asked, "Are you saved?" The next day, as the people left, with her incredible discernment, she asked, "Are you still on the road to destruction?"

Her co-worker wrote: 'Many came to see her and confess their sins, but she sent them away, some as often as three to four times. They were not in a condition of real need. "Pray that God's Spirit may enlighten you concerning your sins," was the admonition they received to take away with them. She never tired of admonishing us, "Do not gather unripe fruit." '

Evangelist Billy Graham, speaking to J. Edwin Orr during the Hollywood for Christ Campaign of September 1951, said, "In the past, evangelists have not always seemed willing to face the fact that the so-called 'converts' passing through their enquiry rooms are not all converts.... Furthermore, many evangelists, including myself, used to spend ninety-five percent of their efforts in persuading men to *decide* for Christ. Now I am convinced that it takes ninety-five percent of evangelistic effort [follow-up] to get men to *follow* Christ, as compared with five percent necessary for decision.'

The Holy Bible plainly declares that 'whoever calls upon the name of the Lord will be saved' (Acts 2:21 and Romans 10:13), but those who confess with their mouths are also called to profess by their changed lives; that is, 'show forth fruits worthy of repentance' (Matthew 3:8). Genuine disciples of Christ can be differentiated from those who come in sheep's clothing, yet inwardly are ravenous wolves, because 'by their fruit you will know them,' for a 'good tree cannot bear bad fruit' (Matthew 7:15-20). *If* we abide in God's Word, we are His disciples and we shall know the truth and it will set us free (John 8:31-32). Also, people will know that we are Jesus' disciples '*if* we have love for one another' (John 13:34-35), and if we 'walk worthy of the Lord, *fully* pleasing Him' and increase in the knowledge of Him which qualifies us to be 'partakers of the inheritance' (Colossians 1:10-12). By the Word of God and His grace we are able to receive the inheritance, but only 'those who are sanctified' (Acts 20:32).

Jesus said that not everyone who calls Him "Lord" will enter the Kingdom of heaven, even though they may have done many miraculous signs and wonders in His name, but He will openly declare, "I never knew you; depart from Me you who practice lawlessness" (Matthew 7:21-23). See Luke 6:46-49.

The tragedy of the twenty-first century is that there are many people who attend church who genuinely believe they are saved and part of God's family (John 1:12), yet they are not. They have had a counterfeit conversion – thus meaning that they are not converted at all, though they sincerely believe they are saved.

Repentance, a renouncing and turning away from the works of darkness with faith in the death and resurrection of Jesus Christ is the foundation of salvation. Are you saved – saved from what? From the wrath to come, the lusts of the flesh? Saved from selfishness, greed, impure thoughts, a deceitful heart – saved from what? Jesus said, "Therefore by their fruits you will know them" (Matthew 7:20), because without holiness no man shall see the Lord (Hebrews 12:4), and we are commanded to be holy because He is holy (1 Peter 1:16).

The righteous one is scarcely saved (1 Peter 4:18), and those who do not do the will of God are not part of Jesus' family (Matthew 7:21 and Mark 3:35). Jesus declared that we are justified and condemned by our words (Matthew 12:37), and our confession of faith in Christ (Romans 10:9-10), is the crux of our faith. If the Lord will say to some, "I never knew you" – to those who even did miracles and cast out demons in His name (Matthew 7:21-23), can you really say you are saved? Jesus said, "Narrow is the gate and difficult is the way which leads to life and there are few who find it" (Matthew 7:14). Jesus said, "You must be born again" (John 3:7).

God knows who His chosen ones are and if we are not wearing the right clothes at the wedding feast we will be caught out and cast out (Matthew 22:11-14). We must accept and live by the Word of God and make Jesus not only our Saviour, but our Lord and Master. Have you? 'Examine yourselves as to whether you are in the faith. Prove yourselves. Do you not know yourselves that Jesus Christ is in you? – Unless indeed you are disqualified' (2 Corinthians 13:5).[11]

- 'Though He was a Son, yet He learned obedience by the things which He suffered. And having been perfected, He became the Author of eternal salvation to all who *obey* Him' (Hebrews 5:8-9).
- 'For if we believe that Jesus died and rose again, even so God will bring with Him those who sleep in Jesus' (1 Thessalonians 4:4).

Appendix D

Scriptures on Intercession and Prayer
- 'For we do not wrestle against flesh and blood, but against principalities, against powers, against the rulers of darkness

of this age, against spiritual hosts of wickedness in the heavenly places. Therefore take up the whole armour of God...' (Ephesians 6:12-17). See also Ephesians 3:10-11.

- 'I have set watchmen on your walls, O Jerusalem, who shall never hold their peace day or night. You who make mention of the Lord, do not keep silent, and give Him no rest till He establishes and till He makes Jerusalem a praise in the earth' (Isaiah 62:6-7).
- God said, "Son of man, I have made you a watchman for the house of Israel [your country or town]..." (Ezekiel 3:17-19).
- 'I exhort first of all that supplications, prayers, intercessions and giving of thanks be made for all men, for kings and all who are in authority, that we may lead a quiet and peaceable life in all godliness and reverence. For this is good and acceptable in the sight of God our Saviour who desires all men to be saved and to come to the knowledge of the truth' (1 Timothy 2:1-4).
- 'The Spirit also helps in our weaknesses. For we do not know what we should pray for as we ought, but the Spirit Himself makes intercession for us with groanings which cannot be uttered. Now He who searches the heart knows what the mind of the Spirit is, because He makes intercession for the saints according to the will of God' (Romans 8:26-27).

For principles of intercession, see *Samuel Rees Howells: A Life of Intercession* by Richard Maton.

Key Scriptural Principles for Answered Prayer
- Confess all known sin – (Psalm 66:18).
- What is our motive in praying for —? Is the Father glorified through your prayers? – (John 16:23 and James 4:3).
- Is it a need or a want? – (Matthew 6:9-13).
- Is it God's will? – (1 John 5:14).
- Ask in Jesus' name – (John 16:23).
- Believe and have faith – (Mark 11:24).
- Be persistent in prayer – (Luke 18:1).

An intercessory prayer team was sent out by the home church to come to the aid of a missionary in the Pacific. Little did the missionary know that the intercessory prayer team had not participated in spiritual warfare before and 'intercessory' was merely a title. It also did not help that there were problems inside the team. It was a recipe for disaster and a Jezebel member of the team brought back an erroneous report. The evaluations and opinions expressed in regards to the situation of which they knew next to nothing about, only caused great tension and was the last string in the bow that led to eventual separation between the sending church and the missionary on the field.

Appendix E

Beneficial Languages
Many former European colonies speak the language of its former colonial power. English is a second language in many countries of the world and widely spoken across South East Asia and down East Africa. French is spoken in two North African countries and in several West African countries. Spanish is widely spoken across South America except in Brazil as they speak Portuguese and English is spoken in Guyana, whilst other local or tribal languages are spoken across South America.

English is the language of business and multitudes of students or those in the tourism industry know the language well and want to practice, but this does not mean that you should not know some basic phrases in the local language. Inevitably, the longer you are immersed in one area, the quicker and easier it is to pick up the language. Some destination are merely passing through points.

In some countries outside of tourist areas (especially in east China) and as I found in Dhaka, Bangladesh, it is increasingly hard to find people who speak (or understand) English, though, at least in the latter, if you give it five minutes or so (as the crowd builds) someone will come along and translate / interpret for you!

Appendix F

Accursed or Defiled Objects
People can unknowingly bring accursed or defiled objects into their homes or churches (Joshua 6:18 and Joshua 7:1). Often these objects are given or bought as presents from foreign destinations. Curses and demons (evil spirits – 1 Timothy 4:1) can be attached to items such as wood carvings, occult objects, face masks, plaques etc. As food can be sacrificed to idols (Acts 15:29 and 1 Corinthians 10:20) and behind all idol worship there are demons, (Deuteronomy 32:17a) then other objects can be defiled (see Genesis 35:1-4 and Psalm 106:36-39). Demons seek a place to dwell and are not just constrained to people, animals or buildings. You can have holy and unholy buildings or land (Exodus 3:5 and Exodus 26:34). Unholy places have become defiled due to sin (often sites of occult or idol worship, see Leviticus 18:25, Psalm 74:7, Psalm 106:36-39 and Jeremiah 16:18). The Canaanites worshiped idols and sacrificed to demons (Leviticus 20:3-5, 2 Chronicles 11:15 and Ezekiel 20:26).

They would hide their idols inside the walls of their homes for protection. These walls and idols were contact points for the demons, thus defiling the homes. Leviticus 14:33-53 is about the cleansing or destruction of defiled homes. Accursed or defiled objects within your possession need to be destroyed (burnt, broken, thrown into a deep lake, or thrown overboard when out at sea) and never sold, regardless of the value (Acts 19:19 and Jude 23).[12]

Appendix G

Famous Missionaries

Famous missionaries from the thirteenth to the twentieth century in chronological order of their arrival on the mission field. Names marked by an asterisk (*) are more readily available though brief biographies can be found online @ www.MissionsNow.co.uk: Raymond Lull (North Africa), Francis Xavier (India and Japan), John Eliot (American Indians), Hans Egede (Greenland), *David Brainerd (American Indians) *William Carey (India), John Williams (South Sea Islands), Theodosius Vanderkemp (Southern Africa), *Adoniram Judson (Burma), *Robert Morrison (China), *Henry Martyn (India and Persia), *Robert Moffat (Southern Africa), *John Gibson Paton (New Hebrides, Pacific), Captain Allen Gardiner (Indians of Chile), Elias Riggs (Turkey), Miss Eleanor Macomber (Burma), Mrs Elizabeth Bowen Thomas (Syria), Titus Coan (Hawaiian islands), Miss Fidelia Fiske (Persia), *David Livingstone (Southern Africa), *Hudson Taylor (China), Guido Fridolin Verbeck (Japan), *Robert Jermain Thomas (Korea), *James Gilmour (Mongolia), Bishop Hannington (Uganda), Mrs A. R. M'Farland (Alaska), *The Cambridge Seven (China), *C. T. Studd (China, India and Central Africa), *Mary Slessor (West Africa), Christina Forsyth (Fingoland, Africa), Martha Croll (Jamaica), *Amy Carmichael (India), Marie Monsen (China), *Gladys Aylward (China), *James 'Jim' Elliot (Ecuador), *Helen Roseveare (Congo), *Jackie Pullinger (Hong Kong) and *Don Richardson (Irian Jaya).

This book is also available as an ebook

www.ByFaith.co.uk

www.MissionsNow.co.uk

www.RevivalNow.co.uk

Sources and Notes

Preface
1. *The Christian Counsellors Pocket Guide* by Selwyn Hughes, Kingsway Publication, 1973, 1977, page 73.
2. *How Christianity Made the Modern World – The Legacy of Christian Liberty* by Paul Backholer, ByFaith Media, 2009, page 251.

Chapter One
1. *From Japan to Jerusalem* by Bishop E. Graham Ingham. Church Missionary Society, 1911, page 209.
2. For more details on the Shanghai Revival (1925) and Andrew Gih, see *Revival Fires and Awakenings* by Mathew Backholer, ByFaith Media, 2009, pages 91-92.
3. For more details on the Pyongyang Great Revival (1907-1910), see *Revival Fire: 150 Years of Revivals* by Mathew Backholer, ByFaith Media, 2010, pages 25-38.
4. See *Charles E. Cowman – Missionary Warrior* by Lettie B. Cowman, The Oriental Missionary Society, 1928.
5. See Missions Links page on www.MissionsNow.co.uk
6. See www.backtojerusalem.com
7. See *Revolution in World Missions* by K. P. Yohannan, gfa books, 1986, 2004.
8. *William Carey The Shoemaker Who Became The Father and Founder of Modern Missions* by John Brown Myers, S.W. Partridge & Co., 1887, pages 26-40.

Chapter Two
1. *Short-term Missions Workbook – From Mission Tourist to Global Citizens* by Tim Dearborn, InterVarsity Press, 2003, pages 10 and 37.
2. *Hudson Taylor and the China Inland Mission – The Growth of a Work of God* by Dr. and Mrs. Howard Taylor, China Inland Mission, 1918, 1940, page 355.
3. *God's Great Ambitions* by Dan & David Davidson & George Verwer, Gabriel Publishing, c.2000, no page numbers.

Chapter Three
1. See also Luke 24:47, John 4:35 and John 20:21-23.
2. *God's Great Ambitions* by Dan & David Davidson & George Verwer, Gabriel Publishing, c.2000, no page numbers.
3. *India Awakening* by Sherwood Eddy, Missionary Education Movement, 1911, pages 171-172.
4. Advice on Money management: www.byfaith.co.uk/paulmoney.htm
5. In *Discipleship For Everyday Living: Christian Growth* by Mathew Backholer, ByFaith Media, 2011, there are three chapters on finances and Christian workers.
6. *Rees Howells Intercessor* by Norman Grubb, 1952, 1986, Lutterworth Press, page 234. See also www.ReesHowells.co.uk
7. *Land of Hope and Glory – British Revival Through the Ages* by Bruce Aitkenson, Dovewell Publications, 2003, page 190.
8. *The Life and Discoveries of David Livingstone – The Pictorial Edition* by J. Ewing Ritchie – Volume I, James Sangster and Co., c.1876, page 519.
9. *Candidates in Waiting – A Manual of Home Preparation for Foreign Missionary Work* by Georgina A. Gollock, Church Missionary Society, 1892, 1898, page 114.

Chapter Four
1. *Hudson Taylor in Early Years – The Growth of a Soul* by Dr. and Mrs Howard Taylor, China Inland Mission, 1911, 1940, pages 372-373.
2. *Guinness of Honan* by Mrs Howard Taylor, China Inland Mission, 1930, page 99.
3. Ibid. page 188.

Chapter Five
1. www.sethbarnes.com/?filename=shortterm-missions-trips-continue-to-boom
2. The cheapest U.K. based STM for one year of which the author is aware costs £3,000 ($4,800) per annum – 2009/10.
3. http://uk.ntm.org/about/history80.php
4. http://uk.ntm.org/go/summit_assist.php
5. *David Hill – Missionary and Saint* by W. T. A. Barber, Charles H. Kelly, 1899, pages 180-181.
6. *Friends Ancient and Modern*, Published for the Friends Tract Association, 1907, No. 9. (Daniel Wheeler) by August Diamond, pages 21-37.
7. Ibid. page 33.
8. Ibid. page 40.
9. *Robert Morrison – The Pioneer of Chinese Missions* by W. J. Townsend, 1892, S. W. Partridge and Co., pages 271 and 272.
10. *An Instrument of Revival – The Complete Life of Evan Roberts 1878-1951* by Brynmor Pierce Jones, Bridge Publishing, 1995, page 205.

Chapter Six
1. www.sethbarnes.com/?filename=shortterm-missions-trips-continue-to-boom
2. *David Livingstone* by Thomas Hughes, MacMillian and Co. 1901, page 23.

Chapter Seven
1. www.MissionsNow.co.uk Links Page (teaching and information regarding STMs) will open up a world of mission opportunities as well as other STMs related websites.
2. *How to Get Ready for Short-Term Missions: The Ultimate Guide for Sponsors, Parents, and THOSE WHO GO!* by Anne-Geri´ Fann and Greg Taylor, Thomas Nelson, 2006, page 56.

Chapter Eight
1. www.direct.gov.uk/en/Governmentcitizensandrights/LivingintheUK/DG_073741

Chapter Nine
1. www.sim.org/index.php/opportunity/shortterm Dec. 2008.
2. www.christianvocation.org 2010.
3. *Stepping Out – A Guide to Short Term Missions* originally edited and compiled by Tim Gibson, Steve Hawthorne, Richard Krekel and Kn Moy, YWAM Publishing, 1992, page 52.
4. *The Personal Life of David Livingstone* by William G. Blaikie, London – John Murray, 1881, pages 115-116.

Chapter Ten
1. See also John 14:15, John 14:21 and 1 John 5:2.
2. *Discipleship For Everyday Living: Christian Growth* by Mathew Backholer, ByFaith Media, 2011, pages 41-58.
3. *The Personal Life of David Livingstone* by William G. Blaikie, London – John Murray, 1881, page 115.

Chapter Twelve
1. *Vacations with a Purpose – A Planning Handbook for Your Short-Term Missions Team* by Chris Eaton and Kim Hurst, Navpress, 1991, page 108.
2. *The Liberating Secret* by Norman Grubb, 1955, Lutterworth Press, pages 193-194.
3. *The Advance Guard of Missions* by Clifford G. Howell, 1912, page 120.

Chapter Thirteen
1. www.dailymail.co.uk/news/article-1191603/One-gap-year-travellers-experience-medical-emergency-crime.html.

2. In the summer of 2009, the World Health Organisation announced that Swine Flu was a pandemic and by the end of July 2009, a minimum of 160 Britons were kept in quarantine around the world.
3. *The Pathways and Abiding Places of Our Lord* - J. Wainwright, 1865, pages 59-60.
4. www.georgeverwer.com/resources_detail.php?id=683.

Chapter Fourteen
1. *Short-term Service Directory 2009*, Christian Vocations, page 10.

Chapter Fifteen
1. www.byfaith.co.uk/paulbyfaithtvmathewthoughts22.htm
2. *David Livingstone* by Thomas Hughes, MacMillian and Co, 1901, page 23.
3. *God Challenges the Dictators – Doom of Nazis Predicted* by Rees Howells, 1939, Simpkin Marshall, Ltd, page 96.

Chapter Sixteen
1. *The Life and Discoveries of David Livingstone – The Pictorial Edition* by J. Ewing Ritchie – Volume I, James Sangster and Co., c.1876, page 718.
2. *Daily Express* newspaper, 27 July 2009, page 29.
3. *The Life and Discoveries of David Livingstone,* c.1876, pages 249, 260 and 273.

Chapter Seventeen
1. Asia Harvest Newsletter #110, July 2011, page 4.

Chapter Nineteen
1. *Mack & Leeann's Guide to Short-Term Missions* by Mack and Leeann Stiles, InterVarsity Press, 2000, page 49.
2. *Seven Pentecostal Pioneers* – C. Whitaker, Marshal Morgan & Scott, 1986, p.30.

Chapter Twenty
1. *Daily Express* newspaper, 19 August 2009.

Chapter Twenty-One
1. *The Advance Guard of Missions* by Clifford G. Howell, 1912, page 154.
2. *Three Miles High – Northward to Tibet* by Leonard Moules, Christian Literature Crusade, 1947, page 26.

Chapter Twenty-Four
1. Please be aware that if a large team takes in numerous bags of clothing into isolated communities then it is possible to wreck the local clothes economy and put individuals out of business. If the items are not good enough for you to wear, should you expect someone else to wear them?
2. *First-Time Around the World – A Trip Planner for the Ultimate Journey* by Doug Lansky, Rough Guides, 2006, page 140.
3. www.which.co.uk/advice/baggage-excess/airlines-compared/index.jsp
4. British and Americans are disliked in some countries because of their countries foreign policies, propaganda by rogue nations and recent wars, which are seen as a personal attack on Islam. Some countries feel oppressed due to unfair trade deals in relation to agricultural subsidies and import duties or because of trade embargoes.

Chapter Twenty-Five
1. *The Life and Discoveries of David Livingstone – The Pictorial Edition* by J. Ewing Ritchie – Volume I, James Sangster and Co., c.1876, page 411.
2. *Unfolding Purpose – An interpretation of the Living Tradition which is C.M.S.* by Max Warren, 1950, Church Missionary Society (CMS), page 9.
3. *Annual Report of the Church Missionary Society, 1948-9,* (Popular Edition), p.13.

4. *Unfolding Purpose* – by Max Warren, CMS, 1950, page 33.
5. *Missionary Education Helps for the Local Church* by Dick Pearson, Overseas Crusades inc., 1966, page 22.

Chapter Twenty-Nine
1. *Successful Mission Teams – A Guide for Volunteers* by Martha VanCise, New Hope Publishers, 1996, 2004, page 115.
2. *Robert Morrison – The Pioneer of Chinese Missions* by W. J. Townsend, 1892, S. W. Partridge and Co., page 95.   3. Ibid. pages 92, 104 and 133.

Chapter Thirty
1. *God Can Be Trusted* by Elizabeth Goldsmith, OM Publishing, 1984, 1993, p.186.

Chapter Thirty-One
1. A hijab is a headscarf worn by Muslim women; concealing the hair and neck and may or may not have a face veil.
2. A jilbab is an Islamic ankle length garment for women (though I have heard the term used to describe the male equivalent), whilst a thawb or thobe is an ankle length garment worn by Muslim men with short or long sleeves.

Chapter Thirty-Two
1. *God Can Be Trusted* by E. Goldsmith, OM Publishing, 1984, 1993, pages 199-200.
2. *Revival An Enquiry* by Max Warren, SCM Press LTD, 1954, page 36.
3. *The Life and Discoveries of David Livingstone – The Pictorial Edition* by J. Ewing Ritchie – Volume I, James Sangster and Co., c.1876, page 404.
4. www.onepoll.com - *Daily Mail* newspaper, 10 November 2008, page 3.
5. *Batak Miracle, The Story of Damai, son of Sumatra* by Elizabeth Goldsmith, Overseas Missionary Fellowship, 1967, pages 35 and 46.
6. *God Can Be Trusted* by Elizabeth Goldsmith, OM Publishing, 1984, 1993, p.195.

Chapter Thirty-Three
1. *Failure Is Never Final* by Lynda Neilands, Christian Focus, 1994, 2000, page 123.
2. *Bottom-Line Faith – Ten Characteristics of Committed Christians* by Larry Kreider, Tyndale House Publishers Inc., 1995, page 73.
3. *The Essential Guide to the Short Term Mission Trip by* David C. Forward, Moody Press, 1998, page 134.

Chapter Thirty-Four
1. *Serving with Eyes Wide Open: Doing Short-term Missions with Cultural Intelligence* by David A. Livermore, Baker Books, 2006, page 128.
2. *David Hill – Missionary and Saint* by W. T. A. Barber, 1899, page 124.

Chapter Thirty-Five
1. *God Can Be Trusted* by E. Goldsmith, OM Publishing, 1984, 1993, pp.178 & 181.
2. *Some want it Tough* by Leonard Moules, Christian Literature Crusade, 1958, 1961, pages 37, 88 and 139.
3. *Candidates in Waiting* by Georgina A. Gollock, CMS, 1892, 1898, pages 74-75.
4. *The Week* – (magazine), Issue 718, (6 June 2009), page 11.

Chapter Thirty-Six
1. *How Christianity Made The Modern World – The Legacy of Christian Liberty* by Paul Backholer, ByFaith Media, 2009, pages 13-14.

Chapter Thirty-Seven
1. See www.byfaith.co.uk/paulni523p.htm (Knowing your Enemy the devil), www.byfaith.co.uk/paulni524p.htm (Standing our Ground and Using our Weapons),

and www.byfaith.co.uk/paulni518p.htm (Our Position in Christ Jesus). Part of a FREE 55 lesson interactive (and printer friendly) basic discipleship course.

Chapter Thirty-Eight
1. Other foods you encounter could be: Monkey, kangaroo, donkey, yak, guinea pig, rabbit, frogs, various rodents, reptiles and insects; grasshoppers, ants, worms, grubs, lizards, snakes, fish, shark, crab, shell fish and a whole host of birds and foul.
2. *The Essential Guide to the Short Term Mission Trip by* David C. Forward, Moody Press, 1998, pages 161-162.

Chapter Thirty-Nine
1. *Vacations with a Purpose – A Planning Handbook for Your Short-Term Missions Team* by Chris Eaton and Kim Hurst, Navpress, 1991, pages 45-46.
2. *Ascent of the Inner Everest* by Leonard Moules, Christian Literature Crusade, 1971, pages 26 and 30.
3. *Equipped for Adventure – A Practical Guide to Short-Term Mission Trips* by Scott Kirby, New Hope Publishers, 2006, pages 160-161.
4. *Hudson Taylor and the China Inland Mission – The Growth of a Work of God* by Dr. & Mrs. Howard Taylor, China Inland Mission, 1918, 1940, page 106.

Chapter Forty
1. Idioms – a manner of speaking that is natural to native speakers of a language or the usage or vocabulary that is characteristic of a specific group of people.
2. *Successful Mission Teams – A Guide for Volunteers* by Martha VanCise, New Hope Publishers, 1996, 2004, pages 148-149.
3. *Merseyside's Great Evangelists – A Biography of William Lockhart, Reginald Radclifffe [and] John Hambleton* by Geoff Green, c.2005, page 7.
4. *Short-term Missions Workbook – From Mission Tourist to Global Citizens* by Tim Dearborn, InterVarsity Press, 2003, pages 21-22.

Chapter Forty-One
1.www.sethbarnes.com/?filename=shortterm-missions-trips-continue-to-boom
2. *Serving with Eyes Wide Open: Doing Short-term Missions with Cultural Intelligence* by David A. Livermore, Baker Books, 2006, page 148.
3. Mack & Leeann's Guide to Short-Term Missions by Mack and Leeann Stiles, InterVarisity Press, 2000, page 122.

Chapter Forty-Four
1. *David Hill – Missionary and Saint* by W. T. A. Barber, 1899, page 180.
2. *How Christianity Made the Modern World – The Legacy of Christian Liberty* by Paul Backholer, ByFaith Media, 2009, page 62.
3. www.asiaharvest.org.
4. See *Discipleship For Everyday Living: Christian Growth* by Mathew Backholer, ByFaith Media, 2011, for more details of the connection between the mind and the body, in chapters 43 and 44 on Inner Healing.
5. *Revolution in World Missions* by K. P. Yohannan, gfa books, 1986, 2004, pages 102, 113 and 114.
6. *A South India Diary* by J. E. Lessie Newbigin, SCM Press Ltd, 1951, pages 6, 53-54 and 57-58.
7. *Yarns on Christian Torchbearers* by Lilian E. Cox and Ernest H. Haynes, The Religious Education Press, 1941, 1954, page 40.
8. Ibid. page 62.

Chapter Forty-Five
1. Mercy Ships pamphlet mercyships.org.uk.

2. Oxfam state: 'Poverty means not having enough money to pay for the things you need. From Oxfam's experience of working with people living in poverty we know that this may involve families and individuals not having enough to eat, being unable to heat their homes, not having adequate warm clothing, and not having enough money to cope with unforeseen events, such as the need to repair a broken washing machine. The 2004/5 Family Resources Survey, published by the Department for Work and Pensions, reported that: 60% of people on low incomes say they are unable to make savings of £10 ($16) a month; 10% cannot afford two pairs of all-weather shoes for each adult in the family; 30% cannot afford household contents insurance; and nearly 30% are unable to have friends or family round for a meal once a month. www.oxfam.org.uk/resources/ukpoverty/morepovertyfacts.html# practice
3. *David Hill – Missionary and Saint* - W. T. A. Barber, Charles H. Kelly, 1899, p.177.

Chapter Forty-Six
1. *In The Steps Of The Master* by H. V. Morton, Rich & Cowan LTD., 1934, pages 112-113.
2. *Candidates in Waiting – A Manual of Home Preparation for Foreign Missionary Work* by Georgina A. Gollock, CMS, 1892, 1898, page 88.
3. www.shorttermmissions.com as quoted in *Short-term Service Directory 2009*, Christian Vocations, page 9.
4. *Stepping Out – A Guide to Short Term Missions* originally edited and compiled by Tim Gibson, Steve Hawthorne, Richard Krekel and Kn Moy, YWAM Publishing, 1992, page 150.
5. *Striking Stories from Real Life* by J. Manton Smith, Passmore & Alabaster, 1894, page 67.

Chapter Forty-Seven
1. *A South India Diary* by J. E. Lessie Newbigin, SCM Press Ltd, 1951, page 77.

Chapter Forty-Eight
1. Available from www.ByFaithBooks.co.uk.

Appendices A-F
1. www.lausanneworldpulse.com/perspectives/265/03-2006?pg=2 (March 2006).
2. *Stepping Out – A Guide to Short Term Missions* originally edited and compiled by Tim Gibson, Steve Hawthorne, Richard Krekel and Kn Moy, YWAM Publishing, 1992, pages 3 and 17.
3. *Vacations with a Purpose – A Planning Handbook for Your Short-Term Missions Team* by Chris Eaton and Kim Hurst, Navpress, 1991, page 15.
4. www.lausanneworldpulse.com/perspectives/265/03-2006?pg=2 (March 2006).
5. www.strategicnetwork.org/index.php?loc=kb&view=v&id=8794
6. www.lausanneworldpulse.com/perspectives/265/03-2006?pg=2 (March 2006).
7.www.benbyerly.wordpress.com/2008/11/13/is-short-term-missions-turning-people-into-beggars-maybe-not/
8.www.barna.org/barna-update/article/20-donorscause/22-despite-benefits-few-americans-have-experienced-short-term-mission-trips (October 2008).
9. *Equipped for Adventure – A Practical Guide to Short-Term Mission Trips* by Scott Kirby, New Hope Publishers, 2006, pages 28-29.
10. *Candidates in Waiting – A Manual of Home Preparation for Foreign Missionary Work* by Georgina A. Gollock, Church Missionary Society, 1892, 1898, page 19.
11. *Revival Fires and Awakenings* by Mathew Backholer, ByFaith Media, 2009, (Appendix F), pages 234-235.
12. See *Discipleship For Everyday Living: Christian Growth* by Mathew Backholer, ByFaith Media, 2011, chapters 48 and 49: Deliverance – The Casting out of Demons and Demonised Places / Territorial Spirits.

ByFaith Media Books and DVDs

Short-Term Missions, A Christian Guide to STMs: *For Leaders, Pastors, Churches, Students, STM Teams...*by Mathew Backholer.

ByFaith – World Mission on 1 DVD is a TV documentary of a Christian short-term mission in Asia, Europe and North Africa.

Global Revival – Worldwide Outpourings: *Forty-Three Visitations of the Holy Spirit – The Great Commission* by Mathew Backholer documents forty-three revivals from more than thirty countries.

Extreme Faith, On Fire Christianity, *Hearing from God and Moving in His Grace, Strength and Power* by Mathew Backholer. Discover the powerful biblical foundations for on fire faith in Christ.

How Christianity Made the Modern World by Paul Backholer. Christianity is the greatest reforming force that the world has ever known, discover its legacy now, and be amazed at its influence!

Jesus Today, Daily Devotional (100 days) by Paul Backholer.

Holy Spirit Power, *Knowing the Voice, Guidance and Person of the Holy Spirit* by Paul Backholer. Inspiration from men of God.

Heaven – A Journey to Paradise and the Heavenly City by Paul Backholer. What will heaven be like? Experience it now!

Great Christian Revivals on DVD is an inspirational and uplifting account of some of the greatest revivals in church history. Filmed in England, Scotland and Wales and drawing upon archive information, the stories of the Welsh Revival (1904-1905), the Hebridean Revival (1949-1952) and the Evangelical Revival (1739-1791) are brought to life in this moving 72-minute documentary.

Revival Fires and Awakenings – *Thirty-Six Visitations of the Holy Spirit: A Call to Holiness, Prayer and Intercession for the Nations* by Mathew Backholer. Biblical teaching on revival, intercession prayer and holiness, with 36 accounts of revival in 18 countries across 6 continents, spanning four centuries.

Understanding Revival and Addressing the Issues it Provokes *So that we can Intelligently Cooperate with the Holy Spirit During Times of Revivals and Awakenings* by Mathew Backholer.

Britain A Christian Country, *A Nation Defined by Christianity and the Bible & the Social Changes that Challenge...*by Paul Backholer.

Revival Fire, 150 Years of Revivals: Spiritual Awakenings and Moves of the Holy Spirit by Mathew Backholer documents in detail, twelve revivals from ten countries on five continents.

Revival Answers, True and False Revivals, Genuine or Counterfeit: Do Not Be Deceived, Discerning Between the Holy Spirit and the Demonic by Mathew Backholer.

Discipleship For Everyday Living – Christian Growth: Following Jesus Christ And Making Disciples of All Nations by Mathew Backholer. A dynamic book covering fifty biblical subjects.

Prophecy Now, Prophetic Words and Divine Revelations: For You, the Church and the Nations by Michael Backholer.

The Holy Spirit in a Man: Spiritual Warfare, Intercession, Faith, Healings and Miracles in the Modern World by R. B. Watchman.

Tares and Weeds in your Church, Trouble & Deception in God's House: The End Time Overcomers by R. B. Watchman.

*Celtic Christianity & the First Christian Kings in Britain: From St. Patrick and St. Columba to King Ethelbert…*by Paul Backholer.

Samuel, Son and Successor of Rees Howells: Director of the Bible College of Wales – A Biography by Richard Maton.

Samuel Rees Howells: A Life of Intercession by Richard Maton is an in-depth look at the intercessions of Samuel Rees Howells & the faith principles that he learnt. With 39 black and white photos.

The Exodus Evidence In Pictures – The Bible's Exodus: The Hunt for Ancient Israel in Egypt, the Red Sea, the Exodus Route and Mount Sinai by Paul Backholer. 100+ full colour photos.

Israel in Egypt – The Exodus Mystery on 1 DVD. A four-year quest searching for Joseph, Moses and the Hebrew slaves in Egypt. The mystery of the biblical exodus. 110+ minutes.

The Ark of the Covenant – Investigating the Ten Leading Claims by Paul Backholer. Join two explorers as they investigate the location of the Ark. 80+ colour photos.

ByFaith – Quest for the Ark of the Covenant on 1 DVD. Exploring Tutankhamun's treasure, Shishak's siege of Jerusalem, the Queen of Sheba's Ethiopia, and the lost gold of Solomon.

www.ByFaithBooks.co.uk – www.ByFaithDVDs.co.uk

The author on the Great Wall of China – July 2011

In Ulaanbaatar, Mongolia – August 2011

Lightning Source UK Ltd.
Milton Keynes UK
UKOW02f0331301116

288804UK00001B/55/P